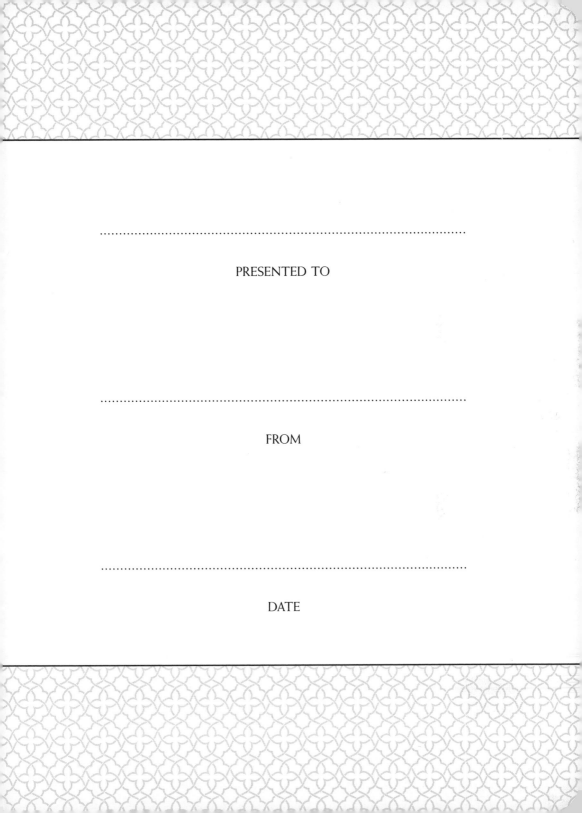

....

PRESENTED TO

....

FROM

....

DATE

MyDaily® DEVOTIONAL

THE GIFT OF

JESUS

COUNTRYMAN®
A Division of Thomas Nelson Publishers

THOMAS NELSON
Since 1798

The Gift of Jesus: MyDaily® Devotional
© 2015 by Thomas Nelson

Published in Nashville, Tennessee, by Thomas Nelson. Thomas Nelson is a registered trademark of HarperCollins Christian Publishing.

Thomas Nelson titles may be purchased in bulk for educational, business, fund-raising, or sales promotional use. For information, please email SpecialMarkets@ThomasNelson.com.

ISBN: 978-0-7180-8641-1

Printed in China

16 17 18 19 20 DSC 5 4 3 2 1

www.thomasnelson.com

INTRODUCTION

The *Gift of Jesus* has been written by fifty-one devoted men of God to guide readers in the way God wants Christians to live. God has given believers the gift of Jesus to live in and through our lives.

With every step you take, every decision you make, every conversation you have, and every thought you entertain, the Lord Jesus desires to live within you. He wants to live out His life through your expression of a perfect blending of His perfection and your unique talents, traits, and personality. It is our prayer that this devotional will open your heart to God's leading as you spend time in His Word and meditate on His truths every day.

Johnny M. Hunt

Dr. Johnny M. Hunt
Senior Pastor
First Baptist Church Woodstock
Woodstock, Georgia

MyDaily® DEVOTIONAL

THE GIFT OF

JESUS

CONTENTS

WEEK 1—MONDAY
The Gift of Hope

The angel said to [the shepherds], "Do not be afraid, for behold, I bring you good tidings of great joy which will be to all people. For there is born to you this day in the city of David a Savior, who is Christ the Lord. And this will be the sign to you: You will find a Babe wrapped in swaddling cloths, lying in a manger."

LUKE 2:10–12

The passage joyfully presents history's great announcement of hope. Whatever area you are struggling in today, whatever concerns for the future are weighing on you, slow down long enough to hear this message of hope. The simple yet profound words "good tidings of great joy" can touch the heart of even the most troubled soul.

This passage shouts of an event and a place, but most of all a Person. And not just any Person! This is Christ the Lord. The long-awaited Messiah, the Promised One, has been born! With His birth comes hope for all humanity, for He is our Savior.

"Jesus is a child born" is a phrase that points to the incarnation, His humanity. But He is "a Son given," are words that allude to His deity and point to the purpose of His coming: to bring salvation to the world. Yes, Jesus Christ is the One appointed to bear our sins on the cross as the sinless and perfect blood sacrifice. Only He could die in our place, take on Himself the punishment for our sins, and He did so voluntarily.

Therefore, rejoice! Jesus is our hope. In fact, He is the hope of all the world. So take the hope of Jesus into your world today and encourage someone who is struggling. You will be amazed at how this hope truly does change others.

....

Lord, I'm grateful for the gift of hope. Thank You! In Jesus' name, Amen.

DR. JOHNNY HUNT, FIRST BAPTIST CHURCH WOODSTOCK, WOODSTOCK, GA

WEEK 1—TUESDAY
The Hope of Heaven

Our citizenship is in heaven, from which we also eagerly wait for the Savior, the Lord Jesus Christ, who will transform our lowly body that it may be conformed to His glorious body, according to the working by which He is able even to subdue all things to Himself.

PHILIPPIANS 3:20–21

After we become followers of Jesus Christ, we come to understand that this world is not our permanent home, that we are just passing through. Our understanding of this truth will very much impact whether or not we live as though we're here to stay or if our focus is on our eternal residence.

If we indeed are citizens of heaven, we can be encouraged today that God has prepared a place for us in eternity and that His Son, Jesus Christ, has prepared us for this place.

In essence, the apostle Paul reminds us that we are to work for Christ as we await His return. The Bible correctly prophesied of His first coming at Bethlehem, and we can rest assured in the promises of God's Word that Jesus is coming again.

How this truth affects each of us has a lot to do with where we are in our pilgrimage and what we are going through right now in our lives. Many of us reading this devotional are facing a physical, spiritual, mental, or emotional challenge. When Jesus returns, He will change us radically. For those suffering with illnesses, for instance, He will give a new, perfect, pain-free body. May God's promise of heaven cause us to turn our faces toward heaven in gratitude and raise our hands in praise to the One who will make all things new.

....

Lord, the hope You give me for the future blesses me. Thank You. In Jesus' name, Amen.

WEEK 1—WEDNESDAY
Sharing the Hope We Have in Christ

I suffer trouble as an evildoer, even to the point of chains; but the word of God is not chained. Therefore I endure all things for the sake of the elect, that they also may obtain the salvation which is in Christ Jesus with eternal glory.

2 TIMOTHY 2:9–10

When I think of the apostle Paul, I think of a passionate man on a mission willing to do whatever it took to accomplish that task. Knowing the price his Savior paid for his forgiveness, knowing that he was in debt to Christ, Paul faced whatever came his way with spiritual tenacity and a Christ-inspired boldness. Paul dug his heels in for the cause of Christ, and he would not be moved.

Even though Paul was a prisoner in chains for the gospel, the Word of God could not be silenced. Paul's passion was fueled by the reality that apart from the gospel, a lost world has no hope. Aware that many people needed to hear Christ's message, Paul made Jesus known anywhere and everywhere he could. Paul allowed nothing to keep him from sharing the gospel.

In Philippians 1:12–13, Paul wrote of the furtherance of the gospel that was happening even while he was imprisoned. Even in chains, he accepted his suffering on behalf of the gospel. We should have the same courage to share the gospel with others in spite of any challenges we face.

Someone in your life needs to hear Jesus' story today. Share it.

....

Lord, what a privilege to be called to share Your life-saving, life-giving message. Grant me, Your servant, boldness. In Jesus' name, Amen.

WEEK 1—THURSDAY
Not by Works

When the kindness and the love of God our Savior toward man appeared, not by works of righteousness which we have done, but according to His mercy He saved us, through the washing of regeneration and renewing of the Holy Spirit, whom He poured out on us abundantly through Jesus Christ our Savior.

TITUS 3:4–6

Did you recognize the central theme in today's passage in which the Lord wants us to understand and build our lives? The truth is this: salvation is from the Lord. His kindness, His goodness, His graciousness, and His love made possible our salvation, our being rescued from sin's power and consequences. Our salvation is a story about what God did for us, not what we did.

How humbling to realize that nothing in me or about me commends me to God. The only Advocate I have—and, truly, the only Advocate I need—is His dear Son, the Lord Jesus Christ. Every day I see more clearly the overwhelming reality that I am hopeless without Jesus. Yet because of Jesus and all He did, I am truly a man of hope.

The phrase "not by works" is a great reminder that I contributed nothing to the cleansing of my sins. Instead, "according to His mercy," He washed me and made me clean. Jesus took on the consequences of my sin and didn't give me what I deserved. He also did a great work through His Spirit and brought me to faith in Him.

The Lord never does anything halfway. He has, for instance, "poured out on us abundantly" His Spirit. Thank God for His super-abounding grace, kindness, and love.

....

Dear Lord, I am forever indebted to You for Your truly amazing grace! In Jesus' name, Amen.

WEEK 1—FRIDAY
Beware!

Beware lest you also fall from your own steadfastness, being led away with the error of the wicked; but grow in the grace and knowledge of our Lord and Savior Jesus Christ. To Him be the glory both now and forever. Amen.

2 PETER 3:17–18

Have you ever had a time in your spiritual journey when you have not walked closely with the Lord? I have—and it was not a pleasant experience. The major problem each day was that I knew in my heart of hearts I was not where I should be with King Jesus.

I am so grateful that I'm not there anymore. And I am so grateful for our Lord's invitation with a promise, spoken by His half-brother James, to "draw near to God, and He will draw near to you" (James 4:8). I have always confessed the truth of 1 Corinthians 15:10: "By the grace of God I am what I am." However, as today's Scripture passage warns us, we can be led astray, or we may choose to disobey and go our own way.

I desire to walk with Jesus. And, because I am aware that I could be "led away with the error of the wicked," I desire to remain teachable. I want to continue to "grow in the grace and knowledge" of my Lord Jesus. Remember, it's not the truth one *knows*, but the truth one *obeys* that impacts our walk and our witness.

Like the apostle Paul, the apostle Peter gave us biblical truth and practical lessons on how to keep growing in one's relationship with Jesus. I have found that the Lord rewards my obedience with His divine enablement: His truth keeps me from falling.

....

Lord, help me to be conscious of Your presence, especially when challenges to my walk with You arise. I want to walk where You want me to walk. In Jesus' name, Amen.

DR. JOHNNY HUNT, FIRST BAPTIST CHURCH WOODSTOCK, WOODSTOCK, GA

WEEK 1—WEEKEND
Spiritual Birthmarks

We know that we abide in Him, and He in us, because He has given us of His Spirit. And we have seen and testify that the Father has sent the Son as Savior of the world. Whoever confesses that Jesus is the Son of God, God abides in him, and he in God.

1 JOHN 4:13–15

Have you ever heard about the spiritual birthmarks of a Christ-follower, about what attitudes and actions are to distinguish the believer from the unbeliever?

The apostle John was aware of the distinctive characteristics of people who truly belong to Jesus. One trait is love: "He who does not love does not know God, for God is love" (1 John 4:8). A second trait of believers is the presence of the Holy Spirit in their lives: "[God] has given us of His Spirit," and His Holy Spirit confirms for us that we belong to Him (Romans 8:16).

John spoke of a personal witness of Jesus because he had seen and touched the Lord (1 John 1:1). As Christ-followers, we can also testify to knowing Jesus personally because of His presence in our lives. We can personally attest to His love because He has poured it into our hearts by His Holy Spirit (Romans 5:5). We can also personally speak of the change He has brought to our hearts. He has changed our sinful choices and given us instead a desire for spiritual things that didn't exist until we began abiding in Him, until we began trusting in His sacrificial death on the cross for our sins and in His glorious resurrection.

Today our life is a testimony to His claims, for if we abide in Him, His nature will indeed shine through us.

....

Lord, thank You for Your love and Your Spirit, our spiritual birthmarks. Use them—use me—to testify to Your glory and grace. In Jesus' name, Amen.

WEEK 2—MONDAY
The Most Important Thing

Jesus answered him, "The first of all the commandments is: 'Hear, O Israel, the Lord our God, the Lord is one. And you shall love the Lord your God with all your heart, with all your soul, with all your mind, and with all your strength.' This is the first commandment. And the second, like it, is this: 'You shall love your neighbor as yourself.' There is no other commandment greater than these."

MARK 12:29–31

What is the most important thing? This is a very good question to ask ourselves when we're beginning a new week. Often we make priority lists so we don't neglect the important things.

But what are the those things? What is *the* most important thing? If we haven't identified what's important, we may be neglecting it!

One day a scribe asked Jesus what was the most important thing in life—the most important commandment to obey—and Jesus gave a clear and profoundly simple answer. Jesus said the most important thing was to love God and love others.

Jesus loved God and loved others flawlessly; He is our perfect example. Loving God and loving others is exactly what Jesus wants us to do. That is the most important thing. We don't need any further explanation. Instead, we need to act. And when we do, our love will show that we know we're doing what God has commanded of His followers.

....

Jesus, thank You for showing me the most important thing. Forgive me for being occupied with lesser distractions. Loving You and loving others—this is what's important. Everything else is a distant second. May Your grace and power and love flow through me. Amen.

WEEK 2—TUESDAY
No Shortcut Savior

The devil said to [Jesus], "All this authority I will give You, and their glory; for this has been delivered to me, and I give it to whomever I wish. Therefore, if You will worship before me, all will be Yours." And Jesus answered and said to him, "Get behind Me, Satan! For it is written, 'You shall worship the Lord your God, and Him only you shall serve.'"

LUKE 4:6–8

Jesus was no shortcut Savior. In today's passage, the devil hurled a temptation at Jesus, and the devil's goal was to try and convince Christ to bypass the cross, but Jesus' mission was ultimately the will of the Father for His Son.

Whenever we experience temptation, Satan has the same goal in mind: to keep us from doing the will of the Father. However, our enemy's weaponry has not changed throughout the ages: the lust of the flesh, the lust of the eyes, and the pride of life. Satan used all three temptations on Jesus, yet He didn't take the enemy's bait. And Jesus gives us His power to resist temptation just as He did.

Remember, most temptations are a shortcut that Satan wants you to take. We can find strength, though, in the Word and in the indwelling Christ. As we abide in Christ and stay grounded in the truth of the Word, we will not be interested in shortcuts. After all, we are on a journey with Jesus! Also, because He didn't take a shortcut in order to avoid the cross, we have a living Savior who is always with us, even in the very moment of temptation. Because Jesus was victorious, we too can be victorious.

....

Lord, I thank You for my victory over temptation through the power You provide me. Your indwelling presence and Your Word keep me victorious. You are so good. I praise You, and I thank You for sharing with me Your victory over sin and death. Amen.

Week 2—Wednesday
There Is Something About That Name

God also has highly exalted Him and given Him the name which is above every name, that at the name of Jesus every knee should bow, of those in heaven, and of those on earth, and of those under the earth, and that every tongue should confess that Jesus Christ is Lord, to the glory of God the Father.

PHILIPPIANS 2:9–11

Every year, a celebrity becomes wildly popular in the media, but before we know it, that name fades into obscurity. Often we see the caption "Where Are They Now?"

Apparently all names have a shelf life. All but one. There is a name that will never fade: the name of Jesus is timeless and without rival. God has exalted Jesus, lifting His name above every name.

Does it seem as though the name of Jesus is being downplayed today? Are the name and fame of Jesus Christ fading? Absolutely not! We shouldn't think we need to "hashtag" or "favorite" the name of Jesus to keep His name relevant! That matter has been settled by God Himself. It is impossible to ignore the exalted name of Jesus. And one day all people will bow at the name of Jesus Christ, confessing Him as Lord.

Celebrities are forgotten. World leaders fade away. Once-famous names inscribed on graveyard headstones become unfamiliar to the living. Yet the eternal Lord Jesus has an eternal name.

I love Your name, Jesus. I confess You as my Savior and Lord. As a Christian, I desire to honor Your name. Please use my life to glorify Your exalted, eternal name. Amen.

Week 2—Thursday
Were You There?

Let all the house of Israel know assuredly that God has made this Jesus, whom you crucified, both Lord and Christ.

Acts 2:36

Have you heard the old spiritual "Were You There When They Crucified My Lord"? Its powerful lyrics take us to the place where Jesus was crucified, and we tremble . . . Just a few weeks after Jesus was crucified, a memorable sermon was preached about His death and resurrection from a perhaps unexpected source. Peter boldly proclaimed, "You crucified Him!" Imagine the faces in the crowd when Peter pointed his finger in accusation.

The truth is that all of us crucified Jesus. We all were "there" that day. Jesus died as the consequence of our sin; He took the punishment we deserved so that we may live. When Peter said "He is Lord and Christ!" the people, under great conviction, asked, "What must we do?" With great clarity, Peter told them to repent of their sins and be baptized. Three thousand repented and trusted in Jesus that day!

Although we were not present that day when the three thousand were saved, we stand with them as the redeemed. The Bible tells of a day when we all will be present: "the number of [angels, living creatures, and elders] was ten thousand times ten thousand, and thousands of thousands, saying with a loud voice: 'Worthy is the Lamb who was slain!'" (Revelation 5:11–12).

All of us were there when Christ was crucified. Will you be there when He is worshipped by His redeemed?

....

Jesus, thank You for dying on the cross. You took my sin and paid my penalty. I can never praise You enough. I will need all eternity with Your redeemed to praise You, Jesus the worthy One, both Lord and Christ. Amen.

Week 2—Friday
Take a Look in the Mirror

If we live, we live to the Lord; and if we die, we die to the Lord. Therefore, whether we live or die, we are the Lord's. For to this end Christ died and rose and lived again, that He might be Lord of both the dead and the living.

ROMANS 14:8–9

Our daily routines may be different, but there's one thing that we all do each morning: we look in the mirror. It's important! We want to look our best.

But the truth is that as the day unfolds, the worst often comes out. All of us struggle with selfishness. Making ourselves number one comes naturally to us. What is everyone's favorite subject? Himself! Who is the first person you look for in a photograph? Yourself! Have you ever noticed that the center letter in the word *sin* is the letter *i*? We all have an "I" problem. We are selfish because we are sinful, and that is why we need Jesus.

Back to the mirror. Each morning when we look in the mirror, it's an opportunity to get things right on this new day. Remind yourself before you walk away from the mirror:

> This life is not about me. It's all about Jesus.
> I belong to the Lord. My entire being is centered in Christ.
> I surrender to Jesus so that He may live through me. Today will be an adventure as Christ shines through me!

....

Lord, what a comfort I have in knowing who You are and whose I am. May the days on this earth not be about me; they are all about You, both now and forever. In the name of the Lord Jesus Christ I pray, Amen.

WEEK 2—WEEKEND
Praise the Lord in All Circumstances

O God, You are my God; early will I seek You; my soul thirsts for You; my flesh longs for You in a dry and thirsty land where there is no water. . . . Because Your lovingkindness is better than life, my lips shall praise You. Thus I will bless You while I live; I will lift up my hands in Your name.

PSALM 63:1, 3–4

Psalm 63 is one of the wilderness psalms written by David, the king of Israel, who was likely in the wilderness of Judah while on the run from his son Absalom. The setting for these words of praise was anything but ideal. Absalom had overthrown his father and taken over the kingdom. Yet the homeless king lifted his voice and hands in praise to the Lord.

The word *lovingkindness* beautifully describes the Lord's unfailing love for His people. Even when life is difficult—David was running for his life in the wilderness, Stephen was stoned to death for his faith, Paul was jailed for talking about Jesus—we need to remember God's ultimate faithfulness and remind ourselves of His eternal lovingkindness. The truth is that "we are more than conquerors through Him who loved us. . . . [Nothing] shall be able to separate us from the love of God which is in Christ Jesus our Lord" (Romans 8:37, 39).

We can therefore praise the Lord in all circumstances because His unfailing love will not let us go. Even in the worst of circumstances, we can stand strong in the truth that the Lord's lovingkindness for eternity is better than anything this life offers.

....

Father, I thank You for Your unfailing love. You are deserving of all praise at all times. I praise You today, not just for what You do, but for who You are as my faithful God. I lift my voice and my hands, and I praise Your great name. Amen.

WEEK 3—MONDAY
Love Gives

"God so loved the world that He gave His only begotten Son, that whoever believes in Him should not perish but have everlasting life."

JOHN 3:16

How completely does God love you? He demonstrated the depth of His love in His gift of Jesus, who is the "author and finisher" of your faith (Hebrews 12:2). Jesus perfectly revealed God's heart by living a sinless life on this earth for you and then dying as the atoning sacrifice for your sins.

From the beginning, our holy God knew that we were incapable of living a pure and sinless life, so He sent Jesus to show us the way. Jesus did not hesitate or say no to the Father, and He gave His life so that we could be forgiven for our sins and be given everlasting life with Him, the Holy Spirit, and the Father.

Because of His love for you, God daily blesses you with life. Because of His love for you, Jesus opens the door to eternal life when you name Him your Savior and Lord. So, acting in God's perfect love, reach out to other people who do not know Him. Think of ways you can share His love with the people around you. Take a moment and write down the names of four people you know.

With those four people in mind, pray this prayer:

Father, thank You for revealing Your complete love for me. Show me how to show Your love to these people. Teach me how to express Your love to them through my words and deeds. Bless them as they go about their daily tasks, and draw them to You for comfort and rest. Meet their deepest needs and heal their hidden hurts so that they will know Your love in a very personal and life-changing way. Thank You, Lord. Amen.

TIM DETELLIS, NEW MISSIONS, ORLANDO, FL

Week 3—Tuesday
Love Completely

Jesus said to [the lawyer who asked], "'You shall love the LORD your God with all your heart, with all your soul, and with all your mind.' This is the first and great commandment."

MATTHEW 22:37–38

Human love is often conditional: we love someone on certain terms, perhaps as long as that person does or doesn't do certain things. God, however, loves us unconditionally.

In response, Jesus called us to love God completely. Jesus' description of how to love God encompasses all of our being—heart, soul, and mind:

Heart denotes the seat of one's conscience.

Soul refers to a person's center.

Mind refers to a person's imagination, thoughts, and understanding.

Jesus' instruction is to devote completely the center of our being, our conscience, our lifetime, our thoughts, and our understanding to loving the Lord: to wholly love Him with all that we are.

When you have given your life to the Lord, then your mind has been set; your decision to love has been made. This is the first and greatest commandment.

Pray this prayer: love God completely.

....

Father, I commit—or recommit—my entire being, my lifetime, my thoughts, and my understanding to You from this moment on. Nothing short of the entirety of me will do. If I grow weary or begin to wander, remind me of this commitment by Your Holy Spirit. I pray in Jesus' name, Amen.

Week 3—Wednesday
The Lord of Love

We have known and believed the love that God has for us. God is love, and he who abides in love abides in God, and God in him.

1 John 4:16

Today's verse makes this truth crystal clear: "God is love." This fact is manifest in the life of Jesus, in the beauty of God's creation, in the immensity of the universe, and in the stars in the heavens. From the tiniest flower to the tallest sequoia, God's power is made real for us all.

Another truth in the verse today is that if we abide in love, then we abide in God and He in us. We should let this truth capture our hearts. We live in an often brutal, heartless world where some governments thwart the dreams, if not take the lives, of their citizens. With God abiding in us, though, we can face any situation with courage, we can find the strength to overcome it, and we can choose to love.

We also see in this verse that God abides in us. Here, *abide* means "to dwell within" or "to live within." Therefore, we see that as we abide in God, He abides in us. In other words, He will never leave nor forsake us! We will never be alone.

Today, recognize the Lord of love who dwells within you. Meditate upon His love. Then think about a situation when you felt completely alone, and ask the Lord to help you see where He was during that time.

As you consider God's faithfulness to you, say this prayer:

Father, I am confident in Your promise never to leave me nor forsake me. I am secure in Your love, willing and able to love others, and looking for opportunities to encourage them. Amen.

TIM DETELLIS, NEW MISSIONS, ORLANDO, FL

WEEK 3—THURSDAY
Love and Life

"The Father loves the Son, and shows Him all things that He Himself does; and He will show Him greater works than these, that you may marvel. For as the Father raises the dead and gives life to them, even so the Son gives life to whom He will."

JOHN 5:20–21

The Father enjoys revealing things to us as we draw near to Him. He delights in seeing our eyes widen with excitement as we learn from Him. As we go further into our relationship with Him, we gain an even greater view of the Lord in all His majesty and splendor, glory and power, and love.

Imagine being with Jesus when He spoke the words above. Would you have marveled at hearing that God wants to show you even "greater works"? Would you have considered yourself worthy of this honor?

Jesus said that God raises the dead and gives them life. We all were dead in our sinfulness, but through Christ, we were forgiven and born again. Through Jesus and by God's grace, we receive new life.

Knowing this, do away with any thoughts that you are unworthy. You are God's new creation, and He delights in revealing Himself to you. He pours His life into you daily, and He longs for you to walk through life with Him. Enjoy the day and look forward to what your loving God has for you.

···

Father, help me stay aware of Your presence with me every moment of the day. Keep me attuned to what You want to show me about Yourself, where You want me to walk, and whom You want me to love with Your love. Amen.

Week 3—Friday
Love One Another

"A new commandment I give to you, that you love one another; as I have loved you, that you also love one another. By this all will know that you are My disciples, if you have love for one another."

John 13:34–35

Jesus' commandment to love one another as He loves us is very challenging. Sometimes people are not very lovable, or they do outrageous and malicious things. What about those people? Are we supposed to love them?

Notice that Jesus does not specify whom we are supposed to love. Instead, He issued the broad command to "love one another." In order to obey this commandment, we must love indiscriminately just as Jesus loves. We are to love the people He puts in our family, our neighborhood, our church, our workplace, and our lives.

God can help us love when we ask Him to enable us to see past people's attitudes or behaviors, to see people as God sees them. In response to this prayer, God can make it much easier for us to love people through our prayers, actions, and words. After all, we have been commanded to love and not to judge other people.

Examine yourself. Are you showing love to others? Are you at the point where you can pray for people whom others have judged or shunned? With one of them in mind, pray this prayer:

Jesus, I ask for Your help in praying for this person. I know that You love him or her, so I need to love him or her as well. Open my eyes to see the person as You do. Also open my eyes to see You, Jesus, and open my heart to receive Your love so I may share it with others. In Jesus' name, Amen.

Week 3—Weekend
Surrender to Love

"As the Father loved Me, I also have loved you; abide in My love. If you keep My commandments, you will abide in My love, just as I have kept My Father's commandments and abide in His love. These things I have spoken to you, that My joy may remain in you, and that your joy may be full. This is My commandment, that you love one another as I have loved you."

John 15:9–12

Jesus invites us to abide in His love. To do so, however, we must surrender to Him as our Lord. While this may sound frightening to some people, the truth is that as we surrender ourselves more and more to Jesus as our Lord, we become more alive than we ever thought possible.

We find abundant life in Christ and only in Christ (John 10:10) but only if we surrender to Him. For many of us, however, surrender is difficult. We have always fought to win, own, or control things, and we like being in charge of our lives. Nevertheless, Jesus wants us to surrender to Him.

What is holding you back? What battle scars can you point to that reinforce your resolve to keep fighting? Tired warrior, it is time to surrender to Jesus. Let yourself learn to rely on His strength, His wisdom, and His guidance. Come now to Him and cast your burdens upon Him. Doing so will free you to live the way God truly created you to live.

Pray this prayer:

Lord Jesus, I come to You weary and ready to surrender myself to You. I want to abide in Your love and drink from Your fountain of life. Receive me, Lord. I am Yours. Amen.

Week 4—Monday
The Pursuit of Peace

Let us pursue the things which make for peace and the things by which one may edify another.

Romans 14:19

On the night before Jesus died, He promised to leave His disciples a wonderful gift. It was the gift of peace. But it was not just any kind of peace, and it was not available from lots of different sources. Jesus said, "My peace I give unto you: not as the world giveth" (John 14:27 KJV). This peace comes only from our Savior and Lord, and it is not at all like the peace this world offers. The peace the world promises is, at best, temporary and, at worst, empty and unfulfilling. The peace Jesus promises is lasting and meaningful.

In our text for today, the apostle Paul reminds us that peace is not only a gift that believers receive, but it is something we must pursue. Paul exhorted us to pursue "the things which make for peace." Far too many people in too many churches pursue their own desires and push their own agendas. The church is not a place for us to work toward getting our individual wills accomplished, but rather a place where God's will is to be done.

The things we pursue must not be divisive, but instead be things that are unquestionably in the will of God. Our personal preferences are not always based on biblical revelation or the promptings of the Holy Spirit. Often our individual biases have nothing to do with honoring the Lord. So let us not waste opportunities for peace by pursuing things that do not matter.

....

Father, give me discernment that I may pursue the things of peace and not the things that satisfy my own desires or preferences. Help me understand that I am to build up others and not tear them down. In Jesus' name, Amen.

DR. ROBERT PITMAN, BOB PITMAN MINISTRIES, MUSCLE SHOALS, AL

WEEK 4—TUESDAY
Peace Under Pressure

"These things I have spoken to you, that in Me you may have peace. In the world you will have tribulation; but be of good cheer, I have overcome the world."

JOHN 16:33

Years ago when I was visiting an unsaved couple in their home, I noticed a large silver tray on the mantle. When I commented on the tray, the lady of the house informed me that the tray was the god of their home. I discovered that these people were part of a shrine cult and that the silver tray was actually the god they worshipped.

I asked her, "Where are your god's eyes?" She replied, "It doesn't have any." When I inquired about the god's ears and mouth, her reply was the same. As I looked at that piece of metal, I thanked God for a Savior who can see, hear, and speak.

In today's text, Jesus spoke about the peace that He has promised. First, He reminded us that it is an *available* peace. He said, "[In] Me you may have peace." Jesus made a promise. This peace is real, and it is available to us through Him.

Second, Jesus told us that His is an *encouraging* peace. He instructed us to "be of good cheer," to be encouraged. We are to be strong in the Lord.

Finally, Jesus told us that His peace is an *overcoming* peace. This world is a place of tribulation, which means loss, disappointment, pain, and pressure. The world constantly tries to press us into its mold. This world wants us to think like it thinks, believe like it believes, and behave like it behaves. But Jesus has overcome this world, and through Him we are victors in the midst of tribulation, not victims of circumstance.

....

Father, thank You for the available, encouraging, and overcoming peace that Jesus has given me. In His precious name, Amen.

WEEK 4—WEDNESDAY
Peace with God

Having been justified by faith, we have peace with God through our Lord Jesus Christ, through whom also we have access by faith into this grace in which we stand, and rejoice in hope of the glory of God.

ROMANS 5:1–2

The Bible teaches that enmity exists between God and unrepentant sinners. Man in his unsaved condition is an enemy of God and at war with Him. But salvation changes that. In Ephesians 2:16, Paul informed us that the enmity between God and man was put to death through the reconciling death of Christ on the cross. As a result of having been justified through our faith that Jesus' death paid for our sins, we now have peace with God.

Now that we have peace with God, two wonderful truths have become realities in our lives. First, we have *access* to God and His grace. When we were lost in our sin, we were separated from our holy God and had no access to Him. But Jesus "made peace through the blood of His cross" (Colossians 1:20). That means Jesus has made possible a relationship between God and man. On the cross Jesus took the hand of God in one hand and the hand of mankind in the other and joined them together. We are no longer strangers to God. We are His children, and He welcomes us into His presence.

Second, because we have peace with God, we have *hope* of future glory. As lost sinners, we were without hope but no longer. We have hope that God is with us in the present and that we will live with Him for eternity. Rejoice in the hope you have in Christ!

....

Father, thank You that we are not enemies but friends. Thank You for the peace You have given to me through Christ. In Jesus' name, Amen.

DR. ROBERT PITMAN, BOB PITMAN MINISTRIES, MUSCLE SHOALS, AL

WEEK 4—THURSDAY
Living in Peace

Finally, brethren, farewell. Become complete. Be of good comfort, be of one mind, live in peace; and the God of love and peace will be with you.

2 CORINTHIANS 13:11

In today's passage, Paul was not writing to the world at large. He was writing to the church at Corinth, and that church was a divided church. The believers were disagreeing about preachers: some liked Paul, some Peter, some Apollos, and some did not like preachers at all (1 Corinthians 3). The Corinthian believers were also divided over how to handle immorality in the church. A man in the church was having an affair with his father's wife (1 Corinthians 5:1). Apparently, some in the church wanted to ignore it; no one seemed to want to confront it. The Corinthian believers were also divided over spiritual gifts, arguing about which gift was the greatest (1 Corinthians 13).

As Paul wrote his final letter to this church, he exhorted them to live in peace. Nothing hinders the cause of Christ more than contention within the church. When there is fussing and fighting in the church, God weeps, Satan laughs, saints are discouraged, and sinners are perplexed. God is a God of love and peace, and we should be people of love and peace.

Paul exhorted the believers to do three things in order to live peaceably. First, they must repair broken relationships. "Become complete" could be read as a picture of a mended fishing net that had been torn. If Christians are to be fishers of men, they must be united. Second, they must listen to godly counsel. Third, they must lay aside their differences and seek to "be of one mind."

....

Father, give me a heart that loves others and seeks to live in peace. In Jesus' name, Amen.

Week 4—Friday
Jesus, Our Peace

In Christ Jesus you who once were far off have been brought near by the blood of Christ. For He Himself is our peace, who has made both one, and has broken down the middle wall of separation.

EPHESIANS 2:13–14

In the ancient world the hatred that existed between Jews and Gentiles was very real. Human history has been plagued by such racial strife from the beginning, and it remains an issue today.

Education is a good thing, but it has not eliminated racism. Legislation can make laws, but it cannot eradicate racial strife. Even religion cannot stop the animosity that exists between the races. Is there any hope? Can different races worship God together, serve Him together, and love one another? The answer is yes!

In our text for today, Paul reminds us that Jesus is both our Peacemaker and our Peace. Through His blood Jesus brought us near to God and near to one another. Jesus destroyed the walls that separate us in our sinfulness from God and from one another: Jesus made us one. All Christians have "one Lord, one faith, one baptism, one God and Father" (Ephesians 4:5–6).

So how can we live out that truth? We can ask Jesus to live in our hearts and to fill us with His love and power. It isn't difficult for Jesus to love people of all races and all backgrounds. If we let Him live through us, our lives become a channel through which His loves flows to others. And more of Jesus' love will mean more of His peace!

....

Jesus, help me to be a channel of peace to others. In Jesus' name I pray, Amen.

DR. ROBERT PITMAN, BOB PITMAN MINISTRIES, MUSCLE SHOALS, AL

Week 4—Weekend
The Prince of Peace

For unto us a Child is born, unto us a Son is given; and the government will be upon His shoulder. And His name will be called Wonderful, Counselor, Mighty God, Everlasting Father, Prince of Peace. Of the increase of His government and peace there will be no end, upon the throne of David and over His kingdom, to order it and establish it with judgment and justice.

ISAIAH 9:6–7

Approximately seven hundred years before Jesus was born, Isaiah wrote about His birth, life, death, and resurrection. The prophet also spoke of Christ's earthly ministry and the eternal nature of His reign.

In today's passage, Isaiah announced the coming of the Messiah and declared that He would be called the "Prince of Peace." What a wonderful thought! Jesus Christ is the Prince who brings peace, and His kingdom is characterized by peace. This Prince is not a tyrant, but a benevolent ruler. He does not hate; He loves. He does not manipulate; He guides. He does not take; He gives. He does not oppress; He encourages. He is the Prince of Peace!

We enter Jesus' kingdom when His kingdom enters us. Once we become a part of His kingdom, we are never out of it again. It begins while we are on earth, and it will last eternally in heaven. Initially, Jesus' kingdom is internal: we can know peace with God who has forgiven our sins, and we can know the peace that "passeth all understanding" in our hearts (Philippians 4:7 KJV). In heaven, peace will be obvious in many ways. Here, for instance, we experience war, sickness, pain, sorrow, and death—and we will never experience any of these things in heaven. Jesus' eternal kingdom is a kingdom of peace!

....

Father, thank You for bringing me into Your kingdom of peace through Your Son, the Prince of Peace. In Jesus' name, Amen.

WEEK 5—MONDAY
Forgiven, Redeemed, and Reborn

[God the Father] has delivered us from the power of darkness and conveyed us into the kingdom of the Son of His love, in whom we have redemption through His blood, the forgiveness of sins.

COLOSSIANS 1:13–14

Did you hear that? In Jesus "we have redemption through His blood, the forgiveness of sins." Paul used this phrase when writing to the church in Colossae. It was a phrase worth emphasizing for the believers long ago, and it's a phrase worth reinforcing in our minds today.

If we are in Christ, we have redemption from the consequences of our sins through His blood. Our sinful state, our deadness apart from Christ, has been given new breath. We have been born again to a new life and a new destiny.

If we are in Christ, our sins are forgiven! Our mistakes and failures are no longer counted against us. We have received a pardon we could not have earned. Not only do we have redemption and forgiveness, not only are we righteous before the Father, but we have been delivered from the power of darkness. By the power of the Holy Spirit within us, we have the ability not to continue in our sins.

Remember when Jesus forgave the adulterous woman brought before Him in John 8:1–12? After forgiving her, He told her to go and sin no more. If we are in Christ, sin no longer has ultimate power over us.

So be encouraged today! You are a new creation. God's mercies are new every day. You have redemption through Jesus' blood, the forgiveness of your sins. The power of darkness will not prevail in your life!

....

Father, help me know the fullness of Your love and grace. Help me to live daily in the victory, forgiveness, and redemption You give. In Jesus' name, Amen.

DR. GRANT ETHRIDGE, LIBERTY BAPTIST CHURCH, HAMPTON, VA

WEEK 5—TUESDAY
Choosing to Forgive

"Whenever you stand praying, if you have anything against anyone, forgive him, that your Father in heaven may also forgive you your trespasses. But if you do not forgive, neither will your Father in heaven forgive your trespasses."

MARK 11:25–26

Forgiving others is difficult. When we've been hurt deeply, we can find it very challenging to extend grace. However, in today's passage, we learn that if we do not forgive others, the Father will not forgive us.

Extending forgiveness may seem impossible at times, and we may feel completely unable to forgive. But know that God is not asking us to do anything He hasn't done. Jesus was betrayed, His friends abandoned Him, He was spit on and physically abused, and . . . He forgave.

On the cross, as He was being crucified, Jesus prayed, "Father, forgive them" (Luke 23:34). At his stoning, Stephen followed Jesus' example (Acts 7:60). Forgiveness is the responsibility of all believers.

And forgiveness is simply supernatural. When our hearts are broken, it can be difficult to offer mercy to the ones who hurt us. With Christ in us, we can find the power to forgive. Christ, the ultimate Forgiver, lives in us, and His Holy Spirit is at work within us.

If you are struggling to forgive someone, tell the Lord. Ask Him to help you; ask Him to work in your heart. He is faithful. It may be a process, but He will empower you. He will work in you and enable you to choose to forgive.

. . . .

Father, thank You for Your forgiveness. Thank You for Jesus and His example of forgiving others. May Your Holy Spirit work in me and help me forgive those who have sinned against me. In Jesus' name, Amen.

WEEK 5—WEDNESDAY
Walking in Forgiveness

In [Jesus] we have redemption through His blood, the forgiveness of sins, according to the riches of His grace which He made to abound toward us in all wisdom and prudence, having made known to us the mystery of His will, according to His good pleasure which He purposed in Himself.

EPHESIANS 1:7–9

A few days ago we looked at the phrase "in Him we have redemption through His blood, the forgiveness of sins." *Redemption* means "to purchase, to release, to repay, to reconcile, to adopt, to vindicate."

Notice words from this passage: "according to the riches of His grace." The apostle Paul did not just say "grace," but "the riches of His grace." God's grace is rich, multifaceted, and as we then read, "abound[ing] toward us." Abounding! In Ephesians 3:8, Paul reminded us of the unsearchable riches of God's grace and glory that He makes known to us "according to His good pleasure."

Acting on His rich and abundant grace, Jesus is pleased to forgive us and redeem us. And these gifts of forgiveness and redemption cost Jesus His blood, His life. Jesus paid the price for our sinfulness, and He purchased us—He redeemed us—from our bondage to sin and death. We please Him, our King, when we walk in the redemption and forgiveness that He offers us.

Your forgiveness of the people who hurt or betray you may not change them, but it will change you! It will not change your past, but it will change your future. May we ask for Jesus' forgiveness, receive it, extend our forgiveness to others, and live as people who have been redeemed!

....

Lord Jesus, thank You for shedding Your blood for me. Help me to walk daily in the forgiveness and redemption You purchased for me. Amen.

DR. GRANT ETHRIDGE, LIBERTY BAPTIST CHURCH, HAMPTON, VA

Week 5—Thursday
Faithful to Forgive

If we confess our sins, He is faithful and just to forgive us our sins and to cleanse us from all unrighteousness.

1 JOHN 1:9

Do you remember if-then statements from school? Let's review. The first part of the statement is conditional: it may or may not happen. But if that condition does happen, whatever is described in the second half of the statement will happen.

Like these if-then statements, mathematical formulas are black and white; there is no gray. Two plus two does not equal four*ish*. It equals four. Three minus one does not equal generally somewhere close to two. It equals two.

Look again at today's passage, a most profound if-then statement: "If we confess our sins, He is faithful and just to forgive our sins and to cleanse us from all unrighteousness." Notice that the statement doesn't say God might be faithful or there's a possibility He will be faithful. It says God *is* faithful. There is never gray area.

Also, sins are not qualified as big sins or little sins—which, after all, is a human construction. This promise simply says "sins," meaning *all* sins. God is faithful and just to forgive all sins if we confess. Whether or not we feel forgiven, whether or not we've forgiven ourselves, if we truly confess our sins as sins before the Lord, He forgives them.

Don't cover your sins. Confess! What guilt or regret are you dwelling on or reliving today? If you've confessed it, God has forgiven it. "There is therefore now no condemnation for those who are in Christ Jesus" (Romans 8:1).

....

Father, thank You for Your forgiveness. Help me to forgive myself as You forgive me. In Jesus' name, Amen.

Week 5—Friday
Forgive as Jesus Forgives

[Bear] with one another, and [forgive] one another, if anyone has a complaint against another; even as Christ forgave you, so you also must do.

COLOSSIANS 3:12–13

Forgiveness is one of the greatest gifts we can ever receive. And being a gift, forgiveness is completely undeserved and unearned. No matter how hard we might work for it, the person we hurt or betray has to choose to give it to us. Then, when that person does forgive us, the act is a great expression of love.

In today's verse, Paul was telling the believers at Colossae how to live as God's chosen people. He listed virtues the believers should possess—compassion, kindness, humility, etc. He then told them to "[bear] with one another, and [forgive] one another" as Christ has forgiven them. Paul followed that thought by saying that love binds all of these virtues together.

One of the most God-honoring acts we can do is to forgive one another. When we forgive, we are doing for others what God has done for us. God's forgiveness of us is a profound demonstration of His love for us, and when we forgive others, the act is a profound demonstration of our love. The second greatest commandment is to love our neighbor, and our forgiveness of someone is an expression of love for that person. Granted, the person we forgive may not care or even know about our forgiveness, but we will know. And Jesus will know.

By God's grace, we have been forgiven of much, and by His grace He enables us to forgive much. May we remember all that Jesus has done for us and reflect that in the way we respond to and forgive others.

Father, help me to forgive those who have wronged me. Thank You for constantly forgiving me when I wrong You. Amen.

DR. GRANT ETHRIDGE, LIBERTY BAPTIST CHURCH, HAMPTON, VA

Week 5—Weekend
A New You

If anyone is in Christ, he is a new creation; old things have passed away; behold, all things have become new.

2 Corinthians 5:17

Have you ever mended an old, worn-out, but much-loved quilt your grandma made? Not long after one repair, the quilt gets a new hole, and you stitch it again . . . and then you stitch the next hole that appears . . . and the next. . . . Soon the quilt is a hodgepodge of patches reflecting all the brokenness and all the repair work done over the years.

We often do the same thing with our lives. We patch over our mistakes, trying to make it look like they didn't happen—and we resolve to try harder to change our ways. Well, the items we continually repair will eventually give out, and so will our efforts to please God with our own strength. It's not possible!

Praise God for His different approach to repairs! God doesn't just cover up our mistakes and make do with our broken parts. He makes us new! He completely changes us from the inside out.

Caterpillars are born as worms, but they are reborn as butterflies. Pinning wings on worms will never make them butterflies. In like manner, the change we need is not to reform on the outside, but redemption on the inside.

In fact, God is able to keep us from falling, and one day He will "present [us] faultless before the presence of His glory with exceeding joy" (Jude v. 24)! Like a father presenting his daughter faultless and pure to her groom, Jesus will present us—not as a hodgepodge of fixes, but as faultless—to the Father. In Christ, "behold, all things have become new."

....

Father, thank You that my old self has passed away and that You make me new daily. Amen.

WEEK 6—MONDAY
The Two Sides of Salvation

The righteousness of God apart from the law is revealed, being witnessed by the Law and the Prophets, even the righteousness of God, through faith in Jesus Christ, to all and on all who believe. For there is no difference; for all have sinned and fall short of the glory of God.

ROMANS 3:21–23

Salvation. The mention of God's gracious intervention on our behalf strikes a chord of gratitude and humility among the faithful. Yet, all too often, our focus rests only on *half* of the sacrificial work that enables us to be born again. Certainly, Jesus died on the cross, substituting Himself for us and taking the punishment for our sins. We celebrate—and rightfully so—the joy of knowing that even though we fall short of God's holy standards, our sins are forgiven. This, however, is only half of the gospel.

Jesus not only removed our guilt, but He also imparted His innocence to us. Our salvation is possible because God takes our sins from us *and* He gives His righteousness to us. In other words, to have faith in Jesus Christ is to stand in righteousness before God. Because of our Savior, our behavior is to be an expression of the righteousness we already possess rather than a means to obtain it.

Do you feel like you cannot live the Christian life? Jesus lived it for you. Are you concerned about those sins that repeatedly entice you? Jesus overcame them. Grace is evident in what God did through Jesus on the cross and in what He continues to do for us, empowering us to be His light and love in this dark and hurting world.

Father, thank You for taking my sins away and for giving me the perfect righteousness of Jesus. Help me become the person You have already declared me to be because of the cross. I yield my life to You today. Amen.

DR. ADAM DOOLEY, SUNNYVALE FIRST BAPTIST CHURCH, SUNNYVALE, TX

WEEK 6—TUESDAY
Seeking God's Righteousness

"Seek first the kingdom of God and His righteousness, and all these things shall be added to you. Therefore do not worry about tomorrow, for tomorrow will worry about its own things. Sufficient for the day is its own trouble."

MATTHEW 6:33–34

Frequent travelers understand the devastation fog sometimes causes on runways, highways, and shorelines. But few people realize that only a small glass of water can create enough fog to cover an entire acre. Similarly, a minimal amount of worry can wreak immense havoc in our lives. Just as thick fog can stop travelers in their tracks, heavy worry can paralyze us with the fear of "what if." Perhaps this is why Jesus spent so much time in the Sermon on the Mount addressing our anxieties.

And what is Jesus' antidote to worry? Trusting God enough to seek His kingdom in all areas of our lives, knowing He will provide for every need we have. When Jesus referred to "these things" being "added" to our lives, He was alluding to His previous statements about food, water, and clothing (6:24–32). Our concern about basics like these is an insult to the loving Father who willingly provides all that His children need.

The issue in verses 33–34 is one of lordship, not provision. Unbelievers seek to provide for themselves (6:32) because they don't view God as a Father who cares for them. Finding security in wealth is not, however, an option for those who belong to Christ (6:24) because they choose not to put their hope in God Himself, rather than in what He gives.

....

Father, forgive me for allowing fear to diminish my trust in You. Increase my faith by enabling me to focus less on life's necessities and more on life's purpose. Help me to live for Your kingdom without distraction or fear. Amen.

WEEK 6—WEDNESDAY
The Power of One

If by the one man's offense death reigned through the one, much more those who receive abundance of grace and of the gift of righteousness will reign in life through the One, Jesus Christ.

ROMANS 5:17

Understanding the magnitude of redemption is impossible apart from the back story of Eden. In the garden, Adam and Eve chose to rebel against God, and the drama of salvation—the divine plan to reclaim what was lost—began. Thus in Romans 5, the apostle Paul identified Jesus as the Second Adam who functions perfectly within the boundaries that God desired for the first man. "Death reigned through the one" refers to the fatal fall and subsequent curse Adam received and passed on to the entire human race. Because of the notorious impact of our oldest ancestor, we are born with a sinful nature, and we naturally rebel against God, ensuring our condemnation.

Juxtaposed against this painful reality, however, is the saving impact of Jesus Christ. One man's sin did result in our death, and by God's grace one Man's righteousness gives us life. If we remain in Adam, damnation awaits. But if we stand in the righteousness of Jesus Christ, salvation and eternal life are ours. Those who receive Jesus' "abundance of grace" and "the gift of righteousness" inherit a new nature and no longer live under Adam's curse. Adam rebelled; Jesus restores. In Adam there is a second death after the grave; in Jesus there is a second birth after we recognize our need for a Savior. Because of Adam's rebellion, our dominion over creation is lost, but through Jesus Christ we will one day reign over creation for the glory of our eternal King!

....

God, help me to lead others to the righteousness that is found through Your Son. In Jesus' name, Amen.

DR. ADAM DOOLEY, SUNNYVALE FIRST BAPTIST CHURCH, SUNNYVALE, TX

WEEK 6—THURSDAY
No Exceptions

Peter opened his mouth and said: "In truth I perceive that God shows no partiality. But in every nation whoever fears Him and works righteousness is accepted by Him. The word which God sent to the children of Israel, preaching peace through Jesus Christ— He is Lord of all."

ACTS 10:34–36

No *exceptions.* Those two words are sometimes painful and isolating. No ticket, no entry. No money, no food. No degree, no job. No pedigree, no accolades. The exclusivity of these claims allows for no exceptions. Ironclad realities with fixed results are not always negative, though. Every person who calls on the name of the Lord will be saved (Romans 10:13). No exceptions. God loves all people (John 3:16). No exceptions. The gospel is for everyone (Romans 10:12). No exceptions. But God's people didn't always realize this truth.

After meeting Cornelius and a large group of Gentiles, the apostle Peter broadened the reach of the gospel beyond the Jewish people. In every nation, God will save those who fear Him and live for Him. The gospel reveals that God shows no partiality among the people of the earth, regardless of skin color, nationality, education, income level, or location. No one is beyond the reach of His grace. All categories of people—without exception—will be present before the throne of God in eternity (Revelation 5:9).

Have you given up on someone who needs to be saved? Or do you wonder if God can change certain "kinds" of people? Do you harbor any racial, social, or economic hatred toward any particular group? God does not show partiality—and neither should we.

....

Thank You, Lord, that Your grace has no boundaries. I worship You for saving me. Use me to lead others to Christ by sharing Your gospel. Amen.

Week 6—Friday
The Surprising Key to Spiritual Growth

Do not present your members as instruments of unrighteousness to sin, but present yourselves to God as being alive from the dead, and your members as instruments of righteousness to God. For sin shall not have dominion over you, for you are not under law but under grace.

ROMANS 6:13–14

The key to life is death. Because Jesus died *for* sin, we must be willing to die *to* sin and follow Him.

Eternal life is more than overcoming death after our earthly lives end; eternal life is walking in Jesus' resurrected power now. The apostle Paul argued that we should die to the wicked tyrant of sin that seeks to control us through unholy desires and temptations. We must so identify with the death and resurrection of Christ that sin loses its power in us and our bodies ("members") become "instruments" for doing good rather than evil.

The presence of this warning reveals three realities about sanctification. First, the battle against sin does not end after a person is saved. Despite some claims to the contrary, moral perfection is impossible until we enter heaven. Left unchecked, sinful impulses will wreak havoc in our lives. Second, the fight against sin is a sign of maturity, not weakness. Growing Christians will actively identify and war against threats to their walks with God. Last, the grace of God is our weapon to overcome sin rather than to excuse it or justify it (Romans 6:15). As God changes our hearts, His grace compels us to live for righteousness rather than wickedness.

....

Father, transform me by Your grace. Sanctify my heart, mind, hands, and feet so that I can live a holy life. Empower me to live victoriously over the temptations that I encounter. In Jesus' name, Amen.

DR. ADAM DOOLEY, SUNNYVALE FIRST BAPTIST CHURCH, SUNNYVALE, TX

Week 6—Weekend
No Greater Glory

But of Him you are in Christ Jesus, who became for us wisdom from God—and
righteousness and sanctification and redemption—that, as it is written, "He who
glories, let him glory in the Lord."

1 CORINTHIANS 1:30–31

Christ crucified. These words prompt thoughts of sacrifice and forgiveness. Rarely, however, do we consider the cross of Jesus the "wisdom of God." Yet after describing the gospel as a stumbling block to some and foolishness to others (1:23), the apostle Paul went on to explain God's insistence that no person boast before Him (1:29). In fact, God chose to save sinners in such a way that all glory belongs to Him. The cross mocks human ideas by boldly declaring that God's wisdom will not bow to human standards of approval.

Thus the wisdom that Christ embodies manifests itself as God's plan for our "righteousness and sanctification and redemption." Apart from the cross, we stand in filthy rags rather than true righteousness. Without the crucifixion, sanctification is more akin to theological fiction than practical reality. If not for the Son's obedient sacrifice, redemption would be nothing more than wishful thinking. Despite our insistence that people are generally good and that a loving God sends no one to hell, Christ crucified shames the wise and nullifies the things we perceive to be true (1:25, 28). Man's wisdom is shattered by the rocks of God's sovereign determination that "He who glories" must "glory in the Lord." This is the wisdom of God. Embrace it, celebrate it, rest in it—and do not dare reject it.

....

Father, thank You for opening my eyes to real wisdom. I am once again awed by
Your sacrificial love and grace-filled plan for my salvation. Help me develop a
greater passion for Your glory rather than for my own. Amen.

Week 7—Monday

Faithful Focus

Blessed be the LORD my Rock, who trains my hands for war, and my fingers for battle—My lovingkindness and my fortress, my high tower and my deliverer, my shield and the One in whom I take refuge, who subdues my people under me.

PSALM 144:1–2

Life is a battle. A constant battle. And many of you reading these words are undoubtedly engaged in various battles that have you feeling fragmented and fatigued. The battles of life are difficult because—among other reasons—they are multifaceted and no two are exactly the same. We fight battles, for our families, for our fitness, for our finances, and even for our faith.

Psalm 144:1–2 teaches us that although the battles we fight are unpredictable and come from various arenas of life, the solution to overcoming them is the same. Regardless of the battles in which we find ourselves, the solution involves a steady focus on and deliberate devotion to God.

On the cross, Christ delivered us from the biggest battle any of us will ever face: the battle against sin. Jesus' victory on the cross proves that He is willing to fight on our behalf to overcome the attack of the enemy. If we find ourselves overwhelmed by the battles we are facing, we should fix our focus on Christ and be encouraged by His ability to deliver us!

....

Heavenly Father, thank You for not leaving me alone in this world to fight my battles with my own strength. Thank You for reminding me through Your Word that You are my Deliverer. When I fail to focus my attention on You, nudge me with the words of this psalm, for in You alone do I have deliverance. Amen.

DR. JAMES MERRITT, CROSS POINTE CHURCH, DULUTH, GA

WEEK 7—TUESDAY
Credible Credentials

"The Spirit of the LORD is upon Me, because He has anointed Me to preach the gospel to the poor; He has sent Me to heal the brokenhearted, to proclaim liberty to the captives and recovery of sight to the blind, to set at liberty those who are oppressed."

LUKE 4:18

Throughout our lives each of us will probably hold several jobs. Each of these jobs will come with a detailed description of responsibilities that we will do our best to fulfill.

In Luke 4, when Jesus picked up the scroll and read from Isaiah 61, He was reading a job description that only He had the ability to fulfill. One word summarizes the job Jesus was to fulfill: *Deliverer*.

Unfortunately, while Jesus offers to anyone and everyone deliverance from sinful, self-centered ways into a Spirit-guided life, not all will be delivered. What separates those who will be delivered by Jesus from those who will not? One simple word: *belief*. Jesus read His job description in the presence of His hometown crowd, but the people would not listen to Him. They refused to believe that Jesus had the power to do what He said—through Isaiah's words—He had come to do.

Jesus has the power to deliver us, but like the people of Nazareth, our unbelief can prevent our deliverance. When we find the toxic thoughts of unbelief creeping into our minds, we must remember that Jesus, who delivered us from our sins, can deliver us from unbelief as well.

....

Lord, when I allow doubt and unbelief to creep into my mind, help me to remember that You have the power to deliver me. Forgive me for my sin of unbelief and allow me to trust that Your mighty hand is at work in my life. Amen.

Week 7—Wednesday
A Collector's Item

The LORD is my rock and my fortress and my deliverer; my God, my strength, in whom I will trust; my shield and the horn of my salvation, my stronghold.

PSALM 18:2

Collectors of classic cars are adamant: they want to purchase vehicles that have original parts. But it's rare to find an old car with original parts that have maintained their usefulness despite the wear and tear of the elements and time. No wonder the most valuable classic cars are those that have survived it all. Weathering the hard times increases a car's value.

Like classic cars, the Christian life gains value when it withstands the harsh elements of this world. We overcome those challenges, however, not because of our own strength, but because God protects us. The writer of Psalm 18 understood this. He believed that when life was hard, God would see him through. God doesn't always deliver us immediately from tough times, but we can trust that He is with us and that He will preserve and protect us. Uncomfortable—even devastating—situations can strengthen our dependence on God.

The apostle Peter also trusted God to bring good out of tough times. Like gold that is tested and purified by fire, our faith in God is tested and purified by the fiery trials of life. And that purified faith brings Jesus praise, honor, and glory (1 Peter 1:6–8).

Father, thank You for watching over me through life's hard times. Although I would choose deliverance, I am grateful that You use challenges and pain to deepen my dependence on You. When I find myself ready to give up, be my strength and my hope. Amen.

DR. JAMES MERRITT, CROSS POINTE CHURCH, DULUTH, GA

WEEK 7—THURSDAY
1st-Round Draft Pick

Let all those who seek You rejoice and be glad in You; let such as love Your salvation say continually, "The LORD be magnified!" But I am poor and needy; yet the LORD thinks upon me. You are my help and my deliverer; do not delay, O my God.

PSALM 40:16–17

Being picked first in the National Football League draft is one of the greatest honors a young football player can receive. Each year only one person can claim that he is the first pick. It is definitely an elite club.

The team that holds the first pick in the draft wants the player who will bring the most to the team. So that team evaluates the player's past performance on the field and interviews as many people related to the player as possible. Weaknesses in character as well as weaknesses in one's game can derail a team. If a player measures up, however, he is then selected as the number-one pick in that year's NFL draft.

Unlike a player selected as the first-overall pick in the draft, the writer of Psalm 40 had no credentials that made him worthy to be selected and delivered by God; however, God mercifully chose to help him who is "poor and needy."

I am eternally grateful that God selects us not based on our merit, but because of His mercy. Indeed, we are all His number-one picks!

....

Father, thank You for choosing to help me and to deliver me even though I am unworthy of the honor. Use me to be Your light in this world and to bring You glory. Amen.

WEEK 7—FRIDAY
Pardon Me

Then I heard a loud voice saying in heaven, "Now salvation, and strength, and the kingdom of our God, and the power of His Christ have come, for the accuser of our brethren, who accused them before our God day and night, has been cast down. And they overcame him by the blood of the Lamb and by the word of their testimony, and they did not love their lives to the death."

REVELATION 12:10–11

In the spring of 2015, a man by the name of Anthony Ray Hinton was released from prison after spending thirty years on death row. Hinton was released because it was discovered that he had been falsely accused and wrongly convicted of committing two murders. The psychological, physical, and emotional toll experienced by Hinton—thirty years of his life stolen from him—is unfathomable.

Hinton was innocent of the crime he had spent thirty years behind bars for, but you and I are 100 percent guilty of the sins for which Jesus took the punishment. Even though we are forgiven, John told us in Revelation 12 that Satan constantly accuses us of wrongdoing. But unlike those who accused Hinton, Satan's accusations are often accurate.

Yet we have one unshakable bit of evidence to present our accuser, and that is the fact that Jesus paid the full penalty for our sins on the cross. The great news of the gospel is that the blood of Jesus delivers us from the punishment we rightfully deserve! What Satan rightfully accuses, God graciously excuses through Jesus' sacrificial death on our behalf!

....

Heavenly Father, thank You for pardoning me and taking on the punishment for my wrongdoings. May I always praise You. Amen.

DR. JAMES MERRITT, CROSS POINTE CHURCH, DULUTH, GA

WEEK 7—WEEKEND
All-Knowing

Oh, the depth of the riches both of the wisdom and knowledge of God! How unsearchable are His judgments and His ways past finding out! "For who has known the mind of the Lord? Or who has become His counselor?" Or who has first given to Him and it shall be repaid to him?" For of Him and through Him and to Him are all things, to whom be glory forever. Amen.

ROMANS 11:33–36

In 2004, *Jeopardy* contestant Ken Jennings went on the longest win streak in the history of the iconic American game show. Jennings won seventy-four games in a row, garnering the attention of the American public. During his win streak, Jennings seemed to have an answer for any question asked. Viewers as well as competitors were mystified and awed by his vast range of knowledge.

Jennings' win streak and the breadth of his knowledge amazed people, but that wide-ranging knowledge shrinks in comparison to the mind of God. While the world was understandably impressed by what Jennings accomplished, all of us who have been delivered by Christ should be far more impressed by what God has accomplished through Jesus on our behalf. We should respond in ecstatic worship of God, thanking Him for His grace.

In Romans 11:33–36, we find a beautiful passage, praising God for His eternal and gracious plan to deliver both Jews and Gentiles from the consequences of their sins. Paul praised God for His plan to deliver all of humanity from bondage to sin and death. Of all of the accomplishments in history, God's deliverance of human beings from their sinful natures and the consequences of their sins stands as the ultimate peace prize.

Father, may I never stop praising You for Your goodness and grace. Amen.

Week 8—Monday
Already Rich

Let a man so consider us, as servants of Christ and stewards of the mysteries of God. You are already full! You are already rich! You have reigned as kings without us—and indeed I could wish you did reign, that we also might reign with you! For I think that God has displayed us, the apostles, last, as men condemned to death; for we have been made a spectacle to the world, both to angels and to men.

1 CORINTHIANS 4:1, 8–9

I recently had the opportunity to travel internationally. I was away from my family for quite some time. As you can imagine, I was overjoyed to see my wife and five children when I returned home. To my great pleasure, they were happy to see me as well.

Before I could make it all the way down the driveway, the older children jumped off the porch and ran to my truck. They all piled in the truck and rode with me the rest of the way—100 feet—to the carport. The little ones squealed with joy, "Daddy! Daddy! Daddy!" while they hugged and kissed me. It was a wonderful scene. I wish I had it all on video.

I had purchased a small souvenir for each of my children during my travels. But I didn't give them their presents that evening. I passed them out the next day. Why? Because that night, it was clear to me that having their father home was what they wanted most. In that moment, I knew how rich I was, how full I was. Not only am I a steward of the Word, but God has also blessed me with a wonderful, loving family who loves me as much as I love them.

What makes you rich? What makes you full?

....

Dear God, help me to see that I am abundantly blessed by You and that I am already rich with Your love, grace, and mercy. Amen.

DR. JIM PERDUE, SECOND BAPTIST CHURCH, WARNER ROBINS, GA

WEEK 8—TUESDAY
God Is Faithful

God is faithful, by whom you were called into the fellowship of His Son, Jesus Christ our Lord.

1 CORINTHIANS 1:9

D o you really believe that God is faithful? The same God who called you into a relationship with Him will always be faithful in that relationship. You will never discover a time when God isn't faithful.

There's a true story about nineteenth-century evangelist, missionary, and orphanage director George Mueller that clearly demonstrates the faithfulness of God. One morning, Mueller was informed that all the children in his orphanage were dressed and ready for school, but there was no food for breakfast. He instructed the three hundred children to be taken into the dining room and seated at the tables.

> He thanked God for the food and waited. Within minutes, a baker knocked on the door. "Mr. Mueller," he said, "last night I couldn't sleep. Somehow I knew that you would need bread this morning. I got up and baked three batches for you. I will bring it in." Soon, there was another knock at the door. It was the milkman. His cart had broken down in front of the orphanage. The milk would spoil by the time the wheel was fixed. He asked George if he could use some free milk. George smiled as the milkman brought in ten large cans of milk. It was just enough for the three hundred thirsty children.[1]

Because of Mueller's fellowship with God, he understood the faithfulness of God. The closer you grow to Jesus, the more you will begin to see how good and faithful He truly is.

....

Faithful Father, help me to trust Your goodness and provision no matter what circumstances I encounter. Amen.

WEEK 8—WEDNESDAY
Getting to Know God

That I may know [Jesus] and the power of His resurrection, and the fellowship of His sufferings, being conformed to His death, if, by any means, I may attain to the resurrection from the dead.

PHILIPPIANS 3:10–11

There are countless things in life that you should know. You should remember your address, your phone number, and your social security number. Don't forget your mom's cell phone number and her maiden name. Your children's birthdays, your wife's birthday, the day you got engaged—and don't you dare forget your anniversary!

These are a few of the many pieces of information you should be able to recall in a moment; these are important things that everyone should know. Beyond that, you have many other things you should remember. Did you forget the milk at the grocery store? Have you changed your oil lately? Did you call the exterminator to schedule that appointment? It seems the list of things you are supposed to know is endless.

But there is one thing you must know that is much more important than the rest. Actually, it's a Someone, not a something. Above all else, you must strive to know Jesus Christ as Savior and Lord. Paul expressed his earnest desire, "That I may know [Jesus]." This passion was the driving force of his life.

While you should know many important things as well as many trivial things, nothing is more important than knowing God. And God has made Himself knowable through His written Word, His Son, and His Spirit.

....

Heavenly Father, I'm grateful that You are a knowable God. In the midst of a world full of endless information, help me to know You better. Help me to know You more. Amen.

DR. JIM PERDUE, SECOND BAPTIST CHURCH, WARNER ROBINS, GA

WEEK 8—THURSDAY
If You Love Me . . .

"If anyone loves Me, he will keep My word; and My Father will love him, and We will come to him and make Our home with him."

JOHN 14:23

M any times in the New Testament Jesus equated loving Him with keeping His Word. In fact, obedience is often the greatest expression of love. Previously in John 14, Jesus said, "If you love Me, keep my commandments" (John 14:15). Jesus equated genuine love with faithful obedience. Obedience is not a condition of God's love for us, but it is the proof of our love for Him.

Those who love Jesus and express that love through faithful obedience will experience the blessings of God's presence: "We will come to him and make Our home with him." Jesus had also promised in John 14:2 that He would go and "prepare a place" for His followers. Here, Jesus enlarged upon that promise. Not only will we have a home in heaven one day, but Jesus will also make His home in our hearts while we are here on earth.

I'm sure you have occasionally traveled and stayed in a hotel. Did you rearrange all of the furniture in the hotel room or hang family pictures on the wall? Of course not! That would be foolish. Hotels are only temporary places to reside. They are not your home.

There are significant differences between having a place to stay and being at home. At home, you have the authority to make changes, rearrange rooms, and paint the walls. Jesus should have this kind of authority in your life since He has come and made His home inside of you. Does He?

. . . .

Dear Jesus, I want to show my love for You by following You faithfully and obediently. Thank You for making Your home in my heart. Amen.

WEEK 8—FRIDAY
Unified in Jesus

If there is any consolation in Christ, if any comfort of love, if any fellowship of the Spirit, if any affection and mercy, fulfill my joy by being like-minded, having the same love, being of one accord, of one mind.

PHILIPPIANS 2:1–2

I remember a science demonstration I saw when I was in middle school. Our teacher dumped all types of different metal shavings onto a table. Some of the shavings were iron, some were steel, some were aluminum, and some were tin. Then the teacher brought out a powerful magnet and passed it over the metal. All of the metals that were magnetic were lifted up and brought together. The metals that were not magnetically charged stayed on the table.

Something similar happens spiritually. When God puts His Spirit inside of us at the point of salvation, we are magnetized. As a result, all kinds of different people are brought together by the magnetic power of the Spirit of God. This is how "every tribe and tongue and people and nation" can gather around the throne (Revelation 5:9). There are many differences but one God. There are many things that separate us, but there is one thing that brings us together. We are united in the Spirit of God.

This is why we can experience love, joy, mercy, compassion, and unity. Jesus unites us in a way that we could never experience apart from Him. We can, for instance, be "like-minded." This doesn't mean that we always think the same thing, but it means we are on the same team. We are "one" in Christ because He brought us together through the power of His Spirit.

....

Holy Spirit, thank You for the unity You provide to Your children. May I live with the peace and joy that You give through Jesus. Amen.

DR. JIM PERDUE, SECOND BAPTIST CHURCH, WARNER ROBINS, GA

WEEK 8—WEEKEND
Abide in Christ

"Abide in Me, and I in you. As the branch cannot bear fruit of itself, unless it abides in the vine, neither can you, unless you abide in Me. I am the vine, you are the branches. He who abides in Me, and I in him, bears much fruit; for without Me you can do nothing."

JOHN 15:4–5

I f you've ever been around anyone who is close to death, you know that someone's last words are very important. Jesus knew that His death was imminent and His time with the disciples was drawing to an end. His words to the disciples during this time are extremely important. These are the teachings He chose to pass along in the last few days of His life. John 15 records the words Jesus spoke to His disciples in the Upper Room the night before His death. Judas had already revealed himself to be a traitor, and the events of Jesus' arrest had been set in motion.

Jesus said, "I am the vine, you are the branches." The strength and the health of the branches are completely dependent upon a vine. Thus we draw all of our strength from Christ. Further, if a branch doesn't bear fruit, it's not because the Vine is bad; it's because the branch is not functioning the way it's designed. If we cut the branch off the Vine, the branch will no longer have any strength for producing fruit. Its source of strength is completely gone.

We quote Philippians 4:13 often, "I can do all things through Christ, who gives me strength" (NLT). Rarely, however, do we quote John 15:5, "Without Me you can do nothing."

....

Gracious Lord, thank You for the strength that comes from abiding in You, the one true Vine. Teach me to rest daily in Your sustenance and support. Amen.

WEEK 9—MONDAY
Christ, the Suffering Servant

To this you were called, because Christ also suffered for us, leaving us an example, that you should follow His steps: "Who committed no sin, Nor was deceit found in His mouth."

1 PETER 2:21–22

S uffering is a mysterious thing. Everyone suffers at some time or another. Maybe we've experienced a major setback in our physical health, the sudden loss of a friend or family member, or being socially isolated by coworkers because of our Christian values. Often we suffer for reasons beyond our control. Suffering is real, and it is painful.

Suffering was even felt by Jesus, the only man ever to live and never commit sin. Scripture teaches that "there is none righteous, no, not one" (Romans 3:10) and that all have fallen short of God's perfect standard (Romans 3:23). Only Jesus lived a perfect, sinless life. And, yes, even Jesus suffered. If the perfect Son of God suffered for us and He is our example for living life, how on earth can we *not* expect to suffer? We suffer because the world has been reeling from the sting of sin since Eden. Frequently we suffer because our adversary, the devil, hates us (John 10:10). Suffering can also be the result of personal pride, greed, an unforgiving attitude, or even our own foolishness.

But the Bible has great news for believers: suffering is temporary. Through the death and resurrection of Christ, eternal suffering was defeated. Like a dead snake that still reflexively thrashes about even though it is dead, suffering may last for today, but it will not last forever. Here's the promise: "[God] will wipe away every tear from their eyes. Death will exist no longer; grief, crying, and pain will exist no longer" (Revelation 21:4 HCSB).

....

Dear God, use my suffering for Your glory and to make me more like Christ. In Jesus' name, Amen.

REV. JEREMY MORTON, CARTERSVILLE FIRST BAPTIST CHURCH, CARTERSVILLE, GA

WEEK 9—TUESDAY
Imitating the Father

Be imitators of God as dear children. And walk in love, as Christ also has loved us and given Himself for us, an offering and a sacrifice to God for a sweet-smelling aroma.

EPHESIANS 5:1–2

It's been said that imitation is the purest form of flattery.

Have you ever seen a small boy trying to walk wearing his father's shoes? Or a young girl dressed in her mother's clothes? Often moments like those are the child's sincere attempt to be like—to imitate—one whom he or she adores.

In today's passage, Paul commanded us to imitate God. Those who are the people of God are commanded to be holy because the Lord is holy (1 Peter 1:15). God's holy, loving character transforms us as we seek Him. The pinnacle of Christian love is the self-giving love of Christ on the cross.

Therefore, the primary way Christians should imitate Jesus today is through their love. When Jesus was asked by a scribe to identify the central teaching of Scripture, Jesus told him the most important commandments were to love God with one's whole being and to love others (Mark 12:28–31). On the night of His betrayal and arrest, Jesus taught the disciples this: "I give you a new commandment: Love one another. Just as I have loved you, you must love one another. By this all people will know that you are My disciples, if you have love for one another" (John 13:34–35 HCSB). The love of Christ is the *what*, *how*, and *why* for reaching the world.

....

Dear heavenly Father, I pray that my speech, attitude, and behavior will reflect Your holy character and gracious love. Make me more like Jesus. In Christ's name, Amen.

Week 9—Wednesday
How Can We Glorify God?

Let this mind be in you which was also in Christ Jesus, who, being in the form of God, did not consider it robbery to be equal with God, but made Himself of no reputation, taking the form of a bondservant, and coming in the likeness of men. And being found in appearance as a man, He humbled Himself and became obedient to the point of death, even the death of the cross.

PHILIPPIANS 2:5–8

Humility is a choice. No one halfheartedly becomes humble. Instead, one determines with his or her mind to embrace the humble character of Christ on a daily basis. Paul told the Philippians to imitate Christ, history's greatest example of humble, selfless love. If believers follow in Christ's footsteps, the church will walk in unity.

Paul explained how Jesus, though He was fully God, humbled himself by leaving His heavenly throne to come to earth as a man. Christ chose the role of a servant when He could have expected people to serve Him: "The Son of Man came not to be served but to serve, and to give his life as a ransom for many" (Matthew 20:28 ESV). Jesus ultimately demonstrated His humility by His brutal death on the cross. He was treated like a common criminal, yet this gruesome, humble act of atonement made it possible for sinners like you and me to receive salvation.

Pause and meditate on the glorious worth of Jesus. The eternal King humbly embraced the role of servant. This is how to glorify your heavenly Father. Today will you walk in humility instead of pride? Will you reject entitlement by embracing the role of a servant?

Dear God, help me to follow the example of Christ. Give me a spirit of humility and selfless love so that it may bring You glory and honor. Amen.

Week 9—Thursday
Running the Race

Since we are surrounded by so great a cloud of witnesses, let us lay aside every weight, and the sin which so easily ensnares us, and let us run with endurance the race that is set before us, looking unto Jesus, the author and finisher of our faith, who for the joy that was set before Him endured the cross, despising the shame, and has sat down at the right hand of the throne of God.

HEBREWS 12:1–2

As a student, do you remember participating in races during physical education class or recess time? There were 100m, 200m, 400m races, and more. As thrilling as it was to perform while your classmates cheered, do you recall how you felt afterward? If you hadn't prepared for the race, your body paid the price! You would have been sore for days. The reason your body might have ached was because of inadequate training beforehand.

The writer of Hebrews compared the Christian life to running a race, but this isn't just any race—it's a lengthy race, like a marathon. Completing this race requires endurance, training, and discipline. In this race, believers often face difficulty. But the author challenged believers to lay aside every weight. In other words, they are to get rid of anything that hinders their relationship with Christ. To run successfully, believers must keep looking to Jesus, the Author and Finisher of their faith. Good runners know that keeping their eyes on the finish line is the ultimate motivation and key to endurance, especially when times are hard. So look to Jesus today! He alone will empower you to run the race all the way to the finish.

....

Dear God, help me run the race with endurance, fixing my eyes on Jesus. Help me resist the temptations of the world so that I may run a strong race. Amen.

Week 9—Friday
True Leaders Serve

"Whoever desires to become great among you shall be your servant. And whoever of you desires to be first shall be slave of all. For even the Son of Man did not come to be served, but to serve, and to give His life a ransom for many."

Mark 10:43–45

Leadership has been the focus of much attention in recent years. There are leadership coaches, leadership conferences, leadership networks, leadership books, leadership podcasts, and more. Everywhere we turn, the world seems desperate for quality leaders. But is it possible we are in greater need of something else? What is the real secret of leadership? Without question, Jesus Christ is the greatest Leader the world has ever known—but, ironically, He is also the greatest Servant the world has ever known.

In today's passage, Jesus taught His disciples the true nature of effective leadership, and that is being a servant. Unlike the leaders who dominate their subordinates through power, money, or authority, Jesus called His followers first to cultivate the heart of a servant. Believers must first learn to serve others rather than to expect to be served. The grand purpose of Jesus' ministry was serving others by suffering on the cross of Calvary to save us from sin (Isaiah 53).

Ask the Lord to show you how truly committed to being a servant you are. Who might directly benefit from your outstretched arms today? An elderly neighbor? A single mom? A struggling coworker? Ask God to open your eyes to the various needs around you. Greater impact may come through greater service. Everyone wins when you serve, including you.

....

Dear God, help me to demonstrate Your love through humble service. May You touch the world through my service. Amen.

REV. JEREMY MORTON, CARTERSVILLE FIRST BAPTIST CHURCH, CARTERSVILLE, GA

WEEK 9—WEEKEND
Nature of Christian Life

"I have given you an example, that you should do as I have done to you. Most assuredly, I say to you, a servant is not greater than his master; nor is he who is sent greater than he who sent him. If you know these things, blessed are you if you do them."

JOHN 13:15–17

Have you ever witnessed a wedding ceremony where the bride and groom washed each other's feet? It is a humbling, beautiful moment to behold as the two seek to portray the dedication, love, and service that a healthy marriage will require. Reminiscent of Paul's words concerning Christian marriage to love one another as Christ loved the church (Ephesians 5:25), Jesus' words here clearly state that the most effective relationships occur when people put others before themselves.

In today's passage, Jesus demonstrated humble service for His disciples: He washed their feet. This lowly act is stunning. Now note the specific word Jesus used to make His point: He called His act an *example*. In other words, what Jesus did to demonstrate authentic humility, His disciples—and believers today—must do as well.

But if your family members, friends, and coworkers were assured of confidentiality and given the opportunity to speak freely about your daily attitude, would any of them describe you as a humble servant? Or, instead, would you be described as proud, egotistical, and too dazzled by your own achievements to notice other people and their needs? One of the marks of a true Christian is a heart of humility.

Since the greatest King in the world—Jesus—was widely described as a humble servant, how could those who call Him "Lord" be any less?

Dear God, help me to be like Jesus. May Your name be glorified as I serve others. Amen.

Week 10—Monday
I Have Called You Friends

"No longer do I call you servants, for a servant does not know what his master is doing; but I have called you friends, for all things that I heard from My Father I have made known to you. You did not choose Me, but I chose you and appointed you that you should go and bear fruit, and that your fruit should remain, that whatever you ask the Father in My name He may give you."

JOHN 15:15–16

Wow! What a statement! "You did not choose me, but I chose you." The Creator of the universe, the great "I AM," the King of kings, the Lord of lords, has chosen you! If you are a Christ follower, God chose you. It doesn't matter what your childhood experiences were, or how weird your teen years were, or how challenging adulthood has been. God chose you!

But what has He chosen you for? "I chose you and appointed you that you should go and bear fruit." God's plan for your life is a life full of fruit.

That sounds like a great plan, but how do you experience it? The answer is in the passage: "I have called you friends, for all things that I heard from My Father I have made known to you." Our friendship with God grows as we pray, study the Bible, and obey what He reveals. This relationship we have with God will shape our lives and bring forth fruit that honors Him.

What will you do today to enrich your friendship with God?

....

Father, please bless and grow my friendship with You as I seek You daily. Help me to cooperate with You and Your Spirit so that You can produce the fruit of life in my life. Amen.

WEEK 10—TUESDAY
God the Father, God the Son

To the Son [God] says: "Your throne, O God, is forever and ever; a scepter of righteousness is the scepter of Your kingdom. You have loved righteousness and hated lawlessness; therefore God, Your God, has anointed You with the oil of gladness more than Your companions."

HEBREWS 1:8–9

In this passage is one of the most amazing and important statements in all the Bible: Jesus is God! Many people of many religions believe Jesus was just a man, or just a prophet of God, or just a good teacher. They like to quote His teachings, but they don't accept His claims of divinity.

Yet throughout His life and ministry Jesus claimed to be equal with God, to be God. Jesus said, "I and the Father are one" (John 10:30 NASB)—and "for this reason therefore the Jews were seeking to kill Him, because He not only was breaking the Sabbath, but also calling God His own Father, making Himself equal with God" (John 5:18 NASB). Jesus made it very clear with His actions and His teaching that He is God.

Here—and this is another astonishing aspect of this verse—the Father said to the Son, "Your throne, O God, is forever and ever." God the Father—God Himself—acknowledged His Son as God, providing us with one of the clearest, most powerful proofs that Jesus is God.

So what does all this mean for us today? It means, among other things, that Jesus' promises can be trusted. Jesus is who He said He is, and He can do what He said He can do. You can live in confidence today that God is on His throne and that His plans and purposes will be fulfilled. No need to worry or fear anything because God's throne will last forever!

Father, thank You that I can have confidence in all of Your promises. Amen.

Week 10—Wednesday
The Secret of Contentment

Let your conduct be without covetousness; be content with such things as you have. For He Himself has said, "I will never leave you nor forsake you." So we may boldly say:"The LORD is my helper; I will not fear. What can man do to me?"

HEBREWS 13:5–6

Webster's defines *contentment* as "a state of satisfaction"—and at times experiencing satisfaction can definitely be difficult. Sometimes I am very content. Life is going as planned, there are no bumps on the road, and I'm grateful and satisfied with all God has for me. But then come those times we all face when things do not go as planned—at least not as *I* had planned!

In those moments—during those seasons of life—can I really be content? That is the message of these words from the book of Hebrews: I am to be content not because of where I am or what I have, but *because of whose I am and what I have in Him.*

No matter what you're facing today, no matter how you feel, remember that you—as a Christ follower—have access to God's power and that He is present with you. Don't allow the enemy or your feelings to make you doubt the one sure thing you have, which is the one thing you need: God.

Whatever you're facing, make this verse personal: "The LORD is my helper; I will not fear." You have the opportunity to experience today with God. If you will trust Him, you can know that He is present, He is your helper, and you have nothing to fear!

....

Father, help me to be aware of Your presence in my life today. May I find comfort and joy in You as I put my faith in Your wisdom, Your promise, and Your presence, and as I trust You to see me through today. Teach me to be content because I am Yours. Amen.

PASTOR CHRIS DIXON, LIBERTY BAPTIST CHURCH, DUBLIN, GA

WEEK 10—THURSDAY
Two Sources of Joy

That which we have seen and heard we declare to you, that you also may have fellowship with us; and truly our fellowship is with the Father and with His Son Jesus Christ. And these things we write to you that your joy may be full.

1 JOHN 1:3–4

I absolutely love these two verses because they have impacted my life in a very powerful way. I lived so many years of my life missing the joy that these verses promise. You may know what I am talking about.

These two verses clearly tell us the source of this joy. It is found in fellowship with God and in fellowship with His followers. Make sure you take notice of the fact that joy is found in both.

When I came to Christ on November 27, 1994, I was at the lowest point of my life. At age nineteen, I had married my pregnant sixteen-year-old girlfriend, and within one year we were already on our way to divorce court. However, we started attending a great church where we began to see people whose lives had been changed. We both surrendered our lives to Christ, and we both began to learn how to walk personally with the Lord.

This past September we celebrated twenty-two years of marriage. We have three beautiful children who are all living for God. I have found a lasting joy in fellowship with God and fellowship with His followers.

Be sure to make time daily to be in fellowship with God and take time regularly every week to be around His people. You'll find the level of joy in your life increase!

....

Father, thank You for the joy and the change You have brought to my life and continue to bring through my relationship with You. Amen.

WEEK 10—FRIDAY
It's a Matter of Perspective

You, LORD, in the beginning laid the foundation of the earth, and the heavens are the work of Your hands. They will perish, but You remain; and they will all grow old like a garment; like a cloak You will fold them up, and they will be changed. But You are the same, and Your years will not fail.

HEBREWS 1:10–12

Have you ever noticed how the troubles and trials of life can sometimes feel like they will never end? Difficulties can come and stay for what seems an eternity.

This text reminds us God has a bigger plan. He created us not just for today but for eternity. The scope of your life and mine is far greater than today's trials and troubles. The writer of Hebrews reminded us that just as we throw out old clothing, Jesus one day will do away with this earth. The Lord is going to create a new heaven and a new earth. The creation will change; the Creator will stay the same. That is why our focus should always be on Him.

God not only has a plan for today; He has plans for all eternity. Read these words by Helen Howarth Lemmel and then heed her advice.

> *Turn your eyes upon Jesus,*
> *Look full in His wonderful face,*
> *And the things of earth will grow strangely dim,*
> *In the light of His glory and grace.*

Father, help me to trust You with the challenges I face. And help me to have Your perspective on those problems. I know You see beyond today and into all eternity. That's one reason I know I can trust You with every area of my life.

PASTOR CHRIS DIXON, LIBERTY BAPTIST CHURCH, DUBLIN, GA

WEEK 10—WEEKEND
Daily Pursuit of the Pursuer

"Behold, I stand at the door and knock. If anyone hears My voice and opens the door, I will come in to him and dine with him, and he with Me. To him who overcomes I will grant to sit with Me on My throne, as I also overcame and sat down with My Father on His throne."

REVELATION 3:20–21

Do you realize that God is pursuing you?

If you have ever felt a million miles away from God—and we all have—the good news is it is just a feeling and not a fact. Christ is in hot pursuit of you.

And why is He pursuing you? The passage says He wants to "dine" with you. The word *dine* speaks of fellowship, communion, and intimacy. God wants more than your Sunday mornings and mealtime prayers; He wants intimacy with you. He wants to lead you and guide you in every area of your life. He wants to mold you into the person He created you to be. He wants you to live in the priorities that will mean abundant life: "Seek first His kingdom and His righteousness, and all these things will be added to you" (Matthew 6:33 NASB).

I pray this week has challenged you to make intimacy with Christ—time alone with Him—a priority in your life. For the Christian, there is no substitute for time alone with God. Make a commitment today to seek Christ on a daily basis.

....

Father, today I commit—I re-commit—myself to daily pursuing Your wisdom and righteousness for my life. When I focus my attention on You and Your Word, may I hear You when You speak to me. I ask You to lead me into the life for which You created me. Amen.

WEEK 11—MONDAY
A Remarkable New Life

For whom He foreknew, He also predestined to be conformed to the image of His Son, that He might be the firstborn among many brethren. Moreover whom He predestined, these He also called; whom He called, these He also justified; and whom He justified, these He also glorified.

ROMANS 8:29–30

Jesus as our brother? The thought is unimaginable. How could we mere humans ever be any sort of peer to the Son of God? Even at our most brilliant moments, at the height of our goodness, we can't approach our Lord's perfection. But God's plan to make this happen has unfolded throughout the centuries. The Almighty set in place a series of events that allows created beings to become His children, His sons and daughters, joint heirs with Jesus. The plan is amazing.

Part 1: The Son of God—the second Person of the godhead—became a fully human man in Jesus and died. He was in the grave for three days and three nights. After that, through the power of the Holy Spirit, Jesus was raised from the dead. He was the firstborn from the dead!

Part 2: This same experience has been made available to every man and woman, all of whom are, at birth, spiritually dead and separated from God. Each individual can be and must be born again. This second birth is a remarkable thing. Just as the Holy Spirit brought life back into the broken body of a crucified Jesus, the Spirit brings the life of God to those who chose to receive Jesus as Lord and Savior. At that moment, the new birth occurs, and we become children of God, brothers and sisters of Jesus.

....

Thank You, Lord, for forgiving me, freeing me, and bringing me into Your family. May I always celebrate my newfound life in You. Amen.

DR. DAVID EDWARDS, CHURCH PROJECT, THE WOODLANDS, TX

WEEK 11—TUESDAY
Speak the Heart of the Father

Do not speak evil of one another, brethren. He who speaks evil of a brother and judges his brother, speaks evil of the law and judges the law.... There is one Lawgiver, who is able to save and to destroy. Who are you to judge another?

JAMES 4:11–12

Being a brother or sister of Jesus means we have spiritual siblings. As in any family, siblings can easily be negative and judgmental of one another. James had this very sobering reminder: *to speak evil of another brother or sister is to speak evil of the Law of God.*

When we judge fellow believers, we imply that the Lord is incapable of adequately dealing with this particular child of His, so we who clearly see the problem will step in and resolve it. After all, since we think we know what's best for that person, what he or she is facing, and all the life details—past and present—we believe we have the right to judge and repair him or her. But this is not so.

Since they aren't receiving love and care, those being judged are often driven away from the community of believers and the healing love that only Jesus Christ can provide through them. Remember, it is the Lord's place to act, and His authority and mercy bring healing to those in need. Our place is to love, care for, be available to, and pray for our brothers and sisters—and allow the Lord Jesus to do His redemptive work.

Be careful about how you treat those who have done wrong. It's not always your place to get involved. Trust God to lead you in the words to say at the right time.

Dear Lord, today help me to be mindful of my words and to speak of others as though You were standing right next to me. Give me the power to let go of petty incidents and to trust You to pour out Your grace through me. Amen.

THE GIFT OF JESUS

Week 11—Wednesday
Family Is What We Do

For both [Jesus] who sanctifies and those who are being sanctified are all of one, for which reason He is not ashamed to call them brethren, saying: "I will declare Your name to My brethren; In the midst of the assembly I will sing praise to You."

HEBREWS 2:11–12

Salvation, sanctification, and family—these go together in God's plan. Because of Jesus' great victory over sin and death, He is able to make humans holy in a process called sanctification. In fact, the New Testament calls those who receive Jesus as Lord and Savior "holy ones" and "saints." As the writer of the book of Hebrews put it, the One who sanctifies and the one who is sanctified are of one Father. Jesus and Christians have the same Father. Jesus is our Brother!

The Lord Jesus desires for each Christian to know the Father as He knows the Father. According to Psalm 22:22 (quoted in the Hebrews passage above), Jesus declares the name of the Father to His brothers and sisters. To know someone's name is to know that person's character and authority. Jesus declares God's name because He desires us to know and love the Father.

Jesus promised not only to declare God's name, but also to sing the praises of the Father. It is one thing to know about various aspects of the Father; it is another altogether to love the Father wholeheartedly. As brothers and sisters of the Lord Jesus, He wants us to love the Father and join with Him in praise. After all, we are family, and praising God the Father is what Jesus and the saints do.

Dear Father, thank You for calling my name and bringing me into Your family. I let go of guilt and shame. This day I choose to live as if I belong to You— because, by Your grace, I do! Amen.

DR. DAVID EDWARDS, CHURCH PROJECT, THE WOODLANDS, TX

Week 11—Thursday
A Holy Temple in the Lord

You are no longer strangers and foreigners, but fellow citizens with the saints and members of the household of God, having been built on the foundation of the apostles and prophets, Jesus Christ Himself being the chief cornerstone, in whom the whole building, being fitted together, grows into a holy temple in the Lord.

EPHESIANS 2:19–21

One afternoon when Jesus was alone with His disciples, He made one of His greatest promises: "I will build My church" (Matthew 16:18). Using that same metaphor, the apostle Paul described the building materials Jesus was using, and they weren't physical stones and boards. Rather, Paul declared that Jesus' church was being built of saints, of holy ones who were "members of the household of God."

This remarkable truth has great consequences. The apostle Paul taught that any person—regardless of age, race, sex, wealth, or power—could enter the household of God. That was radical in Paul's day, and it still is today. Jesus planned for His church to be a place on earth absolutely free of discrimination. Every individual who receives Jesus as Lord and Savior is immediately brought fully into the family of God and recognized as a saint, a fellow citizen of the household of God.

Imagine this fabulous picture: the family of God—you and me and our fellow brothers and sisters of the Lord Jesus—are the building materials. Jesus is the chief Cornerstone, and it is His decision where to place each Christian in position so that each piece fits into its place in the building. The family of believers thus becomes a holy temple in the Lord and able to change the world.

....

Dear Lord, You are the Chief Builder; I am a living stone. Place me in Your community where You see fit, where I can best serve You, Your people, and the lost in this world. Amen.

Week 11—Friday
In the Father's Family

Because you are sons, God has sent forth the Spirit of His Son into your hearts, crying out, "Abba, Father!" Therefore you are no longer a slave but a son, and if a son, then an heir of God through Christ.

GALATIANS 4:6–7

The apostle Paul wrote emphatically that Christians are sons and daughters of God, and, therefore, Jesus is the Christian's brother. Did you hear that? It's truly remarkable! And this position of son and daughter is not just on paper; you enjoy this position every day. If you have accepted Jesus as your Lord and Savior, something supernatural occurred. At the moment of your salvation, the Lord Jesus released His Holy Spirit into your heart, and your spirit came alive. You were born again!

As a result of your new birth, the Holy Spirit is constantly at work bringing you into a fuller, richer relationship with the Lord Jesus and the Father. One of the Spirit's most wonderful works is to give you the unqualified assurance that God is your Father. As you pray, hear a great song of the Lord, or listen to a sermon, the Holy Spirit reminds you again and again that you truly are a child of God—and nothing can ever change that reality. Your spirit rightfully cries out, "*Abba*, Father!"

But there is more. Since you are a son or daughter of God, you are not a slave. In fact, you are a joint heir with Jesus. You are in the family of God.

Almighty God, Your Spirit creates in me an awareness that I am Yours. I now know I am no longer a slave to this world, and my heart is overwhelmed by Your grace. I love You and I thank You for bringing me into Your family. I show my confidence in You with only one word: Abba. Amen.

DR. DAVID EDWARDS, CHURCH PROJECT, THE WOODLANDS, TX

WEEK 11—WEEKEND
There Is More

We are children of God; and it has not yet been revealed what we shall be, but we know that when He is revealed, we shall be like Him, for we shall see Him as He is. And everyone who has this hope in Him purifies himself, just as He is pure.

1 JOHN 3:2–3

The reality of Christianity is to be experienced on this earth and at this very moment. Believers aren't waiting until heaven to know Jesus genuinely and to love Him as Lord and Savior. We're not waiting to receive the ministry of the Holy Spirit, and we're not waiting to experience the incredible blessings of being in God's family. A Christian is a child of God and a member of His family *now*.

But as true and as certain as that fact is, there is still more a Christian will ultimately experience. We do not know all that we will be in the future, but we do know there is life beyond this life. The Bible teaches that at the moment of death, a Christian is immediately with the Lord Jesus (2 Corinthians 5:8). In that next life, there will be no limit to our understanding of or to our relationship with Jesus. He will be fully revealed to us, and we will be like Him. What an amazing thought!

And this amazing truth motivates the way Christians live. As sons and daughters of God, as members of His family, we are to love the Lord Jesus, our heavenly Father, and one another.

....

Dear Jesus, the hope of Your return challenges me to honor You by the way I live. I choose to worship You in my heart. I choose to be faithful to You every day of my life. I choose to focus on living in a way that pleases You. The prospect of living tomorrow with You motivates me to live well for You today. Amen.

WEEK 12—MONDAY
Secure Because of the Resurrection

Blessed be the God and Father of our Lord Jesus Christ, who according to His abundant mercy has begotten us again to a living hope through the resurrection of Jesus Christ from the dead, to an inheritance incorruptible and undefiled and that does not fade away, reserved in heaven for you, who are kept by the power of God through faith for salvation ready to be revealed in the last time.

1 PETER 1:3–5

Peter made several statements in these verses that provide absolute proof that our security is in Jesus and not in ourselves.

First, Peter wrote that we have "a living hope through the resurrection of Jesus Christ from the dead." Today, around the world, people give their lives for a cause in which they believe. Jesus said that He was dying for a cause. In doing so, this cause provided us "a living hope." In the Bible, *hope* means "confident assurance." Jesus claimed He was going to die so that we might have the hope—the confident assurance—of eternal life. When Jesus did not stay dead—when He arose—He served as living hope that we too will experience eternal life! Because He lives, we can live—*and* we can be certain of that. This is great news!

Second, the apostle Peter wrote that we have "an inheritance . . . in heaven." Although we might want to leave a financial inheritance to our children, it may or may not be there for them. We may outlive our savings, or a corrupt financial institution could cause some or all of it to disappear. But praise God that our inheritance in Him is absolutely sure.

Dear God, thank You that my eternal security is not in another human being but in You. Amen.

DENNIS NUNN, EVERY BELIEVER A WITNESS MINISTRIES, DALLAS, GA

WEEK 12—TUESDAY
Secure Because of His Strong Hands

"My sheep hear My voice, and I know them, and they follow Me. And I give them eternal life, and they shall never perish; neither shall anyone snatch them out of My hand. My Father, who has given them to Me, is greater than all; and no one is able to snatch them out of My Father's hand."

JOHN 10:27–29

Sheep just may be the most helpless animals in the world. They can't run fast. They don't have claws or sharp teeth. They can't defend themselves. They are totally dependent upon the shepherd. Their security is based solely on how capable, caring, and strong their shepherd is.

Interestingly, the Bible uses the metaphor of sheep to refer to followers of Jesus. Thankfully, we have a perfect and totally powerful Shepherd. He not only gives us our daily bread, but He gives us eternal life with Him. And notice that eternal life is not something we can earn or purchase. It is a gift.

Not only is eternal life a gift, but it is a gift we possess now. Does that sound like a big responsibility, holding onto eternal life? How can we be sure that we won't forfeit or misplace the gift? Fortunately for us, it is not up to us to keep the gift or keep ourselves secure. We are held securely in the hands of the loving and omnipotent Son and His Father.

A well-known insurance company slogan is "You're in good hands with Allstate." Thankfully, you and I are in the best hands with Jesus.

....

Heavenly Father, thank You for giving me eternal life that is as secure as You are strong. Amen.

WEEK 12—WEDNESDAY
Secure Because of God's Love

I am persuaded that neither death nor life, nor angels nor principalities nor powers, nor things present nor things to come, nor height nor depth, nor any other created thing, shall be able to separate us from the love of God which is in Christ Jesus our Lord.

ROMANS 8:38–39

Paul suffered almost every adversity, pain, and form of persecution we can imagine. His experiences definitely qualified him to speak about security. Second Corinthians tells about the astounding trials Paul endured. This mighty man of God was severely beaten, stoned, shipwrecked, attacked by Jews and by Gentiles, falsely accused, and betrayed by people who claimed to be Christ followers. Paul also suffered hunger, sleeplessness, freezing temperatures without enough clothing, and chronic physical pain. Despite all this, Paul made the amazing declaration, that he was persuaded that nothing in this life or in death, no angel or demonic spirits, nothing in heaven or hell, absolutely nothing—because God created everything—can separate us from the love of God.

As if this truth weren't great enough, God's love for us is unconditional. Unlike the conditional love of humans, God's love is not dependent upon our behavior. We can do absolutely nothing to make Him love us more or less!

So why are we the recipients of such unconditional love? Simply because we accepted the Lord Jesus Christ. Since that moment, the love God has for His Son is the love God has for us.

Do you believe that remarkable truth? Is your belief in Jesus merely an intellectual assent, or have you personally turned from your sins and self-centeredness and received Jesus as your Lord?

....

Heavenly Father, thank You for loving me. Let me relax today, secure in Your love. Amen.

DENNIS NUNN, EVERY BELIEVER A WITNESS MINISTRIES, DALLAS, GA

WEEK 12—THURSDAY
Secure Because of Jesus

This is a faithful saying: For if we died with Him, we shall also live with Him. If we endure, we shall also reign with Him. If we deny Him, He also will deny us. If we are faithless, He remains faithful; He cannot deny Himself.

2 TIMOTHY 2:11–13

Salvation does not come with merely an intellectual acceptance of some historical facts. Neither does salvation mean just declaring what we believe.

Instead, salvation comes when we see ourselves as sinners under God's judgment; believe that Jesus paid with His death on the cross the penalty God established for our sin and then rose from the dead; and call upon Jesus to save us. At that moment a divine, spiritual transaction takes place. We are actually identified with Jesus' death, His burial, and His resurrection. In addition, the water baptism of a new believer offers a picture of the spiritual reality that has taken place. Then comes the promise: since we died with Jesus, we will also live with Him.

Paul went on to tell us that one proof of truly being saved is enduring, continuing to follow Jesus Christ as our Lord no matter what. However, if we do deny Jesus by turning away from Him, our turning is proof that we never really belonged to Him. As a result, He will deny knowing us when we stand before the Father.

Here is my favorite part: Jesus is always faithful even when we aren't! So if we become weak in our faith, if we struggle to believe and stay faithful, Jesus nevertheless stays faithful to us because He cannot deny Himself.

The bottom line is that if Jesus truly lives in us, then He will always be faithful to keep us. Now *that* is security!

....

Jesus, I praise You for Your great faithfulness to me. Amen.

Week 12—Friday
Secure Because of God's Will

"All that the Father gives Me will come to Me, and the one who comes to Me I will by no means cast out. For I have come down from heaven, not to do My own will, but the will of Him who sent Me. This is the will of the Father who sent Me, that of all He has given Me I should lose nothing, but should raise it up at the last day."

JOHN 6:37–39

I am so thankful that it isn't up to me to keep myself saved, to keep myself in the circle of God's family. If that were the case, I would no doubt have lost my salvation long ago. I am all too aware that, in spite of my desire to please God, I have failed Him miserably so many times. I am also thankful that—praise the Lord—I didn't have to clean my life up or promise to keep it clean. Instead, all I had to do was simply go to Jesus. Because I did so, and because He saved me, He is now responsible for keeping me.

It would be blessing enough if our security were solely in Jesus' promise never to cast us out of the family of God. But Jesus went on to tell us that He will never cast us out because He is intent on doing the will of His Father. And that's when Jesus told us what the will of the Father is—that none of the people who come to Jesus would ever be lost.

So have you turned to Jesus? Have you sincerely placed your faith in Him? Do you believe that He forgave you of your sins and has given you eternal life? If so, know that you are actually a special gift the Father has given to His Son.

....

Father, I thank You that You want me to be secure in You. Amen.

WEEK 12—WEEKEND
Secure Because of the Holy Spirit

Let no corrupt word proceed out of your mouth, but what is good for necessary edification, that it may impart grace to the hearers. And do not grieve the Holy Spirit of God, by whom you were sealed for the day of redemption.

EPHESIANS 4:29–30

According to *Merriam-Webster's*, a seal is "something that confirms, ratifies, or makes secure: a guarantee, assurance." The verb *seal* means "to determine irrevocably or indisputably." So the verses above teach that our salvation is confirmed, made secure, guaranteed, and irrevocable! But a seal is only as secure as either the quality of the seal or the person who applied the seal. That being the case, it is glorious that our salvation is confirmed, made secure, and guaranteed by the Holy Spirit!

In light of this unshakable security, some people conclude that they can live any way they want. Paul told the Ephesian believers—and us by extension—that their lives and their lips were to be gracious. Believers are not to live any way they want just because they are saved and secure, but to live in a way that encourages others and builds them up.

Then Paul told the Ephesian believers directly that they were not to do sinful things that "grieve the Holy Spirit." Paul did not say that grieving the Spirit would result in losing one's salvation, but rather that Christians "were sealed for the day of redemption." *Were* is a past tense verb; the event of being sealed has already happened. At the moment of salvation, a person is born into the family of God by the Holy Spirit—and he or she is there to stay.

So the real issue is not just the security Christians have in Jesus, but whether or not they are truly saved. Have you repented and been born into the family?

Father, thank You for putting Your seal on me. I am humbled and grateful. Amen.

THE GIFT OF JESUS

WEEK 13—MONDAY
We Have His Complete Attention

For the eyes of the Lord are on the righteous, And His ears are open to their prayers; But the face of the Lord is against those who do evil." And who is he who will harm you if you become followers of what is good?

1 PETER 3:12–13

We've all done it. We're supposed to be watching someone—a child we know and love—and we get distracted. Maybe our eyes stayed focused, but we found ourselves listening to something other than the little one's voice. Or perhaps we were still within earshot, but our eyes drifted away from our young charge. Isn't it great to know that Jesus never gets distracted? His eyes are watching us continually, and His ears are always open to our prayers. In other words, we have His complete and undivided attention.

What's so amazing is what that fact suggests about how important we must be to Him. Normally, in our world, this kind of attentiveness is lavished only on the most significant of people. This level of personal attention suggests the Secret Service agents' protection of the president.

Let this comforting thought settle in your mind. As you go out to face the day, Jesus is shadowing you, watching your every move, listening to your every word. He is there to guide you, protect you, and answer you when you turn to Him for counsel or cry to Him for help. And unlike even the best of human guardians, Jesus cannot fail. He is almighty God. Nothing can distract Him from caring for you.

....

Dear Lord, it's comforting to know that I have Your complete attention. Since I know You are watching me, I won't be afraid today. I'll focus on living before You a life that will make You smile. And since I know You are listening, I'll want to keep the conversation going all day. In Jesus' name, Amen.

PASTOR MARK HOOVER, NEWSPRING CHURCH, WICHITA, KS

WEEK 13—TUESDAY
Our Faithful Guardian

The Lord is faithful, who will establish you and guard you from the evil one. And we have confidence in the Lord concerning you, both that you do and will do the things we command you. Now may the Lord direct your hearts into the love of God and into the patience of Christ.

2 THESSALONIANS 3:3–5

According to one account, the assassination of Abraham Lincoln, our sixteenth president, occurred because a guard deserted his post. The man assigned to watch the door of Lincoln's box in Ford's Theatre left for a nearby tavern—and we know the rest of the tragic story. Abandoned by his protector, Lincoln was the victim of an assassin.

We, too, have an enemy. First Peter 5:8 tells us that our "adversary the devil walks about like a roaring lion, seeking whom he may devour." But we don't have to face him alone. Our Scripture reading assures us that Jesus will guard us faithfully from the evil one. As our Protector, He will never leave His post.

Is there any characteristic more beautiful in a relationship than faithfulness, than the intense loyalty that says, "I will never abandon you for someone else"? Think about how many times the Bible says God is faithful—faithful to forgive and cleanse us; faithful to keep us from more than we can bear; faithful to keep His promises; even faithful when we fail. And these are but a few of God's commitments to be faithful to you.

Today and always you can stand secure in Jesus' faithful protection.

....

Dear Lord, it's so comforting to know that You are guarding me. Your faithfulness to me inspires me to be loyal to You. In Jesus' name, Amen.

WEEK 13—WEDNESDAY
Guarded Before We Knew It

The Scripture has confined all under sin, that the promise by faith in Jesus Christ might be given to those who believe. But before faith came, we were kept under guard by the law, kept for the faith which would afterward be revealed. Therefore the law was our tutor to bring us to Christ, that we might be justified by faith.

GALATIANS 3:22–24

Long before the newborn child fully knows the mother, the mother knows the child. The child's memory meter isn't running yet, but the mother cares for, shelters, and guards her little one. Only with maturity will the child come to realize the protection and care provided in that unknowable season before awareness.

As we focus today on Jesus' watch over us, let's stop to reflect on something wonderful. Even before we were God's children, He was guarding and taking care of us. The book of Romans says He "foreknew" us (8:29 and 11:2). Even when we didn't know Jesus, He knew us, and God's Spirit was at work bringing us toward an everlasting relationship with Him. Even that overwhelming sense that we had done wrong was part of God's generous plan to show us our need for a Savior.

To a large extent, the specifics will remain something of a mystery until we get to heaven. But today we can celebrate what we do know. Whether we came to Jesus in the tenderness of childhood or after long, painful years, He was guarding us all the time. We survived the close calls and the dangerous moments because He had a plan for us. And He still does.

....

Thank You, Jesus, for guarding me even before I knew You. In Jesus' name, Amen.

PASTOR MARK HOOVER, NEWSPRING CHURCH, WICHITA, KS

WEEK 13—THURSDAY
Advance Guard

"Behold, I send an Angel before you to keep you in the way and to bring you into the place which I have prepared. Beware of Him and obey His voice; do not provoke Him, for He will not pardon your transgressions; for My name is in Him. But if you indeed obey His voice and do all that I speak, then I will be an enemy to your enemies and an adversary to your adversaries. For My Angel will go before you . . . and I will cut them off."

EXODUS 23:20–23

In the days leading up to a major event such as the visit of an important dignitary, an advance team is often dispatched to the site. Members of the team have very special responsibilities as they secure accommodations, assess potential risks, and set the stage for the big occasion.

As you face a new day, God offers to do the same and more for you. But He won't merely send a team; He will *personally* check things out. In fact, many Bible scholars believe the angel God promised to Moses and the Israelites in today's Scripture verses was none other than the pre-incarnate Jesus.

We never know what we're facing when a day begins. We may have the day carefully scheduled and scripted, but a single call or a quick text can turn the day completely upside down. Isn't it comforting to know that Jesus scouts the day ahead of us and that nothing can happen to us that He hasn't already encountered?

Also, we will do well to do as God commanded the nation of Israel: "Beware of Him and obey His voice." And since He's seen what lies ahead, doesn't that make sense?

....

Dear Jesus, thank You for going ahead of me. I trust You completely. In Your name I pray, Amen.

WEEK 13—FRIDAY
Shelter

He shall cover you with His feathers, and under His wings you shall take refuge; His truth shall be your shield and buckler. You shall not be afraid of the terror by night, nor of the arrow that flies by day, nor of the pestilence that walks in darkness, nor of the destruction that lays waste at noonday. A thousand may fall at your side, and ten thousand at your right hand; but it shall not come near you.

PSALM 91:4–7

It was the middle of the night when one of those out-of-nowhere storms that we get in Kansas rolled in, bringing hail the size of ping pong balls. Out among those fiercely bouncing pieces of ice, a mother duck sat on her nest—and she didn't move. She had eggs in that nest, so whatever happened to her would just have to happen. She refused to leave her eggs at the mercy of the storm.

The atheist would have to engage in some serious mental gymnastics to imagine how such a self-sacrificial, altruistic instinct could happen accidentally. That's because the instinct didn't happen accidentally. That hen remained in the storm, faithfully sitting on her eggs, because much of the Creator's handiwork reflects something of His character.

Our Scripture passage today says that you can rest "under His wings." You need not be afraid of the undefined nighttime terror you *can't* see. You don't have to fear the flying arrows you *can* see in the daytime, those hurdles and hardships, those sources of pain and moments of loss. Jesus is doing the watching for you. He has you completely covered and sheltered.

....

Dear Lord, help me to remember You are here with me. Sometimes my fears scream at me so loudly that I forget about Your all-powerful presence. Help me to face this day with calm assurance. In Jesus' name, Amen.

PASTOR MARK HOOVER, NEWSPRING CHURCH, WICHITA, KS

WEEK 13—WEEKEND
Calmed Down

"The LORD your God in your midst, the Mighty One, will save; He will rejoice over you with gladness, He will quiet you with His love, He will rejoice over you with singing."

ZEPHANIAH 3:17

Today's verse is rich with promises from our God. We read that He is in our midst. Our Mighty God will rescue us. He rejoices over us with gladness and singing. And among those wonderful assurances is that line that captures my attention: "He will quiet you with His love."

We've focused this week on Jesus' gifting us with His guardianship. Often, we think of His guarding our physical well-being. But isn't it true that, in our world, our minds and emotions are most frequently under attack? Physical jeopardy, while possible, is inferior to the the attack on our inner person. Pressures, anxieties, and all kinds of threats shriek so loudly that we can find it difficult to function in the daytime and sometimes difficult to sleep at night. Isn't it good to know that our God "will quiet you with His love"?

You've undoubtedly seen a toddler fall down, maybe scrape his knee, and then get up, crying at the top of his lungs. He was probably more scared than hurt. Then the mom comes over, and you know what will happen next. She envelops him in her arms, rocks him a little, and speaks soothing words. In a few seconds, the child calms down, filled with the love of the mother that flowed out of her heart and into his.

If you're hurting today, imagine Jesus enveloping you in His mighty arms. Let Him "quiet you with His love."

....

Dear Lord, when noisy fears scream at me, it's so comforting to know that I can rest in Your arms. In Jesus' name, Amen.

Week 14—Monday
The Lord's Sufficient Grace

[The Lord] said to me, "My grace is sufficient for you, for My strength is made perfect in weakness." Therefore most gladly I will rather boast in my infirmities, that the power of Christ may rest upon me. Therefore I take pleasure in infirmities, in reproaches, in needs, in persecutions, in distresses, for Christ's sake. For when I am weak, then I am strong.

2 CORINTHIANS 12:9–10

One afternoon, I began to feel weak with flu-like symptoms. I thought I'd be tough and sweat it out. Two days later, though, I was in the ER and then admitted into the hospital.

I remember a battery of tests, CT scans, MRIs, bloodwork, and, finally, the diagnosis: spinal meningitis. Then came eight long days quarantined in the hospital, thinking of my wife and children, wondering if I would live.

The doctor said the reason for the sickness was exhaustion. My body was drained. My immunities were down. I had been trying to be everything from the custodian to the CEO of the new church plant. The doctor said, "You're not Superman."

In the end, God gave me a second chance. I realized that Jesus died for the church—and I couldn't grow this church by sheer will or my efforts alone. The members were going to have to be the church together. As the days, weeks, and months unfolded, I watched the members step up, and God grew the church.

We are the body of Christ, and by His grace we will work together for His glory.

....

Lord Jesus, help me to rely on Your grace to enable me to do what You want me to do. And, by Your grace, may the church I'm involved in serve You well. Amen.

REV. BRIAN FOSSETT, FOSSETT EVANGELISTIC MINISTRIES, DALTON, GA

WEEK 14—TUESDAY
A Sufficient Witness Because of God

We have such trust through Christ toward God. Not that we are sufficient of ourselves to think of anything as being from ourselves, but our sufficiency is from God, who also made us sufficient as ministers of the new covenant, not of the letter but of the Spirit; for the letter kills, but the Spirit gives life.

2 CORINTHIANS 3:4–6

As an evangelist, I am honored to see the Spirit give new life. I never want to be lazy about that privileged calling, and I always want to be mindful that I am to do all that I can and trust God to do what I cannot. When I go into a church to preach, I faithfully present the Gospel, but God saves the lost.

I am the chaplain for a high school football team in my hometown. One day after I shared the devotion, I went into the coaches' room, and the middle school coach pointed to my Bible and said, "Hey, will you do that for us? Will you be chaplain for our team too?" Of course I agreed. I asked, "When do you want to start?" He replied, "Six thirty in the morning." I was delighted.

After several weeks of devotions, one day I preached out of James 4:14, "[Your life] is even a vapor that appears for a little time and then vanishes away." I said that obituaries are written for people of all ages, including teenagers. I explained that we are agents of free will who must choose Jesus in order to be saved. More than sixty teenagers gave their lives to Christ that afternoon. Faithfully share the gospel, and be blessed as you watch the Spirit give life.

....

Lord Jesus, by Your grace, make me a sufficient messenger of Your gospel. Help me to make You known at every opportunity. Amen.

Week 14—Wednesday
Cheerfully Invest Your Life in Others

He who sows sparingly will also reap sparingly, and he who sows bountifully will also reap bountifully. So let each one give as he purposes in his heart, not grudgingly or of necessity; for God loves a cheerful giver. And God is able to make all grace abound toward you, that you, always having all sufficiency in all things, may have an abundance for every good work.

2 Corinthians 9:6–8

God wants us to be cheerful givers of the time, talents, and treasures He gives us.

I'm on the road a lot. Once when I was in Missouri, I received a Facebook message from a woman asking me to pray about possibly presenting the gospel at a local skating rink where several lost teenagers hung out. She had grown up going there, and God had burdened her heart for the young people she saw there each day. I told her, "I don't have to pray about it. Let's do it!"

I was excited to go that night. The woman made the arrangements and spread the word, and the rink played Christian music and offered special pricing. Halfway through the night, the rink gave me the mic. I stood in the center of the rink, with skaters all around, and presented the gospel. I told how Jesus came from heaven, was born of a virgin, gave His life for our sins, conquered death, and rose again victoriously. I gave an invitation, and that night thirty-six people gave their hearts and lives to Jesus.

The woman burdened for lost teenagers gave of her time. The skating rink owner gave of his treasure. I was able to give of my talents. Whatever you do, you must do it cheerfully.

....

Lord Jesus, guide my sowing. Show me where you want me to invest my time, talents, and treasures, and help me to do it cheerfully for Your glory. Amen.

REV. BRIAN FOSSETT, FOSSETT EVANGELISTIC MINISTRIES, DALTON, GA

WEEK 14—THURSDAY
He Is Jehovah-Jireh

My God shall supply all your need according to His riches in glory by Christ Jesus.

PHILIPPIANS 4:19

God always supplies our needs. He always comes through. He is, after all, Jehovah-Jireh, the God who provides.

I had just gotten home from being away for a few days and was excited about seeing my family. Holding my son, Jake, in my arms, I walked downstairs to see my daughters, Macey and Kenzey. I missed the last step, awkwardly pulled back to keep from dropping Jake, and tore my quadricep muscle and the tendons in my leg, causing me to need surgery.

Now, my ministry was completely faith-based, and I had no idea how long it would be before I could preach again. After just a few days at home, a supporter in Atlanta called me and said he wanted to send a little something to me in the mail. I told my wife "a little something" could be $50.00 or $500.00. A few days later, I grabbed my crutches and hobbled to the mailbox. There I found a small security envelope addressed to me. The check inside was for $5000.00! No note. No card. Just a check for $5000.00. Needless to say, I praised my very good God! He generously provided for me through a dear brother when I could not provide for myself.

Our faithful God will meet your needs too—your physical, financial, emotional, and, most important, spiritual needs. He alone is able.

....

Jehovah-Jireh, thank You for Your many blessings in my life, but most of all thank You for the gift of my salvation through Your Son. I am humbled by Your love and grateful for Your presence in my life. Amen.

Week 14—Friday
Extravagant Joy

"In that day you will ask Me nothing. Most assuredly, I say to you, whatever you ask the Father in My name He will give you. Until now you have asked nothing in My name. Ask, and you will receive, that your joy may be full."

JOHN 16:23–24

What brings you joy? What brings you joy says a lot about you. If you could ask for anything, what would it be?

We have an extravagant God who loves us beyond measure. Why not ask Him to help you share the gospel? Ask God to make you a soul winner. After all, what could give you greater joy? Being present when the Lord saves another soul brings more joy to a believer's heart than any other thing.

Tragically, in the American church today, we don't see in God's people a hunger for souls or hearts broken for the lost around us. Our passion for the salvation of others has cooled. Proverbs 11:30 says, "He who wins souls is wise." Proverbs 10:5 says, "He who sleeps in harvest is a son who causes shame." We should not be a sleeping church while the harvest awaits. We need to be awake, excited, expectant, and full of joy as we share with people the good news of God's love and grace.

Saved souls bring great joy—extravagant joy—to the very heart of God. So what are you asking Him for? Material things? Prosperity? Fame? Or saved souls that bring true joy?

....

Lord Jesus, help me today to tell others about You. Lay on my heart the names of people who need to hear Your truth and enable me to be loving, articulate, kind, and bold as I share Your story with them. Amen.

WEEK 14—WEEKEND
Becoming More like Jesus

His divine power has given to us all things that pertain to life and godliness, through the knowledge of Him who called us by glory and virtue, by which have been given to us exceedingly great and precious promises, that through these you may be partakers of the divine nature.

2 PETER 1:3–4

To be a Christian means to be like Christ. And in order to be more like Him, we must decrease and He must increase. In other words, we must let Him—not our own wishes—guide our lives. His will for us must become far more important to us than our own desires for ourselves. Of course we can't be sinless this side of heaven, but we can sin less. Is that our desire?

Also key to becoming more like Jesus is our attitude. We do not *have* to go to church; we *get* to go to church. We do not *have* to serve others; we *get* to serve others. We do not *have* to praise Him; we *get* to praise Him. We do not *have* to give; we *get* to give.

Try having the attitude that even if no one else is going to have a great day in the Lord, you will. Choose to delight in the things of God rather than seeing them as duties. Choose every morning to live that new day on fire for God.

So how can you become more Christlike? Here are some basics:

Rest in the Lord: pray throughout the day.
Nutrition: feed your soul with the Word of God daily.
Exercise Your Faith: praise God, spend time with fellow believers, and talk about Jesus with unbelievers every day.

....

Lord Jesus, help me to grow strong in You. Help me to be fit spiritually so that You can use me and so that when others see me, they get a glimpse of You in me! Amen.

Week 15—Monday
Learn to Love as Jesus Loves

Love does no harm to a neighbor; therefore love is the fulfillment of the law. And do this, knowing the time, that now it is high time to awake out of sleep; for now our salvation is nearer than when we first believed.

Romans 13:10–11

We all like being around people who love what we love. Everyday decisions like the food we eat, the entertainment we enjoy, and even the duties we perform become enjoyable when we share them with others who love what we love. Everything seems better in the context of genuine love.

When Jesus died on the cross on the behalf of sinners, He demonstrated God's love (Romans 5:8). But Jesus also commanded several times for us to love.

For example, when asked to rank the commands of Scripture, Jesus did not hesitate. We can summarize His response with these words: love God passionately and love others intentionally. Jesus, who is love, fulfilled the Law when He loved us, and we must love as He loves: selflessly and sacrificially! Doing so will mean a satisfied soul, fulfillment, and peace. Also loving as Jesus loves makes the Christ-following life enjoyable regardless of our circumstances.

Notice, though, that this love is anything but passive! There is purpose in our love for God. We know that His return for His people is drawing near, so there must be an urgency in our love for others. We must live each day in a way that reflects the love of Christ. Learning to love as Jesus loves will impact both our sense of fulfillment today and the eternal future of those in our little corner of the world.

....

Jesus, teach me to love God and love others as You love. Help me to share Your love today, for that is what You created me to do. I love You! Amen.

WEEK 15—TUESDAY
Delight and Desire

Trust in the LORD, and do good; dwell in the land, and feed on His faithfulness. Delight yourself also in the LORD, and He shall give you the desires of your heart.

PSALM 37:3–4

History has often been shaped by the power of simple statements. Whether uttered in a political moment, sung as a catchy slogan, or penned in an historic document, a simple statement can indeed be powerful. However, all of history's great statements pale in comparison to the potency of one biblical truth: "Trust in the LORD." Found more than fifty times in the Bible, this is a life-changing command.

The sequence in Psalm 37:3–4 is clear: God expects us to trust in Him first and foremost and to do good. As we trust and serve, we will find ourselves nourished by God's faithfulness, and as we dwell in the protection of His faithfulness, God will begin to shape our hearts' desires. He conforms us into the image of His Son. In other words, as we faithfully delight ourselves in Him—in His trustworthiness, goodness, faithfulness, and love—He will begin to define, refine, and shape our desires.

God doesn't promise to give us whatever we want. He promises to give us what He wants when we want what He wants.

This process begins with our trust in God. Trust is the first stepping stone along the path that leads to our delighting in Him. And our delighting in God frees Him to do His transformative work on the desires of our hearts. May we trust in the Lord!

....

Heavenly Father, I trust in You and ask that You will shape and transform the desires of my heart so I may want Your will for me and do it. In Jesus' name I pray, Amen.

WEEK 15—WEDNESDAY
My Source, My Satisfaction, My Sustainer, My Security

Jesus said to them, "I am the bread of life. He who comes to Me shall never hunger, and he who believes in Me shall never thirst. . . . All that the Father gives Me will come to Me, and the one who comes to Me I will by no means cast out."

JOHN 6:35, 37

We know fulfillment in the love of Christ and our choice to trust in Him. In this passage, Jesus implied that our fulfillment in Him is inexhaustible.

The beauty of these verses stems from the simple statement Jesus made about Himself and the fourfold promise He made, a promise that we can trust in now and later.

In the very familiar Psalm 23, we learn that the Lord is our Shepherd who keeps us from wanting. In one of His defining statements, Jesus called Himself the Bread of Life, effectively claiming that He is the Source, Satisfaction, Sustainer, and Security of all life. In other words, He is the fulfillment of all our wants.

As our Source, Jesus promised we will never be hungry and that He will always meet our needs according to His riches. As our Satisfaction, He promised we will never thirst for anything that cannot be quenched in Him. As our Sustainer, He promised His very presence with us always. And as our Security, He promised He will never leave us nor forsake us. This is eternal security (1 John 5:13). Today let's trust the One we love to be everything we need.

....

Lord, today I take You at Your word. May I find all that I need in You this day and evermore. Thank You for Your faithfulness! Amen.

WEEK 15—THURSDAY
Unlimited but Conditional

"Whatever you ask in My name, that I will do, that the Father may be glorified in the Son. If you ask anything in My name, I will do it."

JOHN 14:13–14

When you purchase an expensive item—say, a new car—there are two words you desire to see on a warranty: *unlimited* and *unconditional*. An *unlimited warranty* means that regardless of the time since the purchase or the scope of the need, the necessary repair will be made. There's nothing too big, there's nothing too small, and the guarantee never expires. An *unconditional warranty* ensures that no matter what happens, the damage will be repaired. Rarely are the two words found together, and Jesus' words in today's passage are no exception.

Jesus made a promise unlimited in power, but conditional in purpose. We know the promise is unlimited because of the vastness of the word *whatever*, yet the *whatever* of Jesus is conditioned by the phrase *in my Name*. Why?

The answer is found in Jesus' very next words. God is primarily concerned with His glory. Why did Jesus pray to God? Why is God still acting in unexplainable ways around the world? God always works for the spread of His name and His fame. He desires that His glory be known among the nations. So we pray in His Name . . . according to His will and for His desires, so that He might be glorified. And as we pray for God's desires, we soon will experience them as our own.

The strength of the Lord's unlimited power and the strictness of His condition are for our good and God's glory. Pray for big things in His Name and for His glory!

....

Loving God, do Your work in me for my good and for Your glory. In Jesus' name I pray, Amen.

Week 15—Friday
He Is on My Team!

What then shall we say to these things? If God is for us, who can be against us? He who did not spare His own Son, but delivered Him up for us all, how shall He not with Him also freely give us all things?

Romans 8:31–32

Many mornings most of us wake up with "to-do" lists. The lists may be long, they may be loud, and they love to remind us that they are always growing. After all, there's always one more thing to do, right? Some mornings, our minds jump right into an overview of the list as soon as we wake up. We start strategizing, planning, adding items, and subtracting them—and the list can wear us out even before we've walked out the door.

I want to suggest a different approach. Today, rather than focusing on your list, remind yourself of the gospel. Take some time to review all God has done from creation through Jesus' death and resurrection to your birth and your new birth. Remind yourself that God gave His Son for you and that He is the gracious Giver of all things—including the very breath you use to complain about the lists that He's given you the energy, time, and resources to complete. God even made this very day so that you might rejoice and be glad in it. Every day is a blessing!

As the apostle Paul proclaimed in Romans 8, God is for you. When you see your day through the lens of the gospel, hear God say, "I'm on your team. No one can stand against you!" Today rest in the truth of the gospel, the reality of God's grace, and the fact that God is on your team.

....

Heavenly Father, thank You for being for me. Today teach me more about what it is to live for You. In Jesus' name I pray, Amen.

WEEK 15—WEEKEND
Love + Obedience = Fulfillment

"Do not think that I came to destroy the Law or the Prophets. I did not come to destroy but to fulfill. For assuredly, I say to you, till heaven and earth pass away, one jot or one tittle will by no means pass from the law till all is fulfilled. . . . Whoever does and teaches [My commandments], he shall be called great in the kingdom of heaven."

MATTHEW 5:17–19

We tend to look for the quickest way to get things done. We drive in the fast lanes, eat fast food, and complain when our ever-advancing technology is too slow. We want quick fixes and overnight sanctification. But while our salvation was accomplished in an instant, our sanctification is a lifelong process. There are no shortcuts. Though we may wish it were otherwise, we cannot expedite the process of discipleship that contributes to a fulfilling life. God will have His way.

First, our fulfillment is found in Christ alone, and we do not have freedom to look past or skip over His commands. He is consistent and deliberate in His leadership, and He expects our constant diligence as we follow Him. Also note in the passage above that God fulfills each claim He makes. He dots every *i* and crosses every *t*. He is meticulous as He makes good on all of His promises.

We end this week with two points of application. Christ followers are blessed to have a fulfilling, loving relationship with Jesus, which is the basis for our faith. At the same time, we are personally responsible for choosing the fulfillment that comes when we obey God's commands. So serve Him by loving Him passionately and loving others intentionally.

....

Lord, help me to act in ways to bring You glory this weekend—and always! May Your name be praised. Amen.

WEEK 16—MONDAY
The Model Prayer

"In this manner, therefore, pray: Our Father in heaven, hallowed be Your name. Your kingdom come. Your will be done on earth as it is in heaven. Give us this day our daily bread. And forgive us our debts, as we forgive our debtors. And do not lead us into temptation, but deliver us from the evil one. For Yours is the kingdom and the power and the glory forever. Amen."

MATTHEW 6:9–13

Most of us are familiar with the Lord's Prayer. Jesus wasn't teaching that we have to pray these exact words, but He was offering several guidelines. First, He reminded us that prayer is intimate: the very personal name "Father" speaks of His love and provision for us, His children.

Having acknowledged a deep level of intimacy and our trust in Him, we submit our lives in full surrender. "Your kingdom come" refers to God's rule in our daily lives. As our King, God has authority and lordship over us.

Jesus then told us to pray for "our daily bread," symbolizing the basic necessities of daily life. People often say, "I don't want to bother God with the small stuff." God delights in helping His children. You won't be bothering Him.

Then Jesus reminded us that in order for our relationship with God to be right, we must have our earthly ones right as well. Whom, if anyone, do we need to forgive today?

Then Jesus spoke of the devil. A rather inconclusive comment. Satan goes after God's children, but in God's power we can stand strong against him.

Finally, appropriately enough, Jesus' model prayer begins and ends in praise. God is to be our starting point, our endpoint, and our purpose in life.

We call to You, heavenly Father, who loves us. We bless Your holy name. We place Your priorities above our own. We submit to You as Lord. Amen.

PASTOR STEVE FLOCKHART, NEW SEASON CHURCH, HIRAM, GA

WEEK 16—TUESDAY
Passing the Test

Hear a just cause, O LORD, attend to my cry; give ear to my prayer which is not from deceitful lips. Let my vindication come from Your presence; let Your eyes look on the things that are upright. You have tested my heart; You have visited me in the night; You have tried me and have found nothing; I have purposed that my mouth shall not transgress.

PSALM 17:1–3

I love the realness of the psalms. The range of human emotions—love, hate, joy, sorrow, fear, agony, anger—is portrayed in this book, and we see shouting and dancing as well.

The most powerful psalms come out of people's most intense times. King David wrote approximately 75 of the 150 psalms, and he always prayed with heartfelt emotion and intensity.

If we are familiar with the life of David, we know the struggles he experienced. As we see in David's example, when a person goes through the fire and comes out on the other side, this individual has great wisdom to share and greater passion for God's truth.

David declared that God had tested his heart. When gold is tested, the heat causes the dross, the impurities, to rise to the surface. God took David through the fire of purification just as He does each of us. Fire purifies gold, and going through trials purifies, or refines, our character. The entire Christian life is about having our character conformed to the image of Jesus. We will either be transformed in the fire, or we will remove ourselves from our God.

Trust in the One whose hand is on the thermostat and who is working in your life to make you into the person He created you to be.

....

Father, when You bring tests into my life, please help me to pass them. I know You are working all things for my good. I love You. Amen.

WEEK 16—WEDNESDAY
Our Strength

Hear my cry, O God; attend to my prayer. From the end of the earth I will cry to You, when my heart is overwhelmed; lead me to the rock that is higher than I. For You have been a shelter for me, a strong tower from the enemy. I will abide in Your tabernacle forever; I will trust in the shelter of Your wings.

PSALM 61:1–4

Can you think of a time in your life when the pain was so deep and the anguish in your heart so intense you weren't sure you would survive?

That is how King David, the writer of this psalm, felt. As a passionate and emotional man, David was crushed by the weight of his circumstances, and crying out to God, he begged the Lord to hear him. David knew he needed the Lord's help. When we go through difficult times, we need the assurance that God hears us.

We also need the assurance that God is—to use David's words—our strong rock, our shelter, our strong tower, and our fortress. He will protect us.

David stated, "I will abide," and used the word *abide,* which implies "to be a houseguest." David wanted to live in the presence of God. Then he ended his prayer by declaring his trust in the Lord and his confidence that God would shelter him from all harm.

Maybe you're going through a difficult time right now. Let David's psalm remind you of God's constant strength, love, protection, and abiding presence with you.

....

Thank You, Father, for providing me with strength and protection anytime I need You. Amen.

WEEK 16—THURSDAY
Perfect Hope

As for me, my prayer is to You, O LORD, in the acceptable time; O God, in the multitude of Your mercy, hear me in the truth of Your salvation.

PSALM 69:13

No one is immune to the problems of life, and those problems may involve your health, finances, spouse, children, or family matters. Sometimes these situations seem hopeless. Notice, though, what the apostle Paul called Jesus in his greeting to his young friend, Timothy: "the Lord Jesus Christ, our hope" (1 Timothy 1:1). Hope!

Hope in God is not wishful thinking, but rather having great confidence in who God is and then tapping into His sufficiency and power.

In this psalm, David was crying out to God. Here are the words of a broken man who was no stranger to pain—pain that he had brought on himself by getting out of the will of God and living his life the way that he chose as well as pain resulting from other people's actions.

Even in the midst of this great pain, David showed his great confidence in the Lord by crying out to Him in prayer. David's life was in God's hands—God was in charge, and he knew that God is sovereign. David pleaded for mercy; he wanted to rest in God's grace.

Today in the midst of your pain, cry out to God with great confidence in Him who loves you and is ready to help you.

....

Father, in the midst of my pain, I trust You. No matter what comes my way, I will rest in Your promises. Amen.

WEEK 16—FRIDAY
Dressing Up

[Take] the shield of faith with which you will be able to quench all the fiery darts of the wicked one. And take the helmet of salvation, and the sword of the Spirit, which is the word of God; praying always with all prayer and supplication in the Spirit, being watchful to this end with all perseverance and supplication for all the saints.

EPHESIANS 6:16–18

The devil is not threatened by long and eloquent prayers. Nor does he fear idle repetition of words we have memorized. What Satan detests is a man or woman of God who is dressed in the armor of God and knows how to pray. How we pray indicates how we believe.

Writing from a Roman prison cell, the apostle Paul used powerful metaphors to instruct us how to engage in the battle with the forces of darkness.

Paul told us to pick up the shield of faith because the evil one will throw fiery darts at us. This is war! And we all know what it feels like to be attacked by the devil.

Paul also challenged us to think right and to believe right, especially when the battle is raging. We must have God's Word to guide us and protect us from the enemy.

When we wear the armor of God, we are able to pray bold, audacious prayers. We must be praying, believing, standing in the gap for others, and persevering in our prayers.

....

Father, thank You for providing me with armor for the battle. I want to be an active and effective soldier for You. Help me to stand and fight in Your name. I am grateful that Satan has already been defeated and, by Jesus' victory over sin and death, we will win! Amen.

PASTOR STEVE FLOCKHART, NEW SEASON CHURCH, HIRAM, GA

WEEK 16—WEEKEND
No Worries!

*Be anxious for nothing, but in everything by prayer and supplication, with
thanksgiving, let your requests be made known to God; and the peace of God, which
surpasses all understanding, will guard your hearts and minds through Christ Jesus.*

PHILIPPIANS 4:6–7

We worry about many things. Family, finances, and relationships are at
or near the top of the list. Are we feeling restless, agitated, uneasy, and
uncertain? Worrying like that weighs down a person.

In our passage today, we find the apostle Paul in prison, not knowing the
outcome of his life. Paul had every right to worry, but he didn't. In fact, in this
passage he showed us the secret to overcoming worry. Basically, Paul showed
us that our inner attitudes don't have to reflect our outward circumstances.
He told us to "be anxious for nothing." The word *anxious* means "to be pulled
in different directions." All of us have experienced anxiety . . . perhaps while
waiting on that test result or phone call.

Paul told us we have the ability *not* to worry about anything, and that happens when we pray about everything! Paul said we can pray in such a way that
banishes worry, removes anxiety, and releases pressure. After all, when we
pray, we are talking to the Father and the Creator of the world, and we have a
personal relationship with Him. When we pray, we can know peace.

But this kind of peace is not the absence of conflict; it is an internal peace.
It is Christ in you. It is your choosing to trust your Father. That rest—that
inner assurance that God is in control—has its roots in your deep-down confidence that God can handle whatever comes your way.

....

*Father, You are in control of my present and my tomorrow. I will trust You.
Amen.*

WEEK 17—MONDAY
Divine GPS

"When He, the Spirit of truth, has come, He will guide you into all truth; for He will not speak on His own authority, but whatever He hears He will speak; and He will tell you things to come. He will glorify Me, for He will take of what is Mine and declare it to you."

JOHN 16:13–14

I am directionally challenged. Time and time again I've gotten lost when I'm driving. But everything changed with the advent of the Global Positioning System (GPS). Now I can have great confidence in getting to that hard-to-find destination because my GPS guides me.

In the spiritual realm, the Holy Spirit is our divine GPS. He came to be our Helper and our Guide. He wants to guide us "into all truth," so we can make the right decisions and join Him in glorifying Christ.

When it comes to understanding God's truth correctly, we can easily become turned around, twisted, confused, and lost. The Holy Spirit is the One who lets us know the way to go. If and when we take a wrong spiritual turn, He is faithful to convict our hearts of the error. He doesn't berate us for messing up or forsake us because of our wrong turn. Instead, He lovingly says, "Recalculating." He devises another route to get us moving in the right direction again.

Perhaps we're on a dead-end street today. Getting off course like that happens when we stop reading His Word and listening to His voice, but there is good news. We can start following Him once again—and we can start today!

Lord, forgive me for not listening to You. I confess my pride. I want You to lead me. Guide me by the power of Your Holy Spirit. Amen.

WEEK 17—TUESDAY
A Heart like His

"If you extend your soul to the hungry and satisfy the afflicted soul, then your light shall dawn in the darkness, and your darkness shall be as the noonday. The LORD will guide you continually, and satisfy your soul in drought, and strengthen your bones; you shall be like a watered garden, and like a spring of water, whose waters do not fail."

ISAIAH 58:10–11

God cares about the poor and needy. He wants us to care about them too. When we reach out to help those who cannot help themselves, God is both pleased and glorified. He responds by blessing us and satisfying our souls with good things.

It's important to remember who the needy are, though. They are not those who *will* not help themselves. God says, "If anyone will not work, neither shall he eat" (2 Thessalonians 3:10). The truly needy are those who, for one reason or another, *cannot* work or help themselves. God has a special place in His heart for people who find themselves in such circumstances.

Ask yourself: do you need a breakthrough in your life today? Are you spiritually dry, stale, or weak? If so, go and help the poor and needy. Give, serve, and bless people who have little to nothing. God will bless you in return for having a heart like His.

....

Dear Lord, You have given me so much, and I thank You for that. So that I can share those blessings wisely, help me to see true needs and to offer assistance generously, even sacrificially. Help me to be sensitive to the physical and spiritual needs of the people around me. I want to bless You, Lord, as I minister to those around me who genuinely need help. I pray in Jesus' name, Amen.

WEEK 17—WEDNESDAY
Got Peace?

"Through the tender mercy of our God, with which the Dayspring from on high has visited us; to give light to those who sit in darkness and the shadow of death, to guide our feet into the way of peace."

LUKE 1:78–79

Without question, the Lord Jesus is good, loving, and merciful. Approximately two thousand years ago, He came into this dark and sinful world to shine the light of His love and grace upon all mankind. He came to make a way for us to be forgiven and to experience true peace—peace with God and peace within.

In an interview with Barbara Walters, actor Richard Dreyfuss was asked what he wanted most. His answer was short and sweet: he wanted peace. Dreyfuss had fame and fortune, but he didn't have peace. After all, peace is not something you can buy or achieve. Peace is given by God.

Do you have peace today? So many people do not. Peace comes from being right with God. When we bring all of our sins out from the dark recesses of our hearts, when we bring all of the ugliness into His holy light and confess it to Him, and when we receive His forgiveness, then and only then can we experience true peace.

The prostitute in Luke 7:36–50 wept in repentance at Jesus' feet. The Lord graciously forgave her and told her, "Go in peace." Not guilt, but peace. How wonderful! He offers this same peace to you today.

....

Dear God, I have been hiding my sins in the shadows, pretending they are not really there. Today I bring them to the light. I confess all to You. Please forgive me and wash me clean just as You have promised. And then please flood my soul with Your peace. I pray in Jesus' name, Amen.

DR. JEFF SCHREVE, FIRST BAPTIST CHURCH TEXARKANA, TEXARKANA, TX

WEEK 17—THURSDAY
The Bible Is Unique

All Scripture is given by inspiration of God, and is profitable for doctrine, for reproof, for correction, for instruction in righteousness, that the man of God may be complete, thoroughly equipped for every good work.

2 TIMOTHY 3:16–17

Did you know the Bible is not like any other book? It's true! The Bible is the only book that was given by the inspiration of God. That means that the Bible is God-breathed.

But you might ask, "Didn't men write the Bible?" Yes, they did. They were "moved by the Holy Spirit" (2 Peter 1:21). God breathed through them, much like a master musician breathes through a musical instrument. That is why the books are written in various styles, depending on the writer. Paul didn't write like Peter, and a tuba doesn't sound like an oboe even if the same musician is playing both instruments. However, a tuba and an oboe, along with many other instruments, can be used together to play the same beautiful symphony. So it is with the Bible.

The writer of Hebrews told us the Word of God is "living and powerful" (Hebrews 4:12)! And as a living, powerful book, the Bible is critical in the life of a church and in the life of a Christian. There is great profit in spending time reading and studying God's Word. We can't grow without it! The Bible tells us four critical truths: (1) what is right (doctrine); (2) what is not right (reproof); (3) how to get right (correction); and (4) how to stay right (instruction for righteousness). Take time every day to study the Bible. You'll be so glad you did!

....

God, the Bible is truly a treasure. Help me live out this truth by spending time each day reading Your Word and obeying it. In Jesus' name, Amen.

Week 17—Friday
I Will Never Leave You

Nevertheless I am continually with You; You hold me by my right hand. You will guide me with Your counsel, and afterward receive me to glory.

PSALM 73:23–24

One of the greatest promises in the Bible is God's promise to be present in our lives. In Matthew's gospel, "I am with you always" is Jesus' last statement to the disciples (28:20). As followers of Jesus, we can find great comfort knowing that He is always present in our lives, through the good times and the bad. We can count on Him.

Not only is Jesus with us, but He is with us tenderly. He is leading us by the hand, guiding us as a good shepherd does his sheep. He takes us to green pastures and leads us along still waters. He guides us through the dark valleys, so we need not fear, as well as to the blessings of higher ground.

Then when—in His perfect timing—our lives on this earth are complete, He will guide us all the way to heaven! We will be welcomed into glory for one reason: we have received Jesus into our hearts as Savior and Lord.

Be encouraged today! The Lord who died for you is with you always. Although you cannot see Him, you can be assured of His presence with you. He wants you to follow Him humbly and obediently so you can experience all the good things He has for you. Wandering sheep miss out on blessings. May you stay in step with your Shepherd.

. . . .

Dear Lord, thank You for being with me always. Thank You for Your promise to lead me and guide me each day. I choose to follow You humbly, no matter the cost. And, Jesus, I rejoice that my eternal future is secure in You. Hallelujah, what a Savior! Amen.

DR. JEFF SCHREVE, FIRST BAPTIST CHURCH TEXARKANA, TEXARKANA, TX

WEEK 17—WEEKEND
True Success

"This Book of the Law shall not depart from your mouth, but you shall meditate in it day and night, that you may observe to do according to all that is written in it. For then you will make your way prosperous, and then you will have good success."

JOSHUA 1:8

D o you want to succeed in life? Most people do. Most people long to see their efforts bear fruit, whether in academics, sports, business, marriage, family, or the Christian life.

Did you know there is a secret to success? The secret is rather simple. God says true success comes to the one who meditates on His Word . . . and obeys it. As we have learned this week, God's Word is alive and powerful. It has the power to change us from the inside out. As we spend time reading God's Word, we start to see life from His perspective. We start to walk by faith, not by sight. We start to believe Him for big things because we read that He is a big God who delights in doing the impossible.

Maybe you have been struggling with your future. Maybe you have been sensing God wants you to make a major change in your life, but you are too afraid of failing. Fear not! Just keep meditating on God's Word and obeying what He commands. He is faithful to those who are faithful to Him. Joshua 1:8 is not just God's promise to Joshua. It is God's promise to you too.

....

Dear God, help me to meditate on Your Word—and then to do what it says! I want Your Word to change the way I think, act, and react. I thank You that You promise true success for those who obey You. I choose obedience! Amen.

Week 18—Monday
But He Was Here Yesterday . . .

"All flesh is as grass, and all the glory of man as the flower of the grass. The grass withers, and its flower falls away, But the word of the Lord endures forever." Now this is the word which by the gospel was preached to you.

1 Peter 1:24–25

I was eight years old and so excited to get to school early one day. My best friend, Kevin, had promised to let me ride the new bike he received for his birthday. When I arrived at school, I waited and waited, but Kevin never came. I was so disappointed that I didn't see my best friend or get to ride his new bike.

The next day I got up early and raced to school. Kevin wasn't there. At the end of the day, our teacher told us Kevin had moved to another city and would not be returning to our school. I was crying by the time I got home. I told my mom that Kevin had moved and I would never see him again. My mother opened her Bible and read me the Scripture passages you are reading today. She explained that in life we are going to have disappointments. There will be times when people we love will not be with us anymore. But then she told me the good news that Jesus will never leave me and that His Word will last forever.

Have you had friends move away? Maybe someone you love is no longer with you. Remember, Jesus promised you that He would never leave you (Hebrews 13:5) and that you can trust forever what is written in the Bible, and forever is a long time!

. . . .

Lord Jesus, thank You for what friendships teach me about You—and thank You that You are the Friend who will never move away. Thank You too for the foundation for life that You provide in Your unchanging and eternal Word. Amen.

DR. LARRY THOMPSON, FIRST FORT LAUDERDALE, FT. LAUDERDALE, FL

WEEK 18—TUESDAY
You're Out! You Didn't Stay in the Baseline!

The LORD is exalted, for He dwells on high; He has filled Zion with justice and righteousness. Wisdom and knowledge will be the stability of your times, and the strength of salvation; the fear of the LORD is His treasure.

ISAIAH 33:5–6

During one of my first real baseball games, I played second base on the Rancho Village Cobras. The game was tied, and it was our last time at bat. There were two outs, we had a runner on third, and I was at the plate.

The pitcher threw the ball, and I hit it into right field. I ran to first and stopped. I thought we had won the game until the umpire said, "The batter is out! He failed to stay within the baseline." I remember our coach arguing, but he didn't change the umpire's mind. He knew the rules, and apparently I hadn't followed the rules.

God has defined a baseline for every one of us, His children, in the Bible. In its pages God gives us knowledge and wisdom for all of our lives, truth so we can stand strong in our salvation, and opportunity both to know and fear the Lord. What a treasure to have access to the holy Scripture!

But what if we fail to live by God's rules? What if we run outside of His baselines? What if we ignore His Word? We lose something far greater than a baseball game. We lose the treasure of sweet fellowship with God.

....

Lord God, You treasure the fear of Your people. You treasure our reverence, respect, gratitude, and love—treasures forged in my heart thanks to the gift of Your Word and the work of Your Spirit! May my healthy fear of You keep me joyfully in the baselines of life! Amen.

Week 18—Wednesday
How Can 2 Plus 2 Plus 2 Equal 7?

My son, give attention to my words; incline your ear to my sayings. Do not let them depart from your eyes; keep them in the midst of your heart; for they are life to those who find them, and health to all their flesh.

Proverbs 4:20–22

A teacher asked our friend's daughter to answer a math question: "If I give you two rabbits and then give you another two rabbits and then give you another two rabbits, how many rabbits would you have?" The young girl thought, counted on her fingers, and replied confidently, "Seven!"

The teacher said, "Let's try it again, and listen more carefully. If I give you two rabbits and then give you two more rabbits and then give you two more rabbits, how many rabbits would you have?" Without hesitation the little girl again said, "Seven!"

Finally, the teacher took out six pennies and said, "I am going to give you two pennies, and then I am going to give you two more pennies and then two more pennies. Now how many pennies do you have?" The little girl immediately said, "Six!"

"That's right," said her teacher. "So why do you keep getting seven rabbits?"

"Because," the little girl responded, "I already have one rabbit at home. I got it at Easter!"

The little girl was actually doing a great job of paying attention to what her teacher was saying. God wants us to pay close attention to His words as well. His words are very useful, not just for today, but for all of our lives.

....

Lord God, thank You for Your Word. Scripture nourishes my soul, guides my steps, and fuels my love for You. May I therefore be a doer of Your Word, not just a hearer. Amen.

DR. LARRY THOMPSON, FIRST FORT LAUDERDALE, FT. LAUDERDALE, FL

WEEK 18—THURSDAY
I Knew You'd Come Back for Me, Daddy!

"Assuredly, I say to you, this generation will by no means pass away till all these things take place. Heaven and earth will pass away, but My words will by no means pass away."

MATTHEW 24:34–35

When my little girl was five years old, I took her to church with me when I needed to pick up some books. I asked her to sit in the office while I checked on a Bible study class that was having an event at the church. I visited with them for twenty minutes, and then realized I was running late, so I jumped in my car and headed home. My wife had just finished fixing dinner and putting everything on the table. She called for us to come sit down. When we gathered around the table, Cynthia asked, "Where's Taylor?" I gasped. I had left my daughter in my office at church!

I ran to my car and drove the couple of miles back to the church. When I got to my office, she was sitting in the same chair still looking at her books. I told her how sorry I was that I had forgotten her, and she said, "I knew you'd come back for me, Daddy."

Similarly, we can know that our Lord and Savior will come back for us. Jesus reminded us that the "earth will pass away," but His words and His promises will last forever. We can always count on what He has told us in the Bible, and He has said that one day He will come back for us. When He does, we who have trusted Him as our Savior and Lord will live with Him forever.

....

Lord Jesus, I look forward to the day of Your return when I will joyfully say to you, "I knew You'd come back for me!" Amen.

Week 18—Friday
Welcome Home!

Now to Him who is able to keep you from stumbling, and to present you faultless before the presence of His glory with exceeding joy, to God our Savior, who alone is wise, be glory and majesty, dominion and power, both now and forever. Amen.

Jude vv. 24–25

When I was eight, my grandparents took me on vacation to see the California redwoods. Growing up in Oklahoma, I had never seen trees that huge. I couldn't even see the tops of them!

We walked over to one area where there was a deep drop and a fence that kept visitors from falling down the mountain. I climbed onto the fence—only to feel my grandfather's hand immediately grab my arm and pull me back.

He then explained how easy it would be to slip off that fence and how dangerous it was that I had not paid attention. He then picked me up and held onto me as we looked down the mountainside. He smiled and said, "I'm not letting go of you. I want to bring you home safely."

Jesus has made a similar promise to each of us who trusts Him. Jesus said, "I'm going to hold onto you and keep you from falling so I can bring you home safely! There will be great joy in the Father's presence."

Twelve days later, my grandparents' old Pontiac brought me home. The first story my grandfather told was about when he kept me from falling.

It was great to be safely home—but not as great as it's going to be when we go to heaven. And we'll be able to go there because Jesus has kept us safe.

....

Lord Jesus, thank You for keeping me safe. Thank You for intervening when I don't pay attention, for keeping me from stumbling, and for promising to take me safely to my heavenly home. What a joyful day that will be! Amen.

DR. LARRY THOMPSON, FIRST FORT LAUDERDALE, FT. LAUDERDALE, FL

Week 18—Weekend
Do Not Think

"Do not think that I came to destroy the Law or the Prophets. I did not come to destroy but to fulfill. For assuredly, I say to you, till heaven and earth pass away, one jot or one tittle will by no means pass from the law till all is fulfilled."

MATTHEW 5:17–18

What do you think Jesus meant when He told those listening to Him, "Do not think"? Have you ever tried to stop thinking? If I were to tell you to try not to think about anything while I count to thirty, you would keep thinking. (Go ahead and try it if you don't believe me!)

Jesus wasn't really telling us to quit thinking. He told us to quit thinking *the wrong way*. Jesus said, "Don't think that I came to tear things apart. I came to put things back together, and when I am finished, everything will be completely put back together just as God intended in the beginning."

My grandsons love to play with their LEGOs—but I don't. That's because I can't put them together. Whenever I try, I just make a mess of it. Jesus, however, will take the scattered mess of our world, and He will make it just as it was supposed to be.

Again, Jesus didn't tell the people to quit thinking. Instead, He told them—and us—to think about what He was saying: "I will put everything back together just like it's supposed to be."

....

Jesus, thank You for the ways You have already taken sinful, self-centered me and are making me more like You, more the way I'm supposed to be. What a glorious world it will be when You finish putting it back together too! Amen.

WEEK 19—MONDAY
Strengthened to Love

I bow my knees to the Father . . . that He would grant you, according to the riches of His glory, to be strengthened with might through His Spirit in the inner man, that Christ may dwell in your hearts through faith; that you . . . may be able . . . to know the love of Christ which passes knowledge; that you may be filled with all the fullness of God.

EPHESIANS 3:14, 16–17, 19

Today's Scripture passages are a portion of one of Paul's prayers. He was on his knees before the Father, interceding for his beloved church in Ephesus—and for us—to be strengthened through the Holy Spirit in the inner man.

Twentieth-century Christian teacher Watchman Nee often spoke of the outer man, the inner man, and the innermost man. He defined these as the body, the soul (mind, will, and emotion), and the spirit. It is this innermost man—the spirit—about which Paul was praying. That is the part of human beings where divine power resides. God's Holy Spirit then works outwardly through the soul and body. Through faith in Jesus, God works through us when we are in relationship with Him, having received forgiveness for our sins and having submitted our lives to Him. Then the love of heaven works in us and through us to others. The key to being used like this is submission to the God of love.

....

Lord, I ask You today to break me, fill me, and love through me. My love is limited, and I can be self-centered. Enable me to love with Your love that You might be glorified and people around me encouraged. Amen.

DR. TED H. TRAYLOR, OLIVE BAPTIST CHURCH, PENSACOLA, FL

WEEK 19—TUESDAY
Our Inheritance

[We] do not cease to pray for you . . . that you may walk worthy of the Lord, fully pleasing Him, being fruitful in every good work and increasing in the knowledge of God; strengthened with all might, according to His glorious power, for all patience and longsuffering with joy; giving thanks to the Father who has qualified us to be partakers of the inheritance of the saints in the light.

COLOSSIANS 1:9–12

P aul was again praying for Christ followers, for "the saints in the light," and thanking God for the inheritance He has for His people throughout eternity. What do we know about that inheritance?

When we are redeemed from our sinful ways of living apart from God, we receive an inheritance that certainly includes heaven. In addition, we inherit the presence of God in our inner man. In other words, our spirit is made alive in Christ as His might and power work in us. Jesus grants us inner strength "for all patience and longsuffering with joy." The Father has qualified us to be partakers in this inheritance, and clearly that is a reason to—like Paul—give thanks.

One more thought about inheritances: they're not what they used to be! People are living longer, and assisted-care facilities drain retirement funds and inheritances. After we retire, we may not have much to leave to our kids—and even if we did, it wouldn't last.

Two thousand years ago, however, Jesus secured our inheritance. Then when we named Him our Lord, He placed His Holy Spirit within us. And the Spirit strengthens us, fills us with knowledge, and blesses us with wisdom and understanding. And that rich inheritance will never fade.

....

Lord, thank You for my eternal inheritance. Fill me today with Your Spirit that I may know strength and wisdom for this leg of the journey of life. Amen.

Week 19—Wednesday
What Should We Wear Today?

Be strong in the Lord and in the power of His might. Put on the whole armor of God, that you may be able to stand against the wiles of the devil . . . . Take up the whole armor of God, that you may be able to withstand in the evil day, and having done all, to stand.

EPHESIANS 6:10–11, 13

Jesus' followers are fighting a war. The persistent, insidious, and evil schemes of the devil must be combated. We are called to be strong and stand firm. Yet this fight is not physical; it will not and cannot be fought or won in the flesh. That's why Paul called us to be strong "in the Lord and in the power of his might." Paul then went on to describe the armor of God, which is essential for the believer's survival.

I find these six pieces of the armor a great list to pray over each morning as I dress for the day—and after a few weeks of doing so, you'll have the list memorized:

The belt of truth
The breastplate of righteousness
The shoes of peace
The shield of faith
The helmet of salvation
The sword of the Spirit

. . . .

Lord, as I dress for the day, I thank You for providing me with spiritual armor. I am well aware that I am not adequate to win any battle today in my own strength. So I am choosing to trust You to be the Victor in every encounter and to enable me to, in Your strength, stand against the enemy. Amen.

　　　　DR. TED H. TRAYLOR, OLIVE BAPTIST CHURCH, PENSACOLA, FL

Week 19—Thursday
Finding Strength in the Lord

He gives power to the weak, and to those who have no might He increases strength. Even the youths shall faint and be weary, and the young men shall utterly fall, But those who wait on the LORD shall renew their strength; they shall mount up with wings like eagles, they shall run and not be weary, they shall walk and not faint.

ISAIAH 40:29–31

Today's reading offers rich encouragement for us during our most wearying and trying times. Wonderfully, God promises us power and strength to fly, run, and walk, but did you see the two conditions in this text, one even more explicit than the other?

First, we must acknowledge our need for strength and our inadequacy in the face of life's challenges. We are weak and powerless in ourselves. But only when we recognize this reality—only when we recognize our need—will we go to the One who can provide for those needs.

Second—and more explicitly—we are to wait on the Lord. In Psalm 40:1, the psalmist told us he "waited patiently for the LORD; And He . . . heard my cry." Acts 1:4 finds the disciples following the Lord's command to "wait for the Promise of the Father." That promise, which we have received, is the baptism of the Holy Spirit.

We truly do experience power and strength through God's Spirit as we learn to wait on the Lord. Here are a few suggestions to help you in this discipline:

Choose to believe that God is always on time.

Pledge not to move until God says, "Go."

The only place to rush is into the Lord's presence.

Lord, today I choose to wait on You. Give me endurance, Your peace, and godly anticipation of what You will do in Your perfect timing. Amen.

WEEK 19—FRIDAY
Doing All Things

I can do all things through Christ who strengthens me.

PHILIPPIANS 4:13

A text without a context can cause problems, confusion, and the spread of untruths. But sometimes the context does more than prevent those things; sometimes the context adds greater strength and significance to even a single line. Today's often-quoted text gains even more power when you read it in its context.

In Philippians 4:11–12 (context!), we read that Paul has traveled to many places, experienced much hardship, befriended dear people only to have to say "good-bye," took big risks, and stayed faithful to his Lord despite the cost. And God had provided His sufficiency in each and every situation. Maybe that is one reason why, in verses 10–13, the apostle Paul spoke of being content in every situation. In low times as well as in seasons of ease, whether he faced plenty or hunger, abundance, or need, Paul turned to the Lord and found strength in Him. Paul experienced the glory of doing all things in the power of God. And his list of "all things" is a sobering reminder of how much the apostle truly needed the strength of his Lord.

What will you face today? You probably have a general schedule, but you don't know all the people or situations you will encounter. What does your weekend hold? None of us can know for sure. But we do know Jesus Christ. And we know that He is able, that He will not leave you nor forsake you, that He is your strength. So whatever comes your way, know that you can face it, accomplish it, conquer it, and survive it.

....

Lord, thank You for being the source of my true strength. I trust You—and I am confident that I can endure because of who You are. Thank You! Amen.

DR. TED H. TRAYLOR, OLIVE BAPTIST CHURCH, PENSACOLA, FL

WEEK 19—WEEKEND
Whom Shall I Fear?

The LORD is my light and my salvation; whom shall I fear? The LORD is the strength of my life; of whom shall I be afraid? . . . Though an army may encamp against me, my heart shall not fear; though war may rise against me, in this I will be confident.

PSALM 27:1, 3

Fears. We all have them. Some fade as the years go by (I'm no longer dreading recess and fearing I'll be the last person chosen for the kickball game), and too often others step into the void (parenting can mean worries about friends and bullies, teachers and coaches, college admissions and career possibilities). What do you fear?

Maybe you wrestle with one or more of these common fears:

Failure	Intimacy
Sickness	Loss
Embarrassment	Death
Rejection	Finances

In today's text the Bible calls us not to be afraid even if an army rises against us in war. And that is an appropriate metaphor because all of us face battles, and we will no doubt encounter a battle or at least a skirmish or two today. Fear not! The Lord is our strength! We can find our confidence in Him.

Whatever your fears, lay them at the feet of the Lord. Choose to trust God; choose faith whatever the situation looks like. When the army of fear comes at you, remember that your almighty God is the God of angelic armies. Fear not!

....

Lord, today I recognize and confess my fear as a sinful lack of trust. Forgive me—and please enable me to walk by faith. I thank You in advance for defeating the enemies I will encounter. Amen.

WEEK 20—MONDAY
Two Kinds of Light

"I am the light of the world. He who follows Me shall not walk in darkness, but have the light of life."

JOHN 8:12

The Old Testament identifies God as light:

Psalm 27:1 "The LORD is my light and my salvation; whom shall I fear?"
Isaiah 60:19 "The LORD will be to you an everlasting light."
Micah 7:8 "When I sit in darkness, the LORD will be my light."

Jesus stood and said, "I am the light," and this claim—a statement equating Him with God—ultimately caused Him to be arrested and crucified.

An X-ray can reveal what is hidden from the naked eye. It can confirm whether a bone is broken or a tooth needs a filling. Similarly, the Light of the World sees what is inside us, our problems, our hurts, and our sins. Not only can He see our sins, but He reveals them to us so we can confess them and He can cover them with His grace.

Another light we know is the kind that lights our way—and that can be a flashlight or a floodlight. Remember when God delivered Israel from Egyptian bondage? God led His people with a pillar of fire: they were never left in darkness. Jesus, the Light, has promised us that we will never lose our way, even through illness, disease, problems, finances, family, or marriage. He has promised to provide the light we need whenever we need it so we can get through this dark world. What a promise!

....

Father, thank You for shining Your light into my heart so that I can confess my sin and be more the person You want me to be. And thank You for shining Your light onto my path so I can go and do all that You call me to do. In Jesus' name, Amen.

WEEK 20—TUESDAY
Light Has a Purpose

"You are the light of the world. A city that is set on a hill cannot be hidden. Nor do they light a lamp and put it under a basket, but on a lampstand, and it gives light to all who are in the house."

MATTHEW 5:14–15

I had a conversation with a father about Easter with his family. He had enjoyed hiding Easter eggs for his young children and then watching them quickly find each egg. He was, however, puzzled that one egg out of the four dozen had not been found.

Like that unfound Easter egg, our Christian faith—our life-changing acceptance of Jesus as our Savior and our day-to-day walk with Him—was never intended to be concealed. Yes, one's relationship with Jesus is very personal, but we are not supposed to keep it private. We are meant to talk about our faith; we are to be ready to share our salvation stories.

What would you think of a person who planned a trip to Hawaii and, upon arriving, told the desk clerk at the hotel that he wanted the darkest room available? Then he went to the room, closed the blinds, turned off the lights, and sat in the dark for two weeks. He never experienced the sun, the ocean, or the island's beauty. In like manner, we aren't meant to hide our light or hide from the Light!

God extended His light to us so that He may be glorified as He shines light through us to others.

....

Father, thank You that You love me enough not to leave me the way You found me. Give me the desire to tell everyone—especially those still in the dark—what You have done for me. In Jesus' name, Amen.

Week 20—Wednesday
Two Kinds of Eyes

"The lamp of the body is the eye. If therefore your eye is good, your whole body will be full of light. But if your eye is bad, your whole body will be full of darkness. If therefore the light that is in you is darkness, how great is that darkness!"

Matthew 6:22–23

Modern medicine has made cataract surgery an outpatient procedure, and afterward many patients celebrate that objects are no longer dark or cloudy, but clear and plain. In order to see the world as God does, we need to keep the spiritual cataracts from our eyes. Only then will we not be blinded by our self-centeredness and greed. Our healthy spiritual eyes will instead be focused on the things that have eternal value. Spiritually unhealthy eyes are focused on what one can attain for the here and now, the life that someone lives on earth.

Could your vision be one reason life today seems dark? Are you focusing your eyes on the temporary rather than on the eternal?

Father, may Your Holy Spirit help me to have a clear vision of the eternal—and to live for that. In Jesus' name, Amen.

WEEK 20—THURSDAY
Do Not Hide the Light

"Is a lamp brought to be put under a basket or under a bed? Is it not to be set on a lampstand? For there is nothing hidden which will not be revealed, nor has anything been kept secret but that it should come to light. If anyone has ears to hear, let him hear."

MARK 4:21–23

What good is it to have a lamp if we never let anyone see it? What good is it to have a lamp if we never use it for what it's meant to be used for? In both cases, that lamp is of no use at all. Things are created for a purpose, and it makes sense to use them for their specific purposes. Consider now Jesus' life, death, and resurrection. What if Jesus had never revealed the purpose of each event? What if He had paid the ransom for our sins but never communicated it to mankind? We would still be dead in our sins and separated from God.

Before Christ ascended back into heaven, He—who is the Light of the World—declared that His followers are to be the light of the world as well. It is, therefore, our purpose as believers not to hide the light from the world, but instead to allow our light to dispel the world's darkness. Then by God's grace, unbelievers all over the world will see that light of truth and life; choose to forsake the darkness; and commit themselves to serving the Light of the World so that they too can be beacons of light in this world.

....

Lord, deliver me from timidity, fear, laziness, and anything else that keeps my light from shining for You. In Jesus' name, Amen.

Week 20—Friday
This Little Light of Mine

"No one, when he has lit a lamp, covers it with a vessel or puts it under a bed, but sets it on a lampstand, that those who enter may see the light. For nothing is secret that will not be revealed, nor anything hidden that will not be known and come to light. Therefore take heed how you hear. For whoever has, to him more will be given; and whoever does not have, even what he seems to have will be taken from him."

LUKE 8:16–18

Have you ever known a young woman who has just accepted a marriage proposal but didn't tell everyone she knew the good news? Probably not. She usually wants the world to know that she is soon to be a bride.

And that is the kind of joy and passion with which we who follow Jesus are to share our knowledge of Him. The truth He has taught us is a tool to expel the darkness in the world. Jesus didn't share the news of salvation for the disciples' ears only. Rather than hiding what the Teacher had taught, the disciples were to proclaim with their words and display with their behavior the realities of forgiven sins, abundant life, and unshakable joy.

And as Jesus' twenty-first-century disciples, you and I are to do the same today. Who in your path today needs to hear the truth that sins can be forgiven and that, despite the pain and suffering in this world, he or she can know joy? Let your light shine!

....

Father, thank You for calling me to recognize the Light of the World and for helping me walk in the Light. Give me boldness, I ask, so I might share Your life-giving truth with boldness and love. In Jesus' name, Amen.

DR. MIKE WHITSON, FIRST BAPTIST CHURCH INDIAN TRAIL, INDIAN TRAIL, NC

WEEK 20—WEEKEND
Focused and Shining

"The lamp of the body is the eye. Therefore, when your eye is good, your whole body also is full of light. But when your eye is bad, your body also is full of darkness. Therefore take heed that the light which is in you is not darkness."

LUKE 11:34–35

Recently, when I was singing with my brothers and sisters in Christ at a worship service, I found myself extremely distracted by all that was going on around me. The musical instruments, the flashing lights, the words on the screen, the people sitting near me, and seemingly a dozen other things were competing for my attention.

I realized I had to regroup. Why was I in church? Whom was I there to focus on and worship? I was distracted by things that didn't matter.

We can also be distracted by good things, so distracted that we leave the best undone. So let us commit ourselves to being the very best for Christ that we can be. When we keep our eyes focused on the Light of the World, His light can shine through us into a world that desperately needs it.

Examine yourself today: do you have the light of Christ within you? If so, are you letting that light shine so that others may see? If you're not sure about either, remember that a single ember soon goes out; the little bit of light that was shining will fade. Don't be an isolated Christian. Get with others—and not just at a weekly worship service. You need them, they need you, and the world needs that bright light created by your being together.

Father, keep me focused on You, involved with Your people, and shining brightly for Your Son, the Light of the World! In Jesus' name, Amen.

WEEK 21—MONDAY
Enduring and Pursuing

Do not cast away your confidence, which has great reward. For you have need of endurance, so that after you have done the will of God, you may receive the promise.

HEBREWS 10:35–36

Don't give up on the hope of heaven! Don't "cast away your confidence" that Jesus is coming back! Don't defect from your life-giving faith in Jesus Christ! Apparently, the Hebrew recipients of this letter were abandoning the truth of the gospel and returning to their former Jewish practices that were incompatible with their newfound faith in Christ. So this is a clarion call to persevere and stay committed to the truth of our salvation by God's grace through faith in Jesus' death on behalf of our sin and His victory over sin and death.

The Bible clearly teaches the assurance of our salvation: God's power keeps us, the Holy Spirit seals us, and our salvation is sure. This guarantee, however, isn't a license to neglect personal obedience or to sin presumptuously.

Also remember that perseverance doesn't make us Christians. It simply reveals that we are Christians. God wants us to endure in our faith when times are difficult, and He can use our perseverance as a powerful witness to people around us.

Finally, God's Word teaches that we can be confident about our salvation, and that confidence is rooted in God's great faithfulness to us. And there is no greater demonstration of love and faithfulness than Jesus' death on the cross and what His death accomplished for us.

Father, thank You that my salvation is secure in You—and for the confidence that fact instills. Keep me pursuing You with all my heart, soul, mind, and strength. Amen.

DR. STEVE DIGHTON, LENEXA BAPTIST CHURCH, LENEXA, KS

WEEK 21—TUESDAY
The Security We Have in Jesus

Being confident of this very thing, that He who has begun a good work in you will complete it until the day of Jesus Christ.

PHILIPPIANS 1:6

W ho doesn't need encouragement? The apostle Paul wrote these words from a prison cell to people he loved in the Roman province of Philippi. He wanted to give them assurance that God would bring to completion the wonderful work of deliverance that He began that momentous day when they first believed in the Lord Jesus Christ. What a reassuring promise to all of us, though! We are kept by God, through the person of the Holy Spirit, and nothing can separate us from His redemptive love (Romans 8:35–39).

What can you and I do to embrace this assurance? First, we must remember that salvation is ours by grace: "not by works of righteousness which we have done, but according to His mercy He saved us" (Titus 3:5). Second, if we are saved by grace, we will be kept by this same grace (1 Peter 1:5). Third, Jesus promised us that no one can "snatch them out of [His] hand" (John 10:28).

Despite these promises from God, we oftentimes allow our feelings of inadequacy, a sense of guilt, or our ongoing indifference to spiritual things to cause us to doubt the promises God has given to us in His Word.

To counter that doubt today and always, remember that "faith comes by hearing, and hearing by the word of God" (Romans 10:17). So drink in the promises from God and stand strong on His truth. Then you'll discover your confidence being restored.

....

Father in heaven, help me to keep trusting in You and Your promises. May Your love completely overwhelm any doubts that surface, and may my confidence in You be fueled by my renewed and refocused faith in You. Amen.

WEEK 21—WEDNESDAY
Confidence in Prayer

Now this is the confidence that we have in Him, that if we ask anything according to His will, He hears us. And if we know that He hears us, whatever we ask, we know that we have the petitions that we have asked of Him.

1 JOHN 5:14–15

The apostle John wrote this epistle to remind believers of confidence-building truths rooted in their commitment to Jesus Christ. Actually, more than thirty times in five short chapters, John used the word *know*: he wanted us to know with absolute certainty that we can have complete confidence in God's promises.

But what about the promise "If we ask anything according to His will, He hears us"? All of us can list unanswered prayers. How many times have we wondered, "Why doesn't God answer my prayers?" First, are we praying according to the will of God? When we do, He hears us and answers our requests.

Second, what sin has crept into our lives? Isaiah the prophet said our transgressions cause God to refuse to hear us (Isaiah 59:2). Third, even if sin isn't the current problem, our misplaced desires can be. Are we simply praying for superficial needs instead of what we truly need spiritually?

We can be entirely confident, however, that God will answer these prayers:

1. That you will become like Jesus (Romans 8:29)
2. For the spiritually lost to be saved (2 Peter 3:8–9)
3. For spiritual growth and moral purity (2 Peter 3:18; 1 Timothy 5:22)

These requests—definitely God's will—are for our good and His great glory.

Father, help me to pray boldly and always to say as Jesus did, "Not My will, but Yours, be done" (Luke 22:42). Amen.

DR. STEVE DIGHTON, LENEXA BAPTIST CHURCH, LENEXA, KS

WEEK 21—THURSDAY
Confidence in Our Deliverer

Do not be afraid of sudden terror, nor of trouble from the wicked when it comes; for the LORD *will be your confidence, and will keep your foot from being caught.*

PROVERBS 3:25–26

There is much to fear in this fallen world that is populated by sinners like you and me. Black is called white, evil makes the headlines, and people are callous and cruel. The call in Proverbs 3:5 to trust in the Lord remains timely. The chapter also offers insight into how we can eliminate our fears by choosing faith and a confident belief in our all-powerful, all-good, God.

Yet most of us tend to borrow trouble. Honestly, it seems 90 percent of the things that I've feared or worried about never even happened. (And I'm pretty sure that's true for you as well.) Yet I keep borrowing trouble.

But according to this text, we aren't to be fearful because our God is in control. R. C. Sproul says that there is not one maverick molecule in God's universe. Of course the God who orchestrates the rising of the sun and its setting can keep us from being caught in a snare. Yet this promise is contingent on our obedience. God will not bless us when we choose disobedience. That's the essence of Jesus' call to "seek first the kingdom of God and his righteousness, and all these things shall be added to you" (Matthew 6:33).

What exactly will be "added to" us? God will provide for us, His watchful care, and refuge under His wings when the storms of life rage. We build our confidence in God and learn to trust Him more by acknowledging that He is our strength and our ever-present help in times of trouble.

Father, when I feel overwhelmed by trials and difficulties, help me to quit looking around at those circumstances. Doing so always increases my anxiety. Instead, prompt me to look to You and remember that You love me. Amen.

WEEK 21—FRIDAY
Confidence in the Infinite

Now [may] the manifold wisdom of God . . . be made known by the church to the principalities and powers in the heavenly places, according to the eternal purpose which [God] accomplished in Christ Jesus our Lord, in whom we have boldness and access with confidence through faith in Him.

EPHESIANS 3:10–12

It's not easy for a finite human mind to grasp much of our God's infinite wisdom and knowledge. Consider the magnitude and scope of God's redemptive work on our behalf, in our hearts, and through His church. We naturally reduce to our small and simplistic thinking the miracle of rebirth and new spiritual life that Christ accomplished—and to make it worse, we conclude it was just about us.

We have that egocentric way of interpreting everything because, by nature, we're self-centered. However, we see here that God revealed to the powers of heaven His master plan of redemption. God did not keep it a secret that He sent Jesus to atone for our sins and to buy back fallen humanity. The salvation story was developed according to God's wisdom and overseen by His divine orchestration.

Therefore, you and I can be bold when we approach the holy and almighty One. We can also be confident in the power and love of this enormous God who sent His Son to rescue us from the clutches and dominion of sin. Jesus' death and resurrection bring Him glory throughout all time, around the world, and in the details of your sold-out-for-Him life.

....

Father, You are a big God. Help me both to please You with my big confidence in You and glorify You by my obedience. Amen.

DR. STEVE DIGHTON, LENEXA BAPTIST CHURCH, LENEXA, KS

WEEK 21—WEEKEND
Promises and Prayer

"Most assuredly, I say to you, he who believes in Me, the works that I do he will do also; and greater works than these he will do, because I go to My Father. And whatever you ask in My name, that I will do, that the Father may be glorified in the Son. If you ask anything in My name, I will do it."

JOHN 14:12–14

On the eve of His crucifixion, Jesus shared with His disciples a significant promise. He declared that after He had gone away, the disciples would be able to do even greater works than they had seen Him do. That would be possible when the Holy Spirit came to reside in them: the Spirit who raised Jesus from the dead would now enable them to do great things for their Lord.

Then Jesus transitioned to the topic of prayer, explaining to His disciples that by asking in His name—by appealing to God based on Jesus' authority—they can pray with confidence that Jesus "will do it." Wow! What a promise! But its fulfillment is contingent on one key thing: whatever we ask must be God-glorifying and Christ-exalting. (This pretty much leaves out all materialism, selfish desires, sinful motives like greed, and so forth.)

Jesus then mentioned that He would soon "go to My Father." His brutal death on Calvary was imminent; the cross was coming. Yet His death would be both our deliverance from the consequences of our sin and our becoming "the righteousness of God in Him" (2 Corinthians 5:21).

So pray with confidence. Stand on Jesus' promise that His Spirit will enable you to do great things for God.

....

Almighty God, may I believe You today for the challenges I face. May I see my faith increase and my trust in You grow. I want to do great things for You, my heavenly Father. Amen.

Week 22—Monday
The Bible Is a Life-Changer

Faith comes by hearing, and hearing by the word of God.

Romans 10:17

The great preacher D. L. Moody once said that Christians should quit praying for faith and to read their Bibles. If they do this, God will give them faith. I truly believe that everything we need for life is found in the Bible. It is sad that the average American home has four copies, yet only eleven percent of Americans read it daily.

I don't understand why Christians will not make time for God's Word when the Bible is:

1. "A lamp unto our feet" (Psalm 119:105 KJV)
2. Bread for our hunger (Matthew 4:4)
3. A mirror for our life (James 1:22–25)
4. Honey for our soul (Psalm 119:103)
5. Fire for our discouragement (Jeremiah 20:9)

Many times throughout my Christian journey, when I have been walking through difficult days, I would fall asleep at night holding my Bible. You may think I'm a nut! That might be true, but I'm screwed onto the right bolt. God didn't give us the Bible to increase our knowledge but to change our lives.

I want to encourage you to read your Bible every day, even if it means getting up fifteen minutes earlier each morning. You can do it! It's just mind over mattress! And I assure you, it will not be just a game-changer but a life-changer.

....

Father, thank You for Your Word. Thank You that I can speak to You through prayer, and that You speak to me through the Bible. Amen.

DR. BENNY TATE, ROCK SPRINGS CHURCH, MILNER, GA

WEEK 22—TUESDAY
A Picture of Humility

I say, through the grace given to me, to everyone who is among you, not to think of himself more highly than he ought to think, but to think soberly, as God has dealt to each one a measure of faith.

ROMANS 12:3

There is a fable that expresses a great truth about a boastful bird. A woodpecker was pecking away on a tree when it was struck by lightning. The tree split from top to bottom, and the woodpecker flew off. A little while later it came back, proudly leading nine other woodpeckers and saying, "There it is, fellows! Right over there! Look what I did!"[2]

We need to open God's Word and heed its call to humble ourselves. A few years ago, I had an amazing experience that I will never forget. I traveled to Montreat, North Carolina, to visit with Rev. Billy Graham. I sat in a very modest home and visited with a spiritual giant who wore blue jeans, a flannel shirt, tennis shoes, and a Timex watch. At one point, he spoke of his wife's death. He also said that when he gets to heaven, he is going to ask God why He used a rural farm boy from North Carolina to reach so many people. Truly, Mr. Graham was a picture of humility.

Here are some practical ways we can live out humility:

1. Admit your faults (James 5:16).
2. Love your enemies (Matthew 5:44).
3. Don't boast (Proverbs 27:2).
4. Express gratitude to God and others (1 Thessalonians 5:18).
5. Kneel before God (James 4:10).
6. Weep over sin (Psalm 51:17).
7. Serve others (John 13:14).
8. Honor the Lord's Day (Exodus 20:8).

Father, help me to humble myself today so that You will be exalted in my life. Amen.

WEEK 22—WEDNESDAY
God Sticks Out

The fruit of the Spirit is love, joy, peace, longsuffering, kindness, goodness, faithfulness, gentleness, self-control. Against such there is no law.

GALATIANS 5:22–23

A little boy once asked his mother if God lived inside him. She responded, "Yes." Then he asked if God was bigger than he was, and again she said, "Yes." Then the boy said, "Mom, if God is in me and He is bigger than me, shouldn't He stick out?"[3]

I truly believe one of the ways God sticks out in our lives is through the fruit of the Holy Spirit.

When a person names Jesus Christ as Savior, he or she acknowledges God the Father, recognizes Jesus as God the Son, and is filled with God the Holy Spirit. And it is that gift of the Spirit that prompted Jesus to say, "It is to your advantage that I go away" (John 16:7). He explained that when He left, He would send His Holy Spirit—our Helper, Comforter, and Teacher.

The way God sticks out, then, is through the Holy Spirit-sown fruit in our lives. Now understand that we do not produce this fruit. It is produced in us by the indwelling Holy Spirit. Every believer is to bear the full fruit of the Spirit, which involves the list found in Galatians 5:22–23.

One more thing. Yes, we receive the Holy Spirit at the moment of our salvation, but we are leaky vessels that need fresh fillings of God's Spirit. Ask God to fill you afresh with His Spirit today so He can stick out!

....

Father, I want my cup to run over with the love, joy, peace, longsuffering, kindness, goodness, faithfulness, gentleness, and self-control of Your Spirit. Please give me a fresh filling of Your Spirit today and every day. Amen.

DR. BENNY TATE, ROCK SPRINGS CHURCH, MILNER, GA

WEEK 22—THURSDAY
The Jew First

I am not ashamed of the gospel of Christ, for it is the power of God to salvation for everyone who believes, for the Jew first and also for the Greek. For in it the righteousness of God is revealed from faith to faith; as it is written, "The just shall live by faith."

ROMANS 1:16–17

I have had the awesome privilege of leading several pilgrimages to the land of Israel, and after every trip I have a deeper love for the people and for the land. As believers, we have a deep indebtedness to the Jewish people. Have you ever thought about what they gave us?

1. The Scriptures
2. The Prophets
3. The Apostles
4. Jesus Christ

Jesus was born to Jewish parents, dedicated to God in the Jewish tradition, reared in a Jewish home, ministered to the Jewish people, and died with a sign over His head inscribed, "THIS IS JESUS THE KING OF THE JEWS."

With great confidence, I say to you there would be no Christianity without Judaism. Our hearts and prayers should be that Jewish people come to faith in Christ because they are God's original chosen people.

Isn't it interesting that even though Paul was a missionary to the Gentiles, he made a point of first going to the Jewish synagogue in the cities he visited? (Acts 17:1–2). He also shared with the Jews the very same gospel he shared with the Gentiles because he wanted them to be saved.

....

Father, I pray for the peace of Jerusalem and for the Jewish people to see the reality of Jesus as Savior and Lord. Amen.

WEEK 22—FRIDAY
Which Way You Went

We are always confident, knowing that while we are at home in the body we are absent from the Lord. For we walk by faith, not by sight. We are confident, yes, well pleased rather to be absent from the body and to be present with the Lord.

2 CORINTHIANS 5:6–8

A cemetery in New England has the following inscription on a tombstone: *"Stranger, pause as you pass by. As you are now so once was I. As I am so you must be. Prepare for death and follow me.* Someone took a marker and wrote below it: *To follow you, I'll not consent until I know which way you went."*[4]

I am thrilled to report that when Christians die, they enter into the very presence of God because "to be absent from this body" is "to be present with the Lord."

"Present with the Lord." Can you even imagine seeing Jesus in all of His glory, holiness, splendor, and majesty? Standing before the Lord Himself may be beyond our imagination, but we can trust that it will happen—and we are wise if we build our lives on that trust.

Maybe Fanny Crosby's words in her hymn "Saved by Grace" could be yours:

> *I long to see my Savior's face*
> *And sing the story saved by grace.*
> *And there, upon that golden strand,*
> *I'll praise Him for His guiding hand.*

Father, thank You for giving me life—abundant life and eternal life. I long to see Your face and worship You, almighty God, in all Your glory. Amen.

DR. BENNY TATE, ROCK SPRINGS CHURCH, MILNER, GA

WEEK 22—WEEKEND
Pleasing God

By faith Enoch was taken away so that he did not see death, "and was not found, because God had taken him"; for before he was taken he had this testimony, that he pleased God. But without faith it is impossible to please Him, for he who comes to God must believe that He is, and that He is a rewarder of those who diligently seek Him.

HEBREWS 11:5–6

I know of no greater testimony than one's life pleasing God and that is what was said of Enoch. Notice three things from the life of Enoch:

First, take note of his motivation. After Enoch had his son, Methuselah, he began to walk with God (Genesis 5:21–22). The greatest way to train one's child is not to "talk the talk" but to "walk the walk." Actions speak louder than words.

Second, Enoch's method is noteworthy. He walked with God, and that means they spent time together. God cannot do something through us if He is not doing something in us. If we are not careful, we can get so busy doing good things that we miss out on the best thing. I have often said, "If the devil can't make you bad, he will make you busy."

Third, Enoch had a mandate. I have noticed a common quality that I believe all spiritual giants have in their lives. That quality is dynamic faith. Faith sees beyond the obstacles to the opportunities in light of the object of our faith—that being Jesus Christ.

....

Father, help me to please you in my actions and attitudes! Amen.

WEEK 23—MONDAY
Finding the Right Path

Show me Your ways, O LORD; teach me Your paths. Lead me in Your truth and teach me, for You are the God of my salvation; on You I wait all the day.

PSALM 25:4–5

Everyone knows what it's like to be lost. At one time or another we've all been confused. We have deviated from the proper course and found ourselves in unfamiliar territory. Paths do have a way of taking us somewhere, and the wrong path takes us to the wrong place every time.

When you choose a path, you aren't just making a choice; you are setting a course. You aren't just making a decision; you are determining a destination. It's the principle of the path: where you're going determines where you will end up.

That's why we turn to God. When you need to know the right path to take, ask Him. He knows where every path leads. He knows the outcome of every choice and every decision. So ask Him to show you, teach you, and lead you. God leads us in the path that leads to salvation, and He will lead you if you ask.

And remember that asking means waiting. Sometimes we have to wait "all the day," but the wait is worth it. We wait in prayer. We wait in obedience. We wait by studying His Word.

Wait on God. Ask Him to lead you in the right paths. He promises He will if you just slow down and humble yourself long enough to ask Him for directions. Try it today.

．．．

God, I know what it is to take the wrong path, and I want to be on Your path for me. Forgive me for trusting my instincts instead of Your truth. I need You to show me Your path. Teach and lead me today. Amen.

DR. WILLIAM RICE, CALVARY CHURCH, CLEARWATER, FL

WEEK 23—TUESDAY
Dealing with Sin

Christ was offered once to bear the sins of many. To those who eagerly wait for Him He will appear a second time, apart from sin, for salvation.

HEBREWS 9:28

We who follow Christ look both backward and forward.

We look backward into history and see that Christ first came to this earth to deal with our sins. Our world is broken because we are broken: we are sinners. We stand guilty before God, yet the good news of the gospel is that Jesus came to deal with our sins.

The Son of God died on the cross bearing the guilt of our sins, and He died in our place. His sacrificial death atoned for our sins, and we who trust in Christ by faith receive the gracious gift of God's forgiveness.

And now we wait for Jesus to come a second time. He is not coming to deal with our sins—He has already taken care of that—but to bring the culmination of our salvation. Jesus is coming to finish the work of salvation He started and guaranteed He would complete.

Preacher Jerry Vines once said, "We don't fight *for* victory; we fight *from* victory." Our victory is ensured by what Christ did for us when He came the first time. Our eternal victory over sin and death is guaranteed, and our salvation will be completed when Jesus returns.

....

Father, thank You for sending Jesus as the sacrifice for my sins and thank You for the hope that He will return one day to make all things new. I can live in victory and hope today because of Jesus. Amen.

WEEK 23—WEDNESDAY
My Refuge

In God is my salvation and my glory; the rock of my strength, and my refuge, is in God. Trust in Him at all times, you people; pour out your heart before Him; God is a refuge for us.

PSALM 62:7–8

Sometimes we just need a safe place.

Where is your safe place? In our world of criticism and unkindness, deception and deceit, pain and sorrow, and sadness and separation, what is your place of refuge? When your heart is overwhelmed, where do you find refuge? Where is your safe place?

Recently, I spoke with a woman who said, "I feel like I'm drowning." Everything in her life that she had thought was solid was turning to quicksand. Everyone she had thought she could count on was leaving her life. I felt overwhelmed just listening to her. But then I reminded both of us that God is our refuge.

The psalmist proclaimed that God was his refuge and his rock. God never promises us ease and safety in this world, but He does promise to be our refuge when life is difficult or when we need protection. In our heavenly Father we find peace, we find wisdom, and we find strength for life's tumultuous times.

Maybe today you feel overwhelmed by circumstances beyond your control. Remember that whatever is beyond your control is not too big for God. Find your strength and safe place in Him. Pour out your heart to Him.

Father, I praise You for being a safe and strong place I can run to when I need peace and protection. Thank You for always being there for me—and it is really good news that nothing I face is too big for You to handle! Amen.

DR. WILLIAM RICE, CALVARY CHURCH, CLEARWATER, FL

WEEK 23—THURSDAY
The Promise That Will Be Kept

If you confess with your mouth the Lord Jesus and believe in your heart that God has raised Him from the dead, you will be saved. For with the heart one believes unto righteousness, and with the mouth confession is made unto salvation.

ROMANS 10:9–10

P romises. Promises are often made and often broken—by people. Not by God. When God makes a promise, we can stake our lives on His doing exactly what He said He would do. In fact, we can stake eternity on God's promises. And this is the biggest promise: if we confess and believe that Jesus died for our sins and rose again, we will be saved from punishment for those sins.

Despite the fact that Christianity is two thousand years old, people still ask, "How can I be made right with God? How can I be rescued from my own depravity? How can I have eternal life?"

Religions around the world have been designed to address that dilemma, to answer those questions, and the consensus is . . . do something. These religions propose that finding God, righteousness, and eternal life are all about what we must do to earn God's favor, win His love, and gain His acceptance. These religions are like a ladder: adherents must climb up, rung by rung, to try to reach God.

But the message of Jesus turns these other religious systems on their heads. That's because the gospel is spelled "d-o-n-e." Christianity—following Jesus—is not about what we can do for God; Christianity is about what Jesus has already done for us. We don't have to climb anymore; we only have to believe and confess.

If you put your faith in Christ, trusting that He is the perfect offering for your sins, and confess Him as your Lord, you will be saved from eternal punishment for your sins. God promises it—and He always keeps His promises.

....

Father, thank You for the gift of Jesus and the promise of eternal life. Amen.

Week 23—Friday
No Longer Appointed to Wrath

Let us who are of the day be sober, putting on the breastplate of faith and love, and as a helmet the hope of salvation. For God did not appoint us to wrath, but to obtain salvation through our Lord Jesus Christ, who died for us, that whether we wake or sleep, we should live together with Him.

1 Thessalonians 5:8–10

And if I die before I wake . . ." Many childhood prayers contain this line, and it's actually quite frightening. "If I die before I wake"? Who wants children to think about that just before bed?

Yet life is uncertain. We don't know how long we will live. God has numbered our days, and we don't know the number. What we do know is that one day death will indeed come.

But we who follow Christ know more. We know that death is not the end. God has promised us life. The same God who raised Jesus from the dead will also raise us up. When we receive the gift of Jesus, we receive forgiveness of sin and the promise of eternal life. We are no longer "appoint[ed] . . . to wrath." In the person of Jesus, we have received salvation and the promise of eternal life.

So today we can live with courage and peace. Whether we die or awake for another day, we are confident in Christ that we will live together with Him. The hope for tomorrow gives us strength for today.

....

Father, thank You again for Your promise of eternal life. Thank You that I am no longer appointed to wrath, but that You have instead granted me Your glorious salvation. Help me to stand in the strength of that hope today. Amen.

DR. WILLIAM RICE, CALVARY CHURCH, CLEARWATER, FL

WEEK 23—WEEKEND
Such Great Love

Though He was a Son, yet He learned obedience by the things which He suffered. And having been perfected, He became the author of eternal salvation to all who obey Him.

HEBREWS 5:8–9

Jesus suffered. In God's great plan for our salvation, the blessed Son of God, our Lord Jesus, suffered. He suffered rejection. He suffered hunger and thirst. He suffered loneliness and abandonment. He suffered pain and torture. And He suffered complete separation from the Father when He became the perfect sacrifice for our sins. The only One who was ever perfectly innocent, totally free of sin, suffered—and He suffered for you.

And Jesus didn't have to suffer. He was the Son of God and equal with God. But Jesus chose to suffer. He willingly humbled Himself, took upon Himself the role of a servant, and became obedient unto death. Jesus suffered because He had come to earth for this very purpose: to bring us salvation.

But Jesus was innocent and sinless, so why does the Bible say He was "perfected"? The writer of Hebrews didn't mean that at one point in time Jesus was insufficient and He became sufficient at another point in time. Jesus has always been perfect; He has always been sufficient. In this context, *perfected* means that through His suffering, His work on earth was completed. Jesus finished the mission He had been sent to do, and having finished it, He now offers salvation to those who trust in Him.

Humanity's sin brought suffering into the world. Our Savior suffered so that we could be made right with God and one day suffer no more. Yes, the cost of your salvation was high, but the love that God has for you is higher.

....

Father, thank You for Your great love. And thank You, Jesus, for suffering on my behalf so that I could be saved. Amen.

WEEK 24—MONDAY
A Friend of the King

"Greater love has no one than this, than to lay down one's life for his friends. You are My friends if you do whatever I command you. No longer do I call you servants, for a servant does not know what his master is doing; but I have called you friends, for all things that I heard from My Father I have made known to you."

JOHN 15:13–15

Friendship is one of the greatest gifts in life. Friendships allow us to be loved, to love, to give, and to receive. Our friendships with one another and with the Lord may not always be perfect, but His friendship with us is.

In John 15, Jesus referred to Himself as the Vine and His followers as the branches. This vine metaphor illustrates the closeness Jesus desired to have with His disciples. Jesus voluntarily laid down His life so that we might be called friends of God.

We must be careful, however, not to sell short the meaning of the word *friend*. For example, in the context of royalty, the word refers to the inner circle around a king or dignitary. The friends of the king would be close enough to him to listen to his insights and loyal enough to obey his commands.

My mentor Adrian Rogers frequently said, "Each of us is as close to God as we choose to be." The choice is ours: we can draw near to God in prayer and with a thorough reading of His Word, or we can choose to be distant and reserved.

Jesus' unreserved intimacy is not restricted only to His first twelve disciples. He extends it to us, who are also His friends. May our sacrificial love for others and our radical obedience to Christ reflect our friendship with the King and make others desire that friendship too.

....

Father, thank You for the sacrifice of Jesus so that I can be called Your friend. Amen.

　　　　DR. BRAD WHITT, ABILENE BAPTIST CHURCH, MARTINEZ, GA

WEEK 24—TUESDAY
A Friend of God

The Scripture was fulfilled which says, "Abraham believed God, and it was accounted to him for righteousness." And he was called the friend of God. You see then that a man is justified by works, and not by faith only.

JAMES 2:23–24

The lifeblood of friendship is trust. And isn't it remarkable to see how much Abraham trusted God and how much God trusted Abraham? God called Abraham to leave his home in the city of Ur, near the Euphrates River, and travel to Canaan, the promised land. Abraham was required to live by faith each step of the journey, not knowing where he was going. He simply obeyed the Lord's instructions.

In Genesis 18, two angels visited Abraham as they traveled to Sodom to inspect the city's sin. He greeted them and extended to them the best of desert hospitality. He stood by them, waiting to serve them, and then the scene suddenly shifted to Abraham, still standing and communing with the Lord. Abraham was now a friend of God.

Abraham's greatest test would come when God commanded him to sacrifice his son Isaac (Genesis 22). At the last moment—and very pleased by Abraham's obedience—God stopped the sacrifice. Abraham had chosen to believe that the Lord would not let him down. And God didn't.

And the same God who appeared before Abraham that day is the One who stands with you now. He will not let you down. If you are willing to submit to God and be obedient, then you can count on receiving His blessings.

Father, in faith and with obedience I will follow the example of Abraham. I will surrender and sacrifice everything to Your will. Amen.

WEEK 24—WEDNESDAY
The Gift of Community

Two are better than one, because they have a good reward for their labor. For if they fall, one will lift up his companion. But woe to him who is alone when he falls, for he has no one to help him up.

ECCLESIASTES 4:9–10

One of my favorite things to do is share a meal with family and friends (especially if it's barbeque). I find great delight in sitting across the table from people I love and hearing about their joys or concerns. God wired us to need community; He created us to function as social beings, not solitary creatures. In Ecclesiastes, Solomon pointed out that people can accomplish more by working together and that walking with a friend is good when dealing with tough times.

Those tough times are valuable—as Charles Colson knew: "No Christian can grow strong and stand the pressures of this life unless he is surrounded by a group of people who minister to him and build him up in the faith."

Believers need each other, and it is vital for our souls to be active in a faith community. The Lord said, "It is not good that man should be alone" (Genesis 2:18). Following Jesus means following Him into community. At some point along the way, each one of us will need the strength, comfort, and hope that having people close by can offer.

Remember the words of the apostle Paul: "If a man is overtaken in any trespass, you who are spiritual restore such a one in a spirit of gentleness, considering yourself lest you also be tempted. Bear one another's burdens, and so fulfill the law of Christ" (Galatians 6:1–2).

Father, I pray that when I am weak, the community of Your people will help me be strong. Thank You for the gift of community. Amen.

DR. BRAD WHITT, ABILENE BAPTIST CHURCH, MARTINEZ, GA

Week 24—Thursday
Closer Than a Brother

A man who has friends must himself be friendly, But there is a friend who sticks closer than a brother.

PROVERBS 18:24

Are you blessed to have "a friend who sticks closer than a brother"?
Mary and Martha had a brother named Lazarus who did stick with them until he became sick and died. More than likely, he had been the handyman around the house and the one who shouldered many heavy burdens. He probably would have come to their defense in a moment's notice, but he was gone. The hands of death suddenly ended earthly closeness.

But Mary and Martha did have a friend who would come to their aid when their brother couldn't, and He is the same Friend you and I have. Jesus is the Friend who sticks closer than any brother. He will be close in times of grief, and, when we fall, Jesus will lift us up. When Lazarus died, his friend Jesus called him back from death to life. Jesus is the friend who sticks closer than any brother.

God said, "I will never leave you nor forsake you" (Hebrews 13:5). The apostle Paul also shared these glorious words: "Neither death nor life, nor angels nor rulers, nor things present nor things to come, nor powers, nor height nor depth, nor anything else in all creation, will be able to separate us from the love of God in Christ Jesus our Lord" (Romans 8:38–39 ESV).

Do you desire a friend like this? You already have one in Jesus!

....

Father, thank You for Jesus, who celebrates the joys but never leaves me alone in the pains of life. In Jesus' name I pray, Amen.

WEEK 24—FRIDAY
Setting Our Souls Free

The LORD restored Job's losses when he prayed for his friends. Indeed the LORD gave Job twice as much as he had before.

JOB 42:10

Job experienced a horrific day. Satan had sought and received God's permission to subject Job to a whirlwind of intense misery. In one dreadful day, Job lost all seven sons and his three daughters. He lost all his cattle and most of his servants. In just a few hours, Job's children and business were gone.

And when his friends visited, any hope Job had of receiving comfort and condolences quickly faded. The so-called friends shared only words of rebuke and criticism; their thoughts left Job feeling shame and guilt.

Then one day everything changed. Job was set free from pain and blessed with glorious prosperity. What made the difference? "He prayed for his friends." The Lord was not impressed with Job's friends. They were in danger of God's judgment. But when Job prayed for them, God set Job free. Earlier, when Job had prayed for himself, his anguish had not been relieved. After Job showed love for his friends who had wronged him, God gave Job freedom.

Job put into practice what the Lord Jesus taught: "Do good to those who hate you, bless those who curse you, and pray for those who spitefully use you" (Luke 6:27–28). When you pray for others, you release them from any debt they have caused you. And you will find your soul released from the prison cell of bitterness.

I encourage you today to pray for individuals who have hurt you. Allow the healing balm of the Lord to set you free.

....

Father, I pray for _____ . May You bless his or her soul today. In the name of Jesus I pray, Amen.

144   DR. BRAD WHITT, ABILENE BAPTIST CHURCH, MARTINEZ, GA

WEEK 24—WEEKEND
The Friend Who Never Sleeps

I will lift up my eyes to the hills—from whence comes my help? My help comes from the LORD, who made heaven and earth. He will not allow your foot to be moved; He who keeps you will not slumber. . . . The LORD is your keeper; the LORD is your shade at your right hand.

PSALM 121:1–3, 5

There is an old story passed down through the years about a young girl. The four-year-old daughter was afraid of the dark, and tonight, with her husband gone, the mother felt a bit fearful also. When the light was out, the child caught a glimpse of the moon outside the window. "Mother," she asked, "is the moon God's light?"

"Yes," said the mother.

"Will God put out His light and go to sleep?"

The mother replied, "No, my child. God never goes to sleep."

Then the young girl said, "As long as God is awake, we can go to sleep!"

In Psalm 121, the psalmist reminded himself of God's protection. In this psalm, the sun and moon represent all the dangers of day and night. But he wrote, "My strength comes from GOD, who made heaven, and earth, and mountains" (Psalm 121:1–2 THE MESSAGE). We couldn't have a better helper than the God who created this universe! God is higher than the hills, mightier than the mountains, and more powerful than the armies of the earth. He is our Keeper and Protector. We can rest easy because we know the God who never sleeps is protecting us.

Father, You alone are my strength. I want to trust You with my worries, doubts, and fears. Thank You for keeping watch over my soul day and night. In Jesus' name I pray, Amen.

THE GIFT OF JESUS

Week 25—Monday
He Is with Me

"I will pray the Father, and He will give you another Helper, that He may abide with you forever—the Spirit of truth, whom the world cannot receive, because it neither sees Him nor knows Him; but you know Him, for He dwells with you and will be in you. I will not leave you orphans; I will come to you."

JOHN 14:16–18

Jesus spoke these comforting words to the disciples at a dark moment of grief. Jesus had just told Peter that this very night Peter would deny even knowing his Lord. Judas had been sent out of the room earlier as a traitor.

Worst of all, Jesus had just told the remaining eleven that He was leaving them. The disciples had depended on Jesus for everything. When they got up in the morning, they probably looked at Jesus and said, "What do we do today? Where do we go?" When a situation did not go as they planned or imagined, they looked to Jesus to handle the situation. Jesus healed the sick, raised the dead, calmed the storms, and answered the critics. He also calmed His disciples' fears with His words and comforted them with His presence.

So when Jesus said He was leaving, the unspoken question hanging in the air was "Who is going to help us now? The disciples were baffled. Who, they wondered, would encourage them and pick them up when they fell? Who would strengthen them when they were weak or lead them when they did not know where to go? The Holy Spirit has been given to every believer so every believer can have everything he or she would have, if Jesus were still on earth.

....

Lord, thank You for the gift of Your Spirit. May I walk with Him today, comforted, guided, and empowered by His presence with me. May I walk with Him just as Your disciples walked with You. Amen.

PASTOR ROY MACK, GRACE FELLOWSHIP CHURCH, WARREN, OH

WEEK 25—TUESDAY
Unpardoned Sin

"Anyone who speaks a word against the Son of Man, it will be forgiven him; but to him who blasphemes against the Holy Spirit, it will not be forgiven. Now when they bring you to the synagogues and magistrates and authorities, do not worry about how or what you should answer, or what you should say. For the Holy Spirit will teach you in that very hour what you ought to say."

LUKE 12:10–12

As a pastor I am asked occasionally, "What is the unpardonable sin"? Most people assume it is a sin like suicide. Suicide is not the unpardonable sin. Jesus Himself answered this question: blasphemy "against the Holy Spirit . . . will not be forgiven."

Perhaps more relevant on a broader scope is the fact that all sin is unacceptable to God. In other words, any one sin can damn a person to hell. God must forgive all of our sins, or we all are doomed.

But don't panic. Each one of us will die one day with multitudes of sins of which we have not repented or we even remember committing. We need—and we have—a Savior to cover our sins, even those we haven't confessed.

When people have not been born again—when they have not put their faith and trust in Christ—the Spirit of God convicts them of their sin when they hear the gospel. If those individuals refuse the Spirit's invitation to receive Christ as their Savior, they are choosing spiritual death. Their sins will remain unforgiven; they will not receive God's forgiveness.

It's a compelling and chilling truth: once we die, we have no more chances to make things right with God. With whom will you share the gospel?

Lord, thank You for forgiving all my sins. Give me boldness to share my faith with others. Amen.

WEEK 25—WEDNESDAY
By His Spirit

What man knows the things of a man except the spirit of the man which is in him?
Even so no one knows the things of God except the Spirit of God. Now we have received,
not the spirit of the world, but the Spirit who is from God, that we might know the
things that have been freely given to us by God.

1 CORINTHIANS 2:11–12

What does it mean to truly know another person? It means knowing his thoughts, his heart, and his nature, and that knowledge comes when we spend time with someone.

We certainly know ourselves. We know what we like and dislike, what makes us joyful or sad, what we love and whom we love. Now imagine having the ability to place your mind in another person's life so that he or she could come to know you, the real you. Well, that is what God has done for us as believers: He has placed His very Spirit in us so we can know the mind, heart, and nature of God. The Holy Spirit allows us to know God's love, His likes, and His dislikes. When we spend time with God in prayer, when we read His Word and worship Him, His Spirit enables us to come to know Him in an intimate and personal way.

Sadly, what many people know about God is only what someone else has told them about Him. They haven't yet experienced the amazing blessing of letting the Spirit of God reveal to them personally the deep truths of God.

Lord God, I long to know You better. Thank You for sending Your Spirit to help
that happen. From Your Word, may He teach me what You want me to know
about You for my good and especially for Your glory. Amen.

PASTOR ROY MACK, GRACE FELLOWSHIP CHURCH, WARREN, OH

WEEK 25—THURSDAY
I Am His and He Is Mine

If Christ is in you, the body is dead because of sin, but the Spirit is life because of righteousness. But if the Spirit of Him who raised Jesus from the dead dwells in you, He who raised Christ from the dead will also give life to your mortal bodies through His Spirit who dwells in you.

ROMANS 8:10–11

I t is a great truth to know that, as a believer who has trusted in Christ as your Savior, you have the Spirit of God dwelling in you. That is worth saying again: you have the Spirit of God living within you!

But perhaps you should consider this great question: does the Spirit have you? Is the presence of the Spirit in your life impacting how you live? Are you treating your body like the very temple of the Holy Spirit? Are you enjoying the fullness of His presence in your life? That same Spirit who raised Jesus from the dead is able to give you abundant life, and you will discover that living for Christ is the most energizing experience this side of heaven. When the Spirit empowers you to witness for Jesus, to serve, to give, to pray, the experience is more fulfilling than you can imagine.

Preacher D. L. Moody once said of his conversion experience, "I was in a new world. The birds sang sweeter, the sun shone brighter. I'd never known such peace." [5] This is in part what it means to walk in God's kingdom. By the Spirit's indwelling, you will be more alive to His kingdom than to this world in which you dwell physically. It truly is a whole new world when you are His and He is yours.

....

Lord, thank You for Your Spirit. Make me very aware of Your presence within me today. I am Yours. Please use me for Your glory. Amen.

WEEK 25—FRIDAY
Looking for the One Looking for Him

"When the Helper comes, whom I shall send to you from the Father, the Spirit of truth who proceeds from the Father, He will testify of Me."

JOHN 15:26

Knowing that the Holy Spirit is also called the Helper may prompt the question "What is He going to help us do?"

One thing the Spirit helps believers do is fulfill the Great Commission. You and I can't in our own human power help a lost person recognize the need for Christ. We need the help of the Helper.

The Bible tells us that we are all born "dead in trespasses and sins" (Ephesians 2:1), and dead people, as we know, can't see, hear, speak, or make decisions. It is the Spirit of God who enables the spiritually dead to see, hear, confess their sins, and choose to follow Jesus.

The Spirit of God testifies to the spiritually dead not only that what Jesus did—dying on the cross, being buried, and being raised from the dead—actually happened, but also that He did it for them. It is the Spirit who helps people recognize that Jesus died for their personal salvation.

And it is the Spirit of God who enables us to proclaim that truth to others after we have accepted it for ourselves. As the resurrected Jesus promised, "You shall receive power when the Holy Spirit has come upon you; and you shall be witnesses to Me" (Acts 1:8). We are commissioned to be Jesus' witnesses, and we can be assured that when we are witnessing to someone, the Spirit is testifying to that person as well. Purpose today to share the gospel with someone. Perhaps you will find someone who is looking for Him.

Lord, lead me today to a person whose heart in which You are already working.
Use me in Your plan for his or her salvation. Amen.

PASTOR ROY MACK, GRACE FELLOWSHIP CHURCH, WARREN, OH

WEEK 25—WEEKEND
The Great Author

"The Helper, the Holy Spirit, whom the Father will send in My name, He will teach you all things, and bring to your remembrance all things that I said to you."

JOHN 14:26

Maybe you've have heard this old joke: "If my memory were any worse, I could plan my own surprise party."

When we consider sharing our faith or choosing to be God's light, we may oftentimes fear that we won't remember Scripture passages or know what to say. I couldn't count all the times when I didn't know how to answer a question and suddenly the Spirit of God came to my aid. He helped me remember exactly the right passage I needed to give a helpful answer.

We should not be surprised that the Spirit helps us recall biblical truths, sometimes verbatim. After all, holy men of God spoke as they were moved by the Holy Spirit. It is, therefore, not difficult for Him to remind you of something you have read. The Spirit knows the Bible inside and out—but do you?

Imagine you authored a book that took your lifetime to complete. Imagine many people dying because of their efforts to have it published. And then imagine your own children refusing to read it. When God's children don't spend time reading the greatest book ever written, they grieve its Author.

The Spirit dwells in all believers, but He doesn't dwell ungrieved in all believers. Commit to spending time reading, meditating on, and memorizing God's Word. When you do so, you give the Spirit of God more to draw from when you have an opportunity to share the gospel.

....

Spirit of God, make me a student of the Word. Fill my mind and heart with truths that You can use in bringing others to know Jesus. Here I am. Amen.

WEEK 26—MONDAY
Saving Grace

By grace you have been saved through faith, and that not of yourselves; it is the gift of God, not of works, lest anyone should boast.

EPHESIANS 2:8–9

Jesus is your saving grace. Salvation is the ultimate gift of God. He is the Giver of all good gifts, but most of all, He is the Giver of salvation. And what a wonderful gift He has given in the sacrificial death of His Son on our behalf. The gift of our salvation cannot be purchased. Neither is it a wage we can earn or a reward for anything we have done. Our salvation is a gift—purchased by the blood of Jesus—that we can receive only when we admit our sinfulness. And it is a gift of eternal value: it opens heaven to us.

God's grace has no strings attached. Jesus becomes our Savior not because of the good we have done or the good we might do. Jesus becomes our saving grace as an absolutely free and unmerited gift.

Salvation was God's idea, and it was a gift wrapped in Jesus and given because "God so loved the world" (John 3:16). What is your response to God's gift of love for you?

....

Dear God, thank You for the free gift of salvation. Thank You for Jesus. Thank You that He died for me and opened the way for me to be in relationship with You, something I never could have done for myself. Thank You for walking with me through this life and for the promise of eternal life. Amen.

MICHAEL MASON, MICHAEL MASON MINISTRIES, HARTSELLE, AL

WEEK 26—TUESDAY
Guiding Grace

The Word became flesh and dwelt among us, and we beheld His glory, the glory as of the only begotten of the Father, full of grace and truth.

JOHN 1:14

Jesus is your guiding grace. The Son of God came "and dwelt among us." He was light for a dark world. He was peace for a world of chaos. He was joy for a world in despair. He was "full of grace and truth" for a world filled with legalism and confusion. And He still is.

Jesus was filled with grace. No sinner was so sinful that he was beyond Jesus' reach. No one was so lost that he couldn't be saved.

Jesus was filled with truth. He was born into a world filled with half-truths, opinions, and outright lies, but He was truthful with the sinners and the saints.

Jesus lights the way for people throughout history who have, like the disciples, heard His call and followed Him. The multitudes in Jesus' day beheld His glory and followed Him. Today people continue to follow Him, who loves with merciful grace that reaches the outcast, the unbelieving, and the undeserving.

Jesus promised that those who follow Him will not walk in darkness. If you are following Jesus, you know what it is to experience the light of His guiding grace. If you aren't yet following Jesus, it's not too late.

....

Dear God, thank You for Your guiding grace, for Your unseen hand in my life, for Your direction and protection. Help me to trust You to guide me through the dark days and difficult times—and keep me from ignoring You during the good and easy times. Amen.

Week 26—Wednesday
Redeeming Grace

All have sinned and fall short of the glory of God, being justified freely by His grace through the redemption that is in Christ Jesus, whom God set forth as a propitiation by His blood, through faith, to demonstrate His righteousness, because in His forbearance God had passed over the sins that were previously committed.

ROMANS 3:23–25

Jesus is your redeeming grace. Several years ago a pastor friend and his wife welcomed into their home a young boy as a foster child. He wasn't even a year old, yet his leg had been broken in the abuse he suffered at home. The couple immediately fell in love with him and soon adopted him. They showed this boy redeeming grace.

To redeem a slave from slavery was to pay the purchase price to the owner. To redeem us from slavery to sin and Satan, Jesus paid the purchase price with His shed blood. We were orphans with no hope and no future, and then God sent Jesus to redeem us from our sins.

God "set [Jesus] forth as a propitiation." You and I never could satisfy the demands of a holy God, but Jesus could. He redeemed us.

God "demonstrate[d] His righteousness." Sinless Jesus became the guilty sinner on our behalf, and we who were lost became saved.

God "passed over [previous] sins." Thank God that, through the gift of Jesus who suffered our punishment, all our sins are passed over.

Dear God, I thank You today for Your redeeming grace. You knew my sins and saw my need. You let Your Son die; You let Him shed His blood and pass over my sins. Thank You for adopting me as Your child. Amen.

MICHAEL MASON, MICHAEL MASON MINISTRIES, HARTSELLE, AL

WEEK 26—THURSDAY
Sustaining Grace

Through [Jesus] we have received grace and apostleship for obedience to the faith among all nations for His name, among whom you also are the called of Jesus Christ.

ROMANS 1:5–6

Jesus is your sustaining grace. The gift of grace becomes active in our lives the moment we call out to God and receive it from Him. And, thankfully, His grace continues to sustain us long after the trial has passed.

For an illustration of God's saving grace, sit down at a piano. Press the pedal on the right. Then press any key and listen as the sound resonates for what seems like forever. That is what God's sustaining grace does: it keeps resonating in us and empowering us for what seems like forever.

Becoming a Christian is a very simple thing to do. Being a Christian, however, is the most difficult thing we will ever do. In order to persevere in our commitments and our obedience to Christ, we need His sustaining grace.

Paul knew that God had called him to be an apostle and that God would provide the grace he needed to fulfill that calling.

For the apostle Paul, faith and obedience went hand in hand. In his mind—and this is a good example for us—Paul's faith in Christ demanded his obedience.

Paul was eager to take the gospel of Christ to the world. And he would need grace for the journey—sustaining grace.

....

Dear God, thank You for calling me to know You and for enabling me to live a life that pleases You. Thank You for Your grace that sustains me in the difficult times. Amen.

Week 26—Friday
Sufficient Grace

Of His fullness we have all received, and grace for grace. . . . Grace and truth came through Jesus Christ.

John 1:16–17

Jesus is your sufficient grace. Maybe you've been backed into a corner by trouble, weighed down by heartache, or paralyzed by disappointment. If so, I have good news: in Jesus, we have a never-ending supply of grace. As God told the apostle Paul when he prayed about the thorn in his flesh, "My grace is sufficient for you, for My strength is made perfect in weakness" (2 Corinthians 12:9).

In the verse above, the apostle John described God's sufficient grace as "grace for grace." To understand that concept, imagine standing on a sandy shore watching wave after wave come in. Just as each new wave replaces another, we experience wave after wave of grace—"grace for grace"—when we follow Christ.

Jesus is the truth that sets men free from their bondage to sin and death, free from their separation from God, and free from purposelessness and despair. Jesus is "the way, the truth, and the life" (John 14:6). We cannot know God apart from Jesus. No sinful man comes to the holy Father except by accepting Jesus as the One who provides the bridge to Him. Jesus came with the truth that all have sinned and with the grace that believing in Him saves them from eternal separation from God.

In Jesus we have grace that replaces grace and truth that never changes.

....

Dear God, thank You for the never-ending supply of Your grace. Thank You that when I am weak You are strong. Thank You for each new day and for each new wave of grace. Thank You for being the truth that sets me free. Amen.

MICHAEL MASON, MICHAEL MASON MINISTRIES, HARTSELLE, AL

WEEK 26—WEEKEND
Providing Grace

[God] made us accepted in the Beloved [Jesus]. In Him we have redemption through His blood, the forgiveness of sins, according to the riches of His grace which He made to abound toward us in all wisdom and prudence.

EPHESIANS 1:6–8

Jesus is your providing grace. I recently overheard one fellow say to another, "That man has more money than he'll ever need." And that is difficult to imagine, isn't it?

In Christ, you and I have more grace than we'll ever need—and that is wonderfully difficult to imagine! God has grace enough for all who have believed and called on His name and for all who will ever believe and call on His name. Our God is rich in grace.

One aspect of the richness of God's grace is the "redemption through [Jesus'] blood, the forgiveness of sins" we receive. Singer/songwriter Andraé Crouch wrote that the power of Jesus' blood would never lose its power. The blood of Christ erases our sins. And—thank God—our sins are forgiven . . . forgotten . . . forever!

The depth of God's grace is far greater than we can fathom. No amount of sin can ever deplete the riches of His grace. The well of His grace will never run dry. He gives His grace abundantly—the grace of forgiveness that saves, guides, redeems, sustains, is all-sufficient, and provides. God is infinitely generous with His grace, as evidenced in the gift of His Son, our Savior and Lord, Redeemer and Friend.

....

Dear God, thank You for completely forgiving my sin. And thank You for giving Your saving, guiding, redeeming, sustaining, and all-sufficient grace—and for providing all the grace I will ever need. Amen.

WEEK 27—MONDAY
Choosing Faith

I have trusted in Your mercy; my heart shall rejoice in Your salvation. I will sing to the Lord, *because He has dealt bountifully with me.*

PSALM 13:5–6

Have you ever felt abandoned by God? Have you ever wondered, "Where is God when I need Him?" or "Does He even care about me?" or "Why me, God? I can't stand this"?

The psalmist understood these internal struggles, grief, and despair. Sometimes inner turmoil leads to a host of emotions or makes one unable to move forward in life. We ask questions and cry out for relief, but the apparent absence of God overwhelms us and causes us to run either from Him in despair or to Him in desperation.

When God seems conspicuous in His absence, how do we regain a sense of His presence? The psalmist's response was the choice to trust. I heard someone put it this way, "Don't doubt in the dark what God has shown you in the light." God is still God even when we don't see Him or feel Him. He can handle our doubts, frustrations, confusion, and honest grief. Rehearse His promises, remember His past faithfulness, and continue to choose to trust Him.

A song that helps me look beyond my circumstances and focus on Jesus is Israel Houghton's "Jesus, Your Presence Is Heaven." It's a reminder to focus more on who Jesus is and less on what I think I need Him to do for me. After all, Christianity is not about what I do or don't do; it is about what has already been done. Because of His victory over sin and death, I can trust in Jesus and know peace even in the midst of chaotic circumstances.

....

Lord Jesus, help me—as You helped the psalmist—choose to trust You even in the darkness. Help me remember Your past faithfulness in the present chaos. Amen.

DR. RICHARD MARK LEE, FIRST BAPTIST CHURCH MCKINNEY, MCKINNEY, TX

WEEK 27—TUESDAY
The Lord's Path of Mercy

The humble He guides in justice, and the humble He teaches His way. All the paths of the LORD are mercy and truth, to such as keep His covenant and His testimonies.

PSALM 25:9–10

I really like to receive mercy, but I'm not very good at giving it. And maybe that's the fundamental problem: I like to get more than I like to give. Put differently, the pride in my heart hinders my progress on the Lord's path of mercy.

God is looking for the humble of heart, not someone like me who trusts in my own ability, education, background, and life experiences. I need to trust God. And like His people in the Old Testament, I humbly and honestly have to deal with my fears, my limited perspective, my shortsightedness, my confusion, and my doubts. I don't have all the answers. Even Google doesn't have all the answers. At the end of the drama and debates of life, though, I don't need answers—I need God. When I humbly approach Him, I will find what I am looking for and what I need. I will find His mercy!

In Psalm 25:4–5, the psalmist prayed, "Show me Your ways, O LORD; teach me Your paths. Lead me in Your truth." I often pray that prayer for myself. I want to surrender humbly to God so I might walk on the path of His mercy. I want to realize that in Him I find all I need.

....

God, show me, teach me, and guide me on Your paths of truth and mercy. Help me to extend mercy to others in the same way I've received mercy from You. Amen.

Week 27—Wednesday
Reflecting on His Love

Your mercy, O Lord, is in the heavens; Your faithfulness reaches to the clouds. Your righteousness is like the great mountains; Your judgments are a great deep; O Lord, You preserve man and beast. How precious is Your lovingkindness, O God! Therefore the children of men put their trust under the shadow of Your wings.

Psalm 36:5–7

The psalms are raw, real, and full of emotion. They are prayers to God from real people about real life, so they are not always encouraging. The psalms teach us to worship and pray. They teach us that it's okay to cry, doubt, question, struggle, and even rage. They call us to trust, believe, have faith, and remember God's faithfulness throughout the ages.

Psalm 36:5–7 celebrates the greatness of our God. As Creator, God is above, outside of, and apart from His creation, but that doesn't mean He is removed from it.[6] He is deeply involved in caring for us, His most precious creation. He expresses His great love for us in His mercy. He is faithful. He is the Giver and Sustainer of life. He is our Judge, yet also our Advocate. He is our Savior. He paid the debt for our sins. He rescued us from darkness. He knows our name and our needs. He knows all about us and loves us anyway. We can't escape from His presence or from His love.

A friend of mine told me recently, "There are no emergency meetings in heaven over my circumstances." In His sovereignty, God is never surprised by what we encounter. And whatever those circumstances are, we can be sure that His love is unfailing. He is with us. And He is ready to meet you and me at our points of need.

....

Creator God, it is good to meditate on Your greatness and love. May I always be awed by Your kindness and grace. Amen.

DR. RICHARD MARK LEE, FIRST BAPTIST CHURCH MCKINNEY, MCKINNEY, TX

WEEK 27—THURSDAY
To Love Mercy

He has shown you, O man, what is good; and what does the LORD require of you but to do justly, to love mercy, and to walk humbly with your God?

MICAH 6:8

God created us to live in relationship with Him. We experience a life of peace when we live in connection with God. But that connection doesn't come naturally, and one reason is our constant struggle with selfish desires.

But when we humble ourselves and receive God's mercy instead of what we deserve, that choice changes us. Following Jesus changes our perspectives from being focused on ourselves to focusing more on what Jesus would do. Following Jesus changes the way we treat others, the way we plan our calendars, and how we spend the money He entrusts to our care. Our perspectives shift from focusing on what is good for us in this brief life to the impact of our actions and words in light of eternity.

Walking with God is not easy—and He never said it would be. The challenge is maintaining the living, breathing, moment-by-moment connection with our Savior. And to walk humbly is to live in submission and surrender to God in every area of life. In other words, doing justly and loving mercy will take care of itself as an outflow of our personal and humble walk with God.

In what areas of your life are you running on pride instead of surrendering to God in humility and allowing Him to lead you?

....

God, I want to walk humbly with You. I admit I can't do it easily. I'm selfish, often much more concerned about myself than about You. Create in me a pure heart that overcomes my self-centeredness and causes me to do justly, love mercy, and walk humbly with You. Amen.

WEEK 27—FRIDAY
Show and Tell

[God] says to Moses, "I will have mercy on whomever I will have mercy, and I will have compassion on whomever I will have compassion."

ROMANS 9:15

Most of us living on this planet today believe we are basically good. However, the reality is quite different: all of us are fundamentally broken. We are naturally depraved. Left to ourselves, we default to selfishness and sin, and we are prone to wander. We may have some good moments, but we have plenty of bad moments. In fact, when we consider our attitudes, thoughts, and hearts, the bad far too often far outweighs the good!

Thankfully, God is love. And in His love, He is perfectly merciful and just. God's mercy keeps us from experiencing the judgment we deserve. God's grace gives us goodness that we don't deserve. To be specific, God the Father sent the Son to take the punishment for our sins. God withholds from us the penalty of sin, directing it instead to His Son, and then gives us the gift of His Son's righteousness so we can pass the test of holiness. God's mercy to us is one way He displays His love, His grace, and His glory.

Romans 2:4 says, "God's kindness is meant to lead you to repentance" (ESV). And His mercy does lead us back into relationship with Him. As recipients of His mercy, we are to extend His mercy, love, and grace to others. In fact, God may use us as channels of His mercy, love, and grace in their lives to make real His life-changing love for them.

....

God, give me opportunities to show and tell of Your mercy. Give me courage to show and tell of Your love. Amen.

DR. RICHARD MARK LEE, FIRST BAPTIST CHURCH MCKINNEY, MCKINNEY, TX

But God, who is rich in mercy, because of His great love with which He loved us, even when we were dead in trespasses, made us alive together with Christ (by grace you have been saved), and raised us up together, and made us sit together in the heavenly places in Christ Jesus.

EPHESIANS 2:4–6

You were . . . "but God." From Genesis through Revelation, the Scriptures flesh out these pivotal words: "But God."

Adam and Eve were lost forever because of their sin, "but God" . . .

Noah would have been drowned with the people in the world, "but God" . . .

Jonah would never have been given a second chance, "but God" . . .

The same can be said of Peter, who shortly after professing his complete loyalty, denied three times even knowing Christ. "But God" . . .

In Hebrews 11, God's hall of faith, we find a drunkard, a murderer, a prostitute, a husband of a prostitute, a man who ran from God, adulterers, liars, an irresponsible father, a womanizer, and a deceiver. A bunch of moral failures—but their failures were formative, not fatal. Their failures were not the closing act. "But God!"

Think of the comeback! All hope was lost, but then came the grand slam in the bottom of the ninth when we were down by three runs or the three-point shot at the buzzer in overtime when we were down by two. Far better than a Hail Mary pass caught in the end zone as time expires is the truth that we were dead in our sin, "but God" made us fully alive in Christ!

....

Lord, bring to mind, my "but God" moments so that I might live a life of gratitude to You.

Week 28—Monday
Christlike Suffering in the Workplace

Servants, be submissive to your masters with all fear, not only to the good and gentle, but also to the harsh. For this is commendable, if because of conscience toward God one endures grief, suffering wrongfully. For what credit is it if, when you are beaten for your faults, you take it patiently? But when you do good and suffer, if you take it patiently, this is commendable before God. For to this you were called, because Christ also suffered for us, leaving us an example, that you should follow His steps.

1 Peter 2:18–21

What Peter wrote applies to employees today: we are to submit to our employers and supervisors. Our hearts' desires ought to be that we will be honest and glorify the Lord with our work.

Sometimes, though, a Christian employee may be wronged by an unbelieving co-worker or supervisor. When that happens, our attitudes are important. How we respond will reveal much about our faith and about our God. Consider, for instance, that anybody—including unbelievers, can "take it patiently" when they are in the wrong. But it takes dedicated Christians to "take it patiently" when they are falsely accused! Human tendency is to fight back and demand our rights. That is the natural response of the unsaved person, but believers must do much more than nonbelievers do (Luke 6:32–34). Anybody can fight back, but a Spirit-filled Christian will submit to God and let Him fight battles (Romans 12:16–21).

Also Peter reminded us that the Lord suffered for doing what is right and that we should be willing to do the same. Our testimonies and potential relationships are influenced by how we react to being wronged. We should be patient and trust God. He is our defense, and He will be glorified by our Christlike responses not only at work but also in the church and our communities.

....

God, give me the grace to glorify You in my job, regardless of my circumstances. Amen.

DR. ROB ZINN, IMMANUEL BAPTIST CHURCH, HIGHLAND, CA

WEEK 28—TUESDAY
Show Diligence

Beloved, we are confident of better things concerning you, yes, things that accompany salvation, though we speak in this manner. . . . And we desire that each one of you show the same diligence to the full assurance of hope until the end, that you do not become sluggish, but imitate those who through faith and patience inherit the promises.

HEBREWS 6:9, 11–12

This is a complex passage, but understanding the context in which it is written will help.

When we look at verses 1–6, we have to think about how many people today "play" church. There is a huge difference between a person who hears, sees, and has been exposed to the gospel and the person who has been changed by it. Some people act as if they are changed; some have truly been transformed. The gospel is not something to play with: "it is the power of God to salvation" (Romans 1:16). Acknowledging that many have literally walked away from salvation, the writer of Hebrews said to his readers the he was "confident of better things concerning [them]." He was, to be more specific, confident that he would see in their lives the fruit of salvation.

While it is true that God carries us along to maturity and is patient with us, it is also true that believers must do their part. We are to be diligent and not sluggish, for instance. And our lives should exhibit the fruit of the Spirit— and, better yet, continued growth of that fruit. Finally, the writer encouraged us to imitate those believers who have gone before us, and through faith and patience have inherited the promises God had for them.

....

God, help me to be a doer and not just one who hears. I want to glorify You. Amen.

WEEK 28—WEDNESDAY
A Man of God

You, O man of God, flee these things and pursue righteousness, godliness, faith, love, patience, gentleness. Fight the good fight of faith, lay hold on eternal life, to which you were also called and have confessed the good confession in the presence of many witnesses.

1 TIMOTHY 6:11–12

Paul mentioned the danger of false teachers three times in this epistle to Timothy, and each time Paul warned Timothy to resist them. After all, God had called Timothy to the ministry—he was a proclaimed man of God.

In his Grace for You ministries, Pastor John MacArthur pointed out four characteristics that mark the man of God in contrast to the false teacher.

What he flees from: a man of God flees from "these things," such as the love of money, pride, disputes, envy, and strife (verses 3–10).

What he follows after: a man of God will pursue righteousness, doing what is right in God's eyes and man's and living with personal integrity. He will also strive for godliness. While righteousness is manifest in outward behavior, godliness has to do with attitudes and motives. Right behavior flows from right motives (verse 11).

What he fights for: we are called to defend the faith, the body of Christ, truth, and God's Word (verse 12; Jude v. 3).

What he is faithful to: a man of God, unlike false teachers, is faithful to blamelessness, obedience, and the gospel.[7]

....

O Lord, help me to be faithful to You, to follow You, and to live for Your glory. In Jesus' name I pray, Amen.

Week 28—Thursday

Rest in the Lord

Rest in the Lord, and wait patiently for Him; do not fret because of him who prospers in his way, because of the man who brings wicked schemes to pass. Cease from anger, and forsake wrath; do not fret—it only causes harm. . . . The Lord knows the days of the upright, and their inheritance shall be forever.

Psalm 37:7–8, 18

This psalm is just as relevant in the twenty-first century as it was when David wrote it. How many times have you let someone ruin your day? The driver who cut you off? A neighbor who is just being a pain? Watching the news and losing it because if you were in charge, you would do a much better job? Does it bother you that evil people seem to get away with all kinds of things or that people who do illegal things seem to prosper?

If any of those questions ring true for you, note what David said to us:

"Do not fret [worry] because of evildoers" (v. 1 NASB).

"Be not envious toward wrongdoers" (v. 1 NASB).

"Trust in the Lord, and do good" (v. 3 NASB).

"Delight yourself in the Lord" (v. 4 NASB).

"Commit your way to the Lord" (v. 5 NASB).

"Rest (relax; take a deep breath) in the Lord and wait patiently for Him" (v. 7)

Also don't focus on others; focus on God. Focusing on the wrongs people do will only cause your blood pressure to rise. Instead, focus on your Lord and His glory, love, and grace. Know you are His, and you will be with Him forever!

....

O Lord, thank You for Your gracious love and help me to trust You when the world comes at me. I want to rest in You. In Jesus' name I pray, Amen.

WEEK 28—FRIDAY
Count It All Joy

My brethren, count it all joy when you fall into various trials, knowing that the testing of your faith produces patience. But let patience have its perfect work, that you may be perfect and complete, lacking nothing. If any of you lacks wisdom, let him ask of God, who gives to all liberally and without reproach, and it will be given to him.

JAMES 1:2–5

How people handle trouble will reveal whether or not their faith is living or dead, genuine or fake, saving or not. And people all have trials. Make sure you understand what James said: it is not *if*, but "when you fall into various trials."

Trials are not electives in God's school; they are required courses. Sooner or later testing will come. These seasons are not intended to give God an opportunity to see how we are doing, but to let us see how far we have come or failed to come in our journeys of faith.

The bottom line is this: we have trials because God loves us. He is helping us to grow in grace and in faith. So how are we to respond? "Count it all joy." The Greek verb for *count* is an imperative: because joy is not the natural human response to trouble, we need to be commanded to rejoice. Christians are under the divine mandate not simply to be somewhat joyful in our trials, but to look upon them with all joy. Our outlooks impact outcome, and our attitudes impact action.

Since trials can be so productive, it is essential to respond rightly to them. Always remember God loves you and has a plan and a purpose. If you need wisdom, ask Him.

....

Lord, thank You for loving me. Give me the grace to respond wisely and well to trials. Amen.

DR. ROB ZINN, IMMANUEL BAPTIST CHURCH, HIGHLAND, CA

Week 28—Weekend
The Basis of Hope

Whatever things were written before were written for our learning, that we through the patience and comfort of the Scriptures might have hope. Now may the God of patience and comfort grant you to be like-minded toward one another, according to Christ Jesus.

ROMANS 15:4–5

What is the need of all people? Hope! Where do we find hope? In the Word of God.

The goal of the Scriptures is to give us hope, not only for today, but for tomorrow. We find hope in "the patience and comfort of the Scriptures." Our hope is based on what the Bible reveals. Would you have hope in the life to come if you had never read the Scriptures? No. That's why Ephesians 2:12 says that people without the Scriptures are without hope and without God in the world.

Without the Word of God, we have no basis for hope. It is our study and knowledge of the Word of God that gives us hope. The Scriptures give us hope in the middle of a trial and call us to persevere and wait on God (Psalm 27:13–14; 30:5; 34:4; 55:22; Romans 5:3–5; James 5:7–8).

The Word of God teaches us that we can endure any trial, anxiety, or difficulty. We are able to persevere when we are confident in the Scriptures and our knowledge of God. So get in the Word, know the Word, meditate on the Word, and let the Word of God come alive in you.

....

Lord Jesus, give me the desire to meditate on Your Word. Create in me a hunger to fill my heart and mind with the Scriptures. In Jesus' name I pray, Amen.

Week 29—Monday
Be Assured—and Be Committed

Commit your way to the Lord, trust also in Him, and He shall bring it to pass. He shall bring forth your righteousness as the light, and your justice as the noonday. Rest in the Lord, and wait patiently for Him; do not fret because of him who prospers in his way, because of the man who brings wicked schemes to pass.

PSALM 37:5–7

Our world is in turmoil. We can point to many places, politics, and issues, but none of this turmoil would be happening without mankind's sins. According to the Bible, all people are born in sin. Because God is holy and righteous, sinful man is totally separated and without hope in this lost and dying world. Without trusting Christ as Savior and Lord, we have no biblically grounded compass.

David clearly recognized this sin problem. He saw sins in his own life, and he bore witness to sin in the lives of people around him. Furthermore, David didn't miss the fact that many of the wicked prospered despite their sinfulness.

In this psalm, David reminded us that a life committed to God is a trusting life. When we trust God in all our ways, He enables us to accept even those things that are difficult to understand. And He assures us that He is in control.

....

Dear God, I commit my life to You, trusting in Your goodness and resting in Your sovereignty. In Jesus' name we pray, Amen.

DR. DON WILTON, FIRST BAPTIST CHURCH, SPARTANBURG, SC

WEEK 29—TUESDAY
Be Assured—and Be Strengthened

May the LORD answer you in the day of trouble; may the name of the God of Jacob defend you; may He send you help from the sanctuary, and strengthen you out of Zion. . . . May He grant you according to your heart's desire, and fulfill all your purpose.

PSALM 20:1–2, 4

During the reign of King David, the people understood the significance of a person being God's anointed one. There was no doubt in their minds that the Lord Himself had set David apart to be their leader. They had not only heard reports of his gallant feats on the battlefield but they knew God had chosen David from among his many brothers. And God's choices were not to be ignored!

In this psalm of praise and petition, David called for God to send help and strength from "the sanctuary" and "out of Zion," two places symbolizing God's presence. The people who honored their king prayed to God on behalf of him. They wanted God to uphold, support, and sustain their king. They wanted God's blessings poured out on David because they knew if God's anointed king succeeded, they would succeed too. In other words, praying for God's blessings on their king would mean His blessings on them as well. We should be sure to pray for the leaders God has placed over us.

....

Dear God, I pray for the leaders of our nation. Give them wisdom and discernmet. In Jesus' name I pray, Amen.

WEEK 29—WEDNESDAY
Be Assured—and Be Persistent

God is not unjust to forget your work and labor of love which you have shown toward His name, in that you have ministered to the saints, and do minister. And we desire that each one of you show the same diligence to the full assurance of hope until the end, that you do not become sluggish, but imitate those who through faith and patience inherit the promises.

HEBREWS 6:10–12

It is helpful to remember that much of the letter to the Hebrews was written with concern for unbelieving Jews. The writer desired that nonbelievers would realize that their only hope—the only source of assurance for the end of their lives—lies in the Lord Jesus Christ, who is the Author and Finisher of our faith. The readers of this letter were modeling well what it means to live in that hope.

In this passage, the writer was very straightforward: God is not unjust. He will neither forget nor ignore His followers who put their faith in action. As the writer commended the believers' wonderful and faithful ministry to all people, he commented that they were worthy of being imitated. What an affirmation!

Perhaps many of the nonbelieving Jews, however, were so steeped in their traditions that they simply didn't understand this new message, the gospel truth. The writer affirmed to the Hebrews that they were fine examples of love for the nonbelievers, and the writer encouraged them to persist, to follow in their forefathers' footsteps. Serving God in this life—ministering to others—would mean rejoicing in His fulfilled promises for eternity.

....

Dear God, please help me to have assurance enough to persist and persevere in my faith so I may be Your light for nonbelievers around me. Amen.

DR. DON WILTON, FIRST BAPTIST CHURCH, SPARTANBURG, SC

WEEK 29—THURSDAY
Be Assured—and Draw Near

Let us draw near with a true heart in full assurance of faith, having our hearts sprinkled from an evil conscience and our bodies washed with pure water. Let us hold fast the confession of our hope without wavering, for He who promised is faithful. And let us consider one another in order to stir up love and good works.

HEBREWS 10:22–24

I love the time of invitation at the end of our Sunday services. Every time I share the Word of God, I encourage people to respond to whatever the Holy Spirit is calling them to do. Some may believe the invitation is just for the lost to come to Christ, but Jesus continually calls out to His disciples to follow His teachings. Jesus has high expectations for how His followers live in this world as nonbelievers watch.

This passage encourages the faithful to "draw near" to God. When we do, God will draw near to us and strengthen our faith. In fact, the nearer we draw to God, the greater our "assurance of faith."

This assurance of faith—this confidence that one's sins are forgiven and that one will share eternity with God—is rooted in God's amazing grace.

....

Dear God, thank You for enabling me to draw near to You. In Your presence I find complete assurance of my faith in You. In Jesus' name I pray, Amen.

Week 29—Friday
Be Assured—It's Guaranteed!

For we know that if our earthly house, this tent, is destroyed, we have a building from God, a house not made with hands, eternal in the heavens. For in this we groan, earnestly desiring to be clothed with our habitation which is from heaven . . . Now He who has prepared us for this very thing is God, who also has given us the Spirit as a guarantee.

2 Corinthians 5:1–2, 5

Look again at the beautiful word picture in this wonderful passage of Scripture: that heavenly building speaks to us of the assurance we have in Christ.

The older I get, the more I realize just how fragile this body of mine is. For no reason at all, something malfunctions or starts hurting with no explanation. Aches and pains serve as a constant reminder that we live in an earthly "tent." And where would we be without the hope of the resurrection of this tired and getting-more-tired body?

A tentmaker by trade, Paul used the metaphor of a tent to describe the fragile casing that carries the soul of man. The imagery for him was quite natural. Yet he knew that one day he would receive a heavenly body that would never break down or fall apart.

Against this backdrop of bodies and buildings that fade, we can better appreciate the assurance God gives us that one day we will be made perfect in His presence.

....

Dear God, I thank You for the promise of heaven that Your Spirit guarantees. In Jesus' name I pray, Amen.

DR. DON WILTON, FIRST BAPTIST CHURCH, SPARTANBURG, SC

WEEK 29—WEEKEND
Be Assured—and Be Encouraged

Our gospel did not come to you in word only, but also in power, and in the Holy Spirit and in much assurance, as you know what kind of men we were among you for your sake. And you became followers of us and of the Lord, having received the word in much affliction, with joy of the Holy Spirit.

1 THESSALONIANS 1:5–6

I s there anything in this world greater than the gospel of the Lord Jesus Christ? Absolutely not! Paul understood the significance of the gospel and made sure that all people understood, clearly, what the message about Jesus Christ—incarnate God, crucified, and risen—was all about.

Paul called it "our gospel" because it was for him and all people. Planned and executed by God, the gospel teaches the forgiveness of sin available through the shed blood of the Lord Jesus Christ on the cross. We read the gospel in the Scripture, and the Holy Spirit confirms its truth, blesses us with joy, and enables us to share the message.

Paul wanted us to know we can stand strong and confident in this gospel. The validity of the message was confirmed by the lives of those who preached it. To this day, followers of Jesus exemplify the life of Christ and encourage a life of faith in Him through their own witness and even their suffering for their Lord.

....

Dear God, thank You for the encouragement I receive from so many of Your faithful saints, those who have gone before me and those with whom I journey today. In Jesus' name I pray, Amen.

Week 30—Monday
Fool's Gold

Wine is a mocker, strong drink is a brawler, and whoever is led astray by it is not wise.

PROVERBS 20:1

It's a paradigm shift, having as the greatest goal in life not avoiding sin but pursuing Christ and His character.

In our Scripture verses for today, both wine and strong drink are personified: one as a "mocker" and the other as a "brawler." In Hebrew both of these words can mean "foolish." And if one of my goals is for others to see Christlike integrity in my life, I should avoid consuming that which leads to foolishness.

However, we should not judge others. Life is difficult and full of so much pain. Fear and anxiety are ever-present realities for many people. Alcohol can indeed seem like a shelter from the storms of life. If you are using alcohol as your shelter, have you sensed that it is inadequate? I encourage you instead to begin taking refuge in Christ. Pour your heart out to Him in prayer instead of pouring yourself another drink. What you might find is what Jesus promised in Matthew 11:29–30: "Take up My yoke and learn from Me, because I am gentle and humble in heart, and you will find rest for yourselves. For My yoke is easy and My burden is light" (HCSB).

It's easy for people who don't struggle with alcohol use to feel superior to those who do struggle, but other foolish and inadequate things can serve as a refuge or an idol.

What in your life are you trusting to bring you a level of comfort that only God can give?

Father, give me the strength today to run to You as my shelter. Grant me the wisdom to see the foolish things in my life that keep me trapped, and by Your grace set me free today to worship You and You alone. Amen.

PASTOR BRADY COOPER, NEW VISION LIFE, MURFREESBORO, TN

WEEK 30—TUESDAY
Get Coached Up

Exhort the young men to be sober-minded, in all things showing yourself to be a pattern of good works; in doctrine showing integrity, reverence, incorruptibility, sound speech that cannot be condemned, that one who is an opponent may be ashamed, having nothing evil to say of you.

TITUS 2:6–8

I will never forget my first practice as a college baseball player. My coach hit ground balls to me, and he hit me ten or fifteen that I promptly fielded. It was the last hit that I'll never forget. Coach hit it several feet out of my reach. Then he walked out to me and asked what happened. "Coach, I don't have that much range" was my answer. To which he replied, "Not yet, but I'm going to stay on you until you do."

We all need a coach like that, someone who helps us see where we are and exhorts us to do better, to move forward, to grow. Sadly, few of us have invited someone into our lives to exhort us spiritually. In his letter to Titus, Paul talked about how God can use exhortation to produce in us self-control ("be sober-minded" in verse 6) and, ultimately, a life of integrity.

Are you willing to engage with a more spiritually mature person in your church and cultivate a relationship with that person? A simple starting point is asking him or her to hold you accountable each week to memorize one verse of Scripture. As you begin this leg of your spiritual journey, let that individual know you want him or her to coach you and push you to grow in Christ.

Schedule coffee or lunch this week with someone who could potentially be a spiritual coach in your life.

....

Father, lead me today to someone who can exhort me spiritually and help me grow in my knowledge of and love for You. Amen.

Week 30—Wednesday
No More Rearview-Mirror Living

Not that I have already attained, or am already perfected; but I press on, that I may lay hold of that for which Christ Jesus has also laid hold of me. Brethren, I do not count myself to have apprehended; but one thing I do, forgetting those things which are behind and reaching forward to those things which are ahead, I press toward the goal for the prize of the upward call of God in Christ Jesus.

PHILIPPIANS 3:12–14

I am currently teaching my fifteen-year-old son to drive, which is a challenge. His struggle behind the wheel is rooted in his desire to take his eyes off the road and play DJ. I am constantly reminding him to keep his eyes on the road, not on the radio.

Similarly, in Philippians 3, Paul challenged us to keep looking ahead spiritually, not behind. The guilt and shame from our past can keep us looking backward and rob us of our future. Paul put it this way in another letter he wrote: "If anyone is in Christ, he is a new creation; old things have passed away, and look, new things have come" (2 Corinthians 5:17 HCSB).

Because of our new identities as children of God, we can leave our past behind. God has forgiven our past sin. We can quit looking in the rearview mirror and instead live from a place of total forgiveness in Christ. I have always been amazed that Paul, the man who passively witnessed the stoning of Stephen, received a completely new identity in Christ and headed in an entirely new direction.

Memorize 2 Corinthians 5:17 this week so that every time Satan reminds you of a past sin, you can quote this text and find freedom in its truth.

....

Father, teach me today to come wholeheartedly to receive Your transforming grace so I can walk in the total freedom of Your forgiveness. Amen.

PASTOR BRADY COOPER, NEW VISION LIFE, MURFREESBORO, TN

Week 30—Thursday
Know His Schemes

I urge you, therefore, to reaffirm your love for him. Another reason I wrote you was to see if you would stand the test and be obedient in everything. Anyone you forgive, I also forgive. And what I have forgiven—if there was anything to forgive—I have forgiven in the sight of Christ for your sake, 11 in order that Satan might not outwit us. For we are not unaware of his schemes.

2 Corinthians 2:8–11

Being aware of Satan's schemes is a good thing. That awareness is, in fact, key to walking in security or, literally, in freedom. Consider, for instance, how twisted our views on sexuality and marriage are compared to God's original design. This is a direct result of the enemy's schemes, and the result is bondage, not freedom.

Another problem with anything that's twisted is that it loses its strength. When I embrace the enemy's twisted schemes, I become twisted and weak. The perverted ways of my heart "will become known" because I won't have the strength I need to withstand the storms of life.

Integrity, on the other hand, is the God-given ability to see the enemy's schemes and reject them. Walking with integrity means understanding that the enemy's schemes are not shortcuts to be enjoyed, but rather dead-ends to be avoided. A person of integrity knows the truth of God's Word, the heart of the Lawgiver, and the power of the Holy Spirit and, therefore, chooses to live out God's truth in obedience to Him.

In what area of your life, if any, have you settled for a perversion of the truth? Repent right now and begin to walk in freedom.

....

Father, today lead me not into temptation, but deliver me from the evil schemes of the enemy. Amen.

THE GIFT OF JESUS

Week 30—Friday
Leave Your Hiding Place

Be merciful to me, O Lord, for I cry to You all day long. Rejoice the soul of Your servant, for to You, O Lord, I lift up my soul. For You, Lord, are good, and ready to forgive, and abundant in mercy to all those who call upon You.

PSALM 86:3–5

Our views on the nature of God will in many ways determine the courses of our lives.

Consider, for instance, the way we can let past experiences, such as being raised by an overbearing parent, color our understanding of God. If we grew up in a family like that, we may have developed the pattern of hiding our feelings for fear of a harsh response. This kind of faulty understanding of God's nature causes us to develop unhealthy spiritual patterns, such as hiding from our heavenly Father. Our Scripture passage today, however, reminds us that God is nothing like an overbearing parent. Our God is rich in mercy and very willing to forgive.

When we let the Scripture form our understanding of the nature of God, we are transformed. Ephesians 1:8 says that He lavishes His grace upon His children (HSCB). Our text today says our God is ready to forgive. We don't have to hide our mistakes and our fears from a God like this. Instead, we can cast all our cares on Him because He cares for us (1 Peter 5:7).

With this fresh understanding of God's grace, what area of your life are you now willing to uncover in confession to Him?

....

Father, I know that You are rich in grace and mercy and willing to forgive. Help me to know Your Word better so that I learn more about Your true nature. Amen.

PASTOR BRADY COOPER, NEW VISION LIFE, MURFREESBORO, TN

WEEK 30—WEEKEND
Glass Bottles

As for me, I will walk in my integrity; redeem me and be merciful to me. My foot stands in an even place; in the congregations I will bless the LORD.

PSALM 26:11–12

As a kid I frequently visited redemption racks for glass soda bottles. My mom often let me keep the cash we received when we redeemed the bottles. Those days are long gone, but the principle of redemption is still in play.

Part of walking in integrity is understanding that God is able to redeem all things. Joel 2:25 says that God can restore the years the locusts have eaten. In other words, we don't have to be prisoners of the past. We must let God forgive us for our past sins, and then watch Him redeem them. He will use our past for good.

Too many people, though, miss the life that could be theirs because they let themselves remain prisoners of the past. But some of their greatest ministry in the future could come out of God redeeming their past—and that is true for us too. God can redeem a painful divorce or devastating bankruptcy and enable us to minister to others because of that experience.

A person of integrity recognizes that God redeems the past by making it a tool he or she can use for ministry. A person of integrity, therefore, walks in wholeness, realizing that even the painful parts of his or her past don't have to be stumbling blocks any longer, but can instead be stepping stones to greater intimacy with God and richer ministry to others.

Is there an old glass bottle hidden in your heart that you need to take to the Father to be redeemed for His glory and for your good?

....

Father, thank You that because of Your grace and power, my past doesn't have to sideline me but can instead position me to minister to others. Amen.

WEEK 31—MONDAY
When Troubles Come

Blessed be the God and Father of our Lord Jesus Christ, the Father of mercies and God of all comfort, who comforts us in all our tribulation, that we may be able to comfort those who are in any trouble, with the comfort with which we ourselves are comforted by God.

2 CORINTHIANS 1:3–4

Every single one of us is either in trouble, just getting out of trouble, or about to encounter trouble. Heartaches, disappointments, sorrow—troubles like these are all part of life. "How can I avoid trouble in life?" is not a question we need to ask because we simply can't avoid it. The question should be how you will respond when trouble comes.

A good first response is to praise the Lord. Paul knew much about trouble firsthand, yet he counseled, "In everything give thanks" (1 Thessalonians 5:18). Choosing to thank our Father and praise Him in the midst of trouble helps shift our focus from ourselves and to Him, the Source of all we need.

In addition to being the Source of all compassion and all comfort, our Father knows exactly what we are going through, and He cares about us. Nothing in this world—not drugs, religion, philosophy—can bring comfort. Only Jesus can bring us real comfort.

Another response to trouble is to take the comfort you have received and pass it on to others when they have those same troubles. Don't waste the lessons you learned in Trouble 101. The Father wants to use you to comfort someone out there. Will you allow Him?

....

Father of all my comfort, I thank You for the troubles You allow to come my way because they turn my focus to You and teach me how to comfort others. Use me as a channel of Your comfort for others. Amen.

DR. MICHAEL CLOER, ENGLEWOOD BAPTIST CHURCH, ROCKY MOUNT, NC

WEEK 31—TUESDAY
Recognize Those Who Labor

Comfort each other and edify one another, just as you also are doing. We urge you, brethren, to recognize those who labor among you, and are over you in the Lord and admonish you, and to esteem them very highly in love for their work's sake. Be at peace among yourselves.

1 THESSALONIANS 5:11–13

Most companies, organizations, clubs, governments, teams—almost every group in the world—honors hardworking and faithful members. And we are to recognize those same qualities in the church.

Scripture teaches that all Christ-followers have an obligation to encourage and build up other followers. Comforting fellow believers, though, doesn't mean we simply pat them on the head or heartily shake their hands. Instead, we are to put strength into them for their responsibilities and support them so they will grow stronger in their faith.

While we must comfort and edify every believer, we must show special recognition to those among us who are our spiritual authorities, those who "labor among [us]." That word *labor* does not imply just an hour or two on Sunday, but toiling to the point of weariness and exhaustion. Honor these leaders for their work and for their worth in the body of Christ.

God says we are to "esteem them very highly in love": we must give them the respect that their love and service deserve. We should ask ourselves today, "Do we *dis*courage or *en*courage our spiritual leaders?" The result will be harmony in the church. As we encourage one another and show respect to our spiritual leaders, we will enjoy greater peace in our family of believers.

....

Precious Lord, please help me use my words and actions to cause Your church and our spiritual leaders to be encouraged and strengthened. Amen.

Week 31—Wednesday
God Is with You

"Have I not commanded you? Be strong and of good courage; do not be afraid, nor be dismayed, for the LORD your God is with you wherever you go."

JOSHUA 1:9

Next to "bless this food to the nourishment of our bodies," perhaps the most repeated prayer is "Lord, be with me as I . . ." But why would you ask someone who is constantly with you to be with you?

Maybe because you haven't yet grasped one of the most glorious realities in the Christian life: "Christ in you, the hope of glory" (Colossians 1:27). When you gave your life to Jesus Christ, you were placed in Him; and at that same moment, He gave His life to you and came to live within you. The Christian life is not your asking, "What would Jesus do if He were here?" He *is* here, and He lives inside of you!

You are the house of God today. Your body is His holy temple, not a hotel. He did not come to visit. When you welcomed Jesus to be Lord of your life, He moved in to stay—forever. He promised that when He came to live inside you, He would "abide with you forever" (John 14:16).

You do not need to *pray* for His presence; you need to *practice* His presence. There is not a place you go without Him. What you watch, He watches through your eyes. What you hear, He listens to through your ears.

At times you may be lonely, but you are never alone. The living Lord Jesus Christ is closer to you than you realize.

....

Blessed Lord, I praise You for Your faithfulness to me. I thank You that because You are with me in every situation, I will face nothing that You can't handle. Amen.

DR. MICHAEL CLOER, ENGLEWOOD BAPTIST CHURCH, ROCKY MOUNT, NC

WEEK 31—THURSDAY
Here! Take My Seat!

Let love be without hypocrisy. Abhor what is evil. Cling to what is good. Be kindly affectionate to one another with brotherly love, in honor giving preference to one another.

ROMANS 12:9–10

What blood is to our physical bodies, love is to the body of Christ. Love enables all the members of the church to function in a harmonious, healthy way when this love is honest, "without hypocrisy," humble, and willing to put other people before us.

Jonathan knew that as Saul's son he was rightful heir to the throne and that David was God's choice as the next king. Nevertheless, Jonathan showed brotherly love to David and, despite the personal cost, respected him as Israel's future king. Never forgetting these generous actions, King David showed kindness to Jonathan's family and especially to his grandson (2 Samuel 9).

"Giving preference" or stepping aside so someone else can benefit or be honored instead of you does not come naturally. What *is* natural is putting yourself first, thinking of yourself, protecting yourself, and promoting yourself. This countercultural "take my seat!" attitude will require the divine love of the living Jesus Christ inside of you, loving people through you.

Jesus' love—expressed through you—will cause you to put everything you have into pleasing the Lord and serving Him. Not casually or when it is convenient, but wholeheartedly. Allowing Him to love others through your life and lips will result in His praise, greater patience with others, and faithful praying for them. It will also prompt you to use your material resources to benefit others in practical ways.

Heavenly Father, You are a loving God. I want to put You first today and every day, and I want to serve others too. Amen.

Week 31—Friday
All in the Family

I, therefore, the prisoner of the Lord, beseech you to walk worthy of the calling with which you were called, with all lowliness and gentleness, with longsuffering, bearing with one another in love, endeavoring to keep the unity of the Spirit in the bond of peace. There is one body and one Spirit, just as you were called in one hope of your calling.

Ephesians 4:1–4

Someone has said:

> *To live there above with those that we love,*
> *Oh, that will be glory!*
> *But to dwell here below with those that we know,*
> *Now, that's another story.*

The two bars of the cross remind us of the two dimensions of the Christian life: our relationship with God and our relationship with others. The more difficult area is relating to other people. Why? Because God is perfect, but other people are not—and neither are we.

How can we live with others in a way that honors the name of Christ? By choosing humility, gentleness, and meekness. By quietly enduring people's quirks and faults. By not retaliating when someone wrongs us. This assignment is not easy, which is why God's Word calls us to work hard at it and persevere.

Jesus Christ is our role model for every aspect of the Christian life. He endured mistreatment with love and longsuffering. Believers may have different preferences as to styles of music, clothes, or politics, but if a person is a Christ follower like us, we are in the same family. Choose to love your fellow believers today.

....

My Lord, I ask You to love every person through my life and actions. For Jesus' sake, Amen.

DR. MICHAEL CLOER, ENGLEWOOD BAPTIST CHURCH, ROCKY MOUNT, NC

WEEK 31—WEEKEND
Calmness in the Storm

Above all these things put on love, which is the bond of perfection. And let the peace of God rule in your hearts, to which also you were called in one body; and be thankful. Let the word of Christ dwell in you richly in all wisdom, teaching and admonishing one another in psalms and hymns and spiritual songs, singing with grace in your hearts to the Lord.

COLOSSIANS 3:14–16

Peace. It doesn't come in a pill. It can't be found in a bottle or bought. But peace is something all of us want and need. Peace is not the absence of problems, but the awareness of the presence of Jesus. He is the Peacemaker, the Peace Speaker, the Prince of Peace.

Peace is part of the legacy Jesus left to His followers: "I am leaving you with a gift—peace of mind and heart!" (John 14:27 NLT). However, we can never have the peace *of* God until we have peace *with* God through a relationship with Jesus Christ. His peace then becomes not only a precious gift, but also a helpful guide in life.

How can you know you are making the right decisions? When there is peace ruling in your heart. The word *rule* means "to arbitrate" or "to umpire." Whatever the sport, as long as you are playing correctly, the umpire is silent. Only when you go out of bounds or break a rule does the umpire speak up. So if you have a decision to make, allow God's Word to dwell in your heart, pray, seek counsel from other Bible-believing Christians, and if there is no whistle, go for it!

....

Father, guide my choices today by Your Word and by Your peace. For Jesus' sake, Amen.

WEEK 32—MONDAY
A Prescription for Hope

I know the thoughts that I think toward you, says the LORD, thoughts of peace and not of evil, to give you a future and a hope. Then you will call upon Me and go and pray to Me, and I will listen to you. And you will seek Me and find Me, when you search for Me with all your heart.

JEREMIAH 29:11–13

When I am sick, I go to the doctor. The doctor performs certain tests, examines the results, and prescribes a remedy for what ails me. During the days of the prophet Jeremiah, the nation of Israel needed a remedy for its sickness. And like Israel then, we find our souls sick today, and we long for healing.

Based on the eternal purposes of His heart, God has prescribed a future for us. Like Israel in Jeremiah's day, we have caved to the pressures of sin and we have rebelled against God, resulting in a whirlwind of tattered souls and scuttled dreams. Yet God's heart beats for a hope-filled future for us.

The future we crave is made possible because of God's merciful love: He sent Jesus to pay the penalty for our sin and overwhelm our rebellion through His death and resurrection. Through Jesus we have forgiveness as well as hope for each day.

Jesus is God's prescription for hope. To find healing, we must call upon God. We must seek Him with our whole hearts. We must abandon ourselves into His gracious grip today, so that we can taste the hope of God's glorious love.

Glorious God! I call upon You today. I abandon myself into Your hands. Through Jesus I am fully committed to following Your heart and being blessed by the future You have planned for me. Amen.

　　　　DR. ERIC J. THOMAS, FIRST BAPTIST CHURCH, NORFOLK, VA

WEEK 32—TUESDAY
Hard-Hearted Hearing

Trust in the LORD with all your heart, and lean not on your own understanding; in all your ways acknowledge Him, and He shall direct your paths.

PROVERBS 3:5–6

Much of my life, I have been hard of hearing. When I was a little boy, my parents would tell me to clean my room or take out the trash, and I would respond with "Huh?" But the "Huh?" of my hearing was too often the result of my not listening well the first time.

I'm still hard of hearing. When God calls me to adjust my life to better fit His will and to seek His pleasure, I respond with "Huh?" I hear, but I don't want to obey. I have a case of hard-hearted hearing, and that always means a crooked path to catastrophe where I plummet to despair and am pummeled with pain.

Yet the opposite is also true. If we give ourselves—hearts, souls, bodies, and minds—to the Lord in absolute trust, we will experience joy. When we place our past, present, and future into the hands of the One who knows best, He will direct our steps to security and satisfaction.

So today, trust in the Lord, yield to His control, and get rid of hard-hearted hearing. Jesus, the Light of the world, shines brightly in the shadowy haze of this day to lead us to abundant living. Trust Him and live!

....

Lord, today I reject hard-hearted hearing. I look to You for direction. I submit myself to Your control. I pray that You will shine brightly in my life today so that I may live fully for Your glory. Amen.

WEEK 32—WEDNESDAY
Patient Love

Beloved, do not forget this one thing, that with the Lord one day is as a thousand years, and a thousand years as one day. The Lord is not slack concerning His promise, as some count slackness, but is longsuffering toward us, not willing that any should perish but that all should come to repentance.

2 PETER 3:8–9

Life's journey is difficult. Too often piercing winds chase away comfort. Life's journey is also filled with sadness. And life's journey is painful, like the nose-numbing wind that freezes our minds and clouds our vision with stinging tears.

Yet God comes alongside us during the journey of life and offers us the joy of His patient love. God, who is eternally present, sees our lives from beginning to end. God, who is forever faithful, sent Jesus to the world to thaw the wintry chill of sin and isolation with His rescuing love. Even when we stubbornly ignore God's love, He persistently offers rescue. Even when we trust our inadequate ability to navigate the arctic wasteland of our lives, God continually opens His arms to us.

God is patient in His love and persistent in offering life to sinners. The reason is that He desires all His creation to taste His grace, to choose genuine repentance, and to put life-giving faith in Jesus. In Jesus, the brilliant light of victory over darkness and death consumes the gloom of sin with the power of new life. Jesus is the promise of God's patient love warming me after freeing me from the shivering embrace of my sin and shame.

....

God, thank You for loving me. Thank You for sending Jesus to rescue me and to provide a path of joy on which I can walk each day. Amen.

DR. ERIC J. THOMAS, FIRST BAPTIST CHURCH, NORFOLK, VA

WEEK 32—THURSDAY
Set Free

"Most assuredly, I say to you, whoever commits sin is a slave of sin. And a slave does not abide in the house forever, but a son abides forever. Therefore if the Son makes you free, you shall be free indeed."

JOHN 8:34–36

Regardless of the color of the skies above, a slave lives in the deep darkness of defeat and despair. Regardless of the road he travels, a slave longs for the clattering chains that bind his soul to be shattered. Regardless of the songs in the air around him, a slave's soul sobs out a hymn of hopelessness.

In our sins, we were slaves shackled to sorrow. But Jesus came to set us free. He tore the veil of death's dark shadows with the hope of His resurrection. He untangled our souls from the curse of sin's chain, purchasing our freedom with the price of His own death. He pours His Spirit into our hearts, constantly giving us His love.

In Jesus Christ, we are no longer slaves to sin and death. We are now sons and daughters of the King. We live in the majestic mansion of His life-giving love. We walk in the glorious pleasure of our Father in heaven, who has forgiven us, accepted us, who loves us, and makes us complete. Today we live in victorious salvation under the banner of God's grace. No longer constrained to the march of mourning, our souls delight in the dance of victory.

Jesus has set us free!

....

Heavenly Father! I rejoice in the freedom You have given me through Jesus Christ, my Lord. Grant me the vision to embrace my liberty and live as Your son or daughter—fully pleasing to You, totally accepted by You, forever forgiven, thanks to Your Son. Amen.

Week 32—Friday
Afraid of the Dark

God is light and in Him is no darkness at all. If we say that we have fellowship with Him, and walk in darkness, we lie and do not practice the truth. But if we walk in the light as He is in the light, we have fellowship with one another, and the blood of Jesus Christ His Son cleanses us from all sin.

1 John 1:5–7

Monsters come out at night." These terror-filled words grip most children when the sun's glow has slipped past the horizon. After the bedtime prayers have been said and the lamp is switched off, children's hearts may fill with fear. For them, darkness isn't good.

In like manner, we should all be afraid of spiritual darkness, of all that is bad, including our sins. When we are swallowed up by darkness, we live a chaotic, nightmarish life. We are the monsters in our own horror story when we aren't living in fellowship with God. The message of today's verses is that God is light. He is pure, perfect, grand, and good, heavenly, and holy. He is light, and light cannot coexist with darkness.

Here is the good news: Jesus came to obliterate the darkness, to end our nightmare, to cleanse us from our sin. The blood of Jesus covers our sins (justification), and He works in us to conquer our sins (sanctification). Our monstrous selves have been killed: the darkness of our sins has been swallowed up by God's holy light.

....

Lord God, I pray that I do not return to the horror of my sins; I don't want darkness to be a way of life. So I ask You to help me conquer the sin that plagues me. Amen.

DR. ERIC J. THOMAS, FIRST BAPTIST CHURCH, NORFOLK, VA

WEEK 32—WEEKEND
Dehydrated Souls

On the last day, that great day of the feast, Jesus stood and cried out, saying, "If anyone thirsts, let him come to Me and drink He who believes in Me, as the Scripture has said, out of his heart will flow rivers of living water."

JOHN 7:37–38

Thirst is the body's way of telling us that we need water, and Jesus speaks to us about our thirst in His Word. He spoke to those who are suffering under the oppressive heat of sin and dying of soul dehydration. In our sin and out of sync with God, we migrate to any moisture, like the animals in the Serengeti, looking for even a miniscule mudhole in which to quench our spiritual thirst. Tormented by our need, we find ourselves dying of thirst.

Jesus is the only Source of satisfaction for a soul dehydrated by sin. We need more than a casual encounter with something or someone who makes us feel good. We need to be nourished from the inside out. Jesus is the One who answers our thirst and satisfies us completely. He is the Servant who suffers for our salvation, the Sinless One who is fully pleasing to God, the Son of God, who is the fulfillment of God's plan for our salvation, and the Lamb of God, who takes away the sin of the world.

If we will believe in Jesus, then our dehydrated souls will spring to life with rivers of life-giving water flowing from hearts fully entrusted to Jesus.

....

Lord God, my sin has dehydrated my soul. I'm dying of thirst. I believe Jesus is my only hope for life. I confess my sin and turn to Jesus so that I may be satisfied in Him. Amen.

WEEK 33—MONDAY
What Are You Saying to Me Now?

"Is it not to share your bread with the hungry, and that you bring to your house the poor who are cast out; when you see the naked, that you cover him, and not hide yourself from your own flesh? Then your light shall break forth like the morning, Your healing shall spring forth speedily, and your righteousness shall go before you; the glory of the LORD shall be your rear guard."

ISAIAH 58:7–8

The context of today's passage from Isaiah is a discussion of true and false worship. The passage, however, suggests that our healing is not just about us, but that it's about others too. We are to feed the hungry, clothe the naked, and house the poor. We are blessed by God to be a blessing to others. Doesn't it make sense that this principle would apply to healing?

As we look at Jesus, our Healer, let's first consider the most important healing Jesus offers us. Physical healing is temporary; emotional healing is fleeting; but spiritual healing is eternal. Everyone in the Bible who was healed physically eventually died, but everyone who is healed spiritually lives forever. Thus the point of every physical healing was to point people to the One who offers spiritual healing.

Our inner righteousness and spiritual healing will eventually manifest themselves in our lifestyles. And our light, our healing, and our righteousness—all gifts of God, all blessings secured for us by Jesus—will enable us to bless others.

....

Dear heavenly Father, help me to hear Your voice. I want to know what You are saying to me now. Show me too how You want me to participate in the healing You have for me and whom You want to bless through my blessings. Amen.

DR. ALEX HIMAYA, THECHURCH.AT, BROKEN ARROW, OK

WEEK 33—TUESDAY
Prosperity Is . . .

"I will bring [this city] health and healing; I will heal them and reveal to them the abundance of peace and truth. . . . I will cleanse them from all their iniquity by which they have sinned against Me, and I will pardon all their iniquities by which they have sinned and by which they have transgressed against Me. Then it shall be to Me a name of joy, a praise, and an honor before all nations of the earth, who shall hear all the good that I do to them; they shall fear and tremble for all the goodness and all the prosperity that I provide for it."

JEREMIAH 33:6, 8–9

The passage from Jeremiah 33 teaches that prosperity is characterized by peace and truth, cleansing from sin, and joy. Many of us tend to think of prosperity in physical terms, but every physical blessing that God provides is first and foremost for peace and truth, for joy, and for His praise and honor, so that we can bless others and bring them to peace with God.

Out of great healing comes great growth. Healing can only begin with God's unwavering forgiveness of our sins and iniquities. We must ask Him to heal us of our brokenness, and then rest in the truth of His promised cleansing power. Then we will begin to see the fulfillment of God's promises revealed in our lives as God blesses us with prosperity. As a result, we will find ourselves joyfully praising and honoring our good God.

....

Lord Jesus, help me to think of healing as You do, in terms of inner healing, of peace and truth, and of cleansing from sin and iniquity. May I joyfully praise and honor You for these blessings. And may I find healing for my soul in You and You alone. Thank You, Jesus, for Your healing work in my life! Amen.

WEEK 33—WEDNESDAY
God's Unconditional Love

The LORD builds up Jerusalem; He gathers together the outcasts of Israel. He heals the brokenhearted and binds up their wounds. He counts the number of the stars; He calls them all by name. Great is our Lord, and mighty in power; His understanding is infinite. The LORD lifts up the humble.

PSALM 147:2–6

God desires to heal the wounded and bring them to Himself. You can trust that God is at work as you deal with a wound, a broken heart, or difficult circumstances.

Have you ever looked into the night sky to find the constellations? The heavens are beautiful and overwhelming! I wish my stargazing success went beyond finding the Big and Little Dippers. Just as God designed the stars, He also knows how He uniquely designed you. He completely understands your circumstances and wants you to rely on His healing touch. You might feel small and insignificant in comparison to the stars, but the Creator of the universe wants to be involved in your life. He loves you more than all of the stars combined.

What pain, brokenness, or wound are you carrying alone? Lay it at God's feet today. Allow Him to work in your life and heal you. God has a master plan for you, and it involves your having a relationship with Him. He longs to be a part of life, and He can offer you spiritual healing.

God, You are amazing. I stand in Your presence today, humbled by Your mighty power, Your infinite wisdom, and Your great compassion and mercy. You are my Healer. I give You all of my wounds and ask that You heal each and every one of them. I trust You for my healing. Amen.

DR. ALEX HIMAYA, THECHURCH.AT, BROKEN ARROW, OK

Week 33—Thursday
Pray and Trust

Is anyone among you sick? Let him call for the elders of the church, and let them pray over him, anointing him with oil in the name of the Lord. And the prayer of faith will save the sick, and the Lord will raise him up. And if he has committed sins, he will be forgiven. Confess your trespasses to one another, and pray for one another, that you may be healed. The effective, fervent prayer of a righteous man avails much.

JAMES 5:14–16

When my youngest son was two years old, we left him with a babysitter for a few hours and headed to a beach half an hour away. As we sat down to eat lunch, we received a frightening phone call. "Ben fell into the pool!" the babysitter screamed.

While making the twenty-five-mile trip back to the beach house, I was able to get the sheriff on the phone. He told me that my baby would be life-flighted to the hospital. I asked the sheriff to wait on us so that one of us could ride in the helicopter with Ben, but they could not wait. As we turned the corner toward the helipad, the helicopter took off over the trees! So we drove two hours to the nearest hospital that could help our son, only knowing that his prognosis was not good. During those long minutes, we prayed, we worried, and we prayed and worried more. One of our prayers was asking the Lord to heal our son. Later that night, we watched a miracle happen. The Lord healed our son physically.

I've read some commentators, though, who say this passage from James isn't about physical healing. But why limit God? Why not pray the prayer of faith and see what He does? I've seen "the effective, fervent prayer of a righteous man" accomplish much!

....

Lord, I want to take You at Your Word. I want to pray in faith. I will pray and trust the results to You. Amen.

WEEK 33—FRIDAY
By His Stripes

Surely He has borne our griefs and carried our sorrows; yet we esteemed Him stricken, smitten by God, and afflicted. But He was wounded for our transgressions, He was bruised for our iniquities; the chastisement for our peace was upon Him, and by His stripes we are healed. All we like sheep have gone astray; we have turned, every one, to his own way; and the LORD has laid on Him the iniquity of us all.

ISAIAH 53:4–6

The tenses of the verbs in this passage are very interesting. The perfect tense in Hebrew grammar indicates a completed action, and all but one of these verbs is in the perfect tense. In other words, these actions are already done, completed, finished:

He *has* borne our griefs.
He *was* wounded.
He *was* bruised.

The imperfect tense in Hebrew grammar indicates a progressive action: it happened, is happening, and will continue to happen. The verb in the imperfect tense is here: "by His stripes we *are* healed."

Look at all that God has done and finished for us. As we deal with our current realities and consider our futures, we can see how much God has already accomplished on our behalf. We need to live aware of the provisions that Jesus has already made for us. By His stripes we have been saved. We are healed. Jesus has already born your grief and died for your sins so that you can be healed and set free. Where do you need healing—emotional, relational, physical, or spiritual? Jesus can start your healing today.

....

Lord Jesus, thank You for all that You went through and for all of Your blessings.
I choose to live in the healing that is available to me in You alone. Amen.

DR. ALEX HIMAYA, THECHURCH.AT, BROKEN ARROW, OK

Week 33—Weekend
Soul, Listen Up!

Bless the LORD, O my soul; and all that is within me, bless His holy name! Bless the LORD, O my soul, and forget not all His benefits: Who forgives all your iniquities, who heals all your diseases, who redeems your life from destruction, who crowns you with loving kindness and tender mercies, who satisfies your mouth with good things, so that your youth is renewed like the eagle's.

PSALM 103:1–5

In the psalm above, David is blessing the Lord's name with all his heart and soul. David knows the Lord is worthy of all of his worship. David is reminding himself not to forget how the Lord has ministered to him in the past. David knows that God forgives, heals, redeems, and crowns us in His glory.

David was not a perfect man, but he had a heart that loved God. Sometimes you might feel as though you are not worthy of God's love. When your past sins come to mind, when your body aches, when the doctor's report is negative, or when all signs point to bad news, you might find it difficult to believe that God loves you. In those moments, you must be like David and bless the Lord and believe in Him. The Lord heals both body and spirit, resulting in wholeness.

God, help me to see who I really am in You. Let me always remember how You have graciously dealt with me in the past. May I bless the Lord with all that is within me! Amen.

WEEK 34—MONDAY
The Joy We Receive

Let all those rejoice who put their trust in You; let them ever shout for joy, because You defend them; let those also who love Your name be joyful in You. For You, O LORD, will bless the righteous; with favor You will surround him as with a shield.

PSALM 5:11–12

Everything we receive in the Christian life we receive by faith. Faith is the hand that reaches out to accept what the grace of God gives. One of those gifts from God is joy.

In a single verse here—Psalm 5:11—the psalmist used three different ways to describe the joy of the Lord. "Rejoice" means to show gladness. To "shout for joy" means to cry out in triumph. To "be joyful" means to experience and express the deep emotions of joy.

Doesn't everyone want a life typified by a joy so rich it takes a dictionary to describe it? All of us can have that joy if we believe God. The psalmist said those who trust in the Lord are blessed recipients of an almost indescribable joy. The Hebrew word for *trust* in verse 11 is used sometimes to describe a person seeking shelter, a place of security. Once we find that resting place in Christ, we will truly know joy.

....

Lord Jesus, You are my joy! Today I reaffirm my trust in You and with gratitude receive afresh the precious gift of Your joy. In Jesus' name, Amen.

DR. J. KIE BOWMAN, HYDE PARK BAPTIST CHURCH, AUSTIN, TX

WEEK 34—TUESDAY
Lasting Joy

"These things I have spoken to you, that My joy may remain in you, and that your joy may be full. This is My commandment, that you love one another as I have loved you."

JOHN 15:11–12

N ot many good things in life last. In fact, life itself is temporary and fleeting. So when something good comes along, we want it to last as long as possible.

On the last night of His life, Jesus assembled His followers for the final lessons they would learn as a group. He taught them about heaven, prayer, and persistence in their walk with God. Jesus also made it clear that He was going to the cross and that they would face trouble in the world. In addition, He reminded them of their mission to take His message to the world, and there was one thing they could count on through it all—joy!

Jesus promised His disciples in the Upper Room (and He promises you and me) His joy, and His joy is permanent. Jesus said His joy would remain. Whenever Jesus taught about the things that remain, apparently the apostle John listened carefully. In fact, the Greek word for *remain* occurs in John's gospel almost three times more often than in the other three gospels combined!

The word for *remain* describes the difference between a permanent dwelling like a house and a temporary shelter like a tent. Jesus promised that His joy would move into our lives and take up permanent residence. Unlike other good things in life that we can only enjoy for a short time, the joy of the Lord remains forever.

For the Christian, joy has come to stay!

....

Lord, I am so thankful for Your abiding joy today and every day. Amen.

Week 34—Wednesday
The Joy of Salvation

Do not cast me away from Your presence, and do not take Your Holy Spirit from me.
Restore to me the joy of Your salvation, and uphold me by Your generous Spirit.

PSALM 51:11–12

E ven faithful Christians can sometimes act unfaithfully. Although it's a difficult and sometimes painful lesson to learn, if we are going to live by faith, we have to accept that the people we look up to can let us down, that leaders can stumble and fall, and that, thankfully, God won't do either.

King David was a man after God's own heart. He enjoyed the kind of favor from God that few men had ever known, but even David stepped into a downward spiral of deceit, disobedience, and depression. His life story will always include the night his lust led him to commit adultery, which in turn led to lies, murder, and shattered fellowship with God. Finally, the prophet Nathan boldly confronted the spiritually defeated king, and a change took place.

Psalm 51 is David's prayer of repentance. In it, David revealed the one thing he missed the most during his time out of fellowship with God. "Restore to me the joy" was the discredited king's prayer. He had power, wealth, and pleasure, but when he refused to fulfill his responsibilities as a follower of God, he lost the one thing money can't buy. David lost his joy.

Fellowship with God comes with a benefit found nowhere else. If you walk with God in the power of the Spirit, you will experience joy. If you turn away from God, you burn the bridge to joy.

Do you still have joy in the Lord? If not, what's changed?

....

O Lord, restore the joy of my salvation. Forgive my sins and bring me back to
the life of knowing joy in Your presence. In Jesus' name, Amen.

DR. J. KIE BOWMAN, HYDE PARK BAPTIST CHURCH, AUSTIN, TX

WEEK 34—THURSDAY
Jesus, Our Rest

"Come to Me, all you who labor and are heavy laden, and I will give you rest. Take My yoke upon you and learn from Me, for I am gentle and lowly in heart, and you will find rest for your souls. For My yoke is easy and My burden is light."

MATTHEW 11:28–30

I f you have ever driven across the country on the highways of America, you know how welcome a rest area can be. Families needing a break can get out of the car to stretch, the kids can play, you can check the map, or sit down at a picnic table for a quick meal before hitting the road again.

Along the journey of life, we also reach a point when what we need most of all is a break. And what is true of our physical life is equally true of our spiritual life. Living every day with constant demands and our pressing schedules can be exhausting. In fact, the demands of life are too great to handle if we don't take a break to refresh and renew. No one knew that better than Jesus. That's why in one of Jesus' most well-known calls to discipleship He invited us to rest.

The Greek word *rest* in Jesus' invitation is an encouraging one. It means "to permit a person to stop moving in order to seek refreshment or regain strength." Are you spiritually fatigued or emotionally spent? The best news in Jesus' invitation is found in a pronoun. He said, "Come to Me." The rest He promised is not so mystic or spiritual that physically exhausted people can't find it. Jesus Himself is our Rest.

....

Precious Lord, You always have been and always will be my only true Rest. Thank You for always welcoming me into Your refreshing, renewing presence. Amen.

WEEK 34—FRIDAY
Eternal Joy

"His lord said to him, 'Well done, good and faithful servant; you were faithful over a few things, I will make you ruler over many things. Enter into the joy of your lord.'"

MATTHEW 25:21

Someday life as we know it will end, and eternity will begin. When that happens, Jesus promised, God will conduct a review of every moment of our lives. Are we ready for that day? Now is the time to prepare.

Have you ever been the focus of a job performance review? If so, you were probably nervous before it started. Most of us dread criticism of any kind, but we do relish commendation. When God reviews their lives, followers of Jesus can expect honesty (what else could He be?), but His grace will also be on display that day.

What else do we know about the review? Jesus promised that if we are "faithful over a few things," God will declare us "ruler over many things." Because Jesus was talking about heaven, it's difficult for us to imagine what He meant. We do know this, though: on that day God will reward His people for their faith and service. And what will the reward be? Jesus told us: it's joy!

The joy Jesus knows in heaven right now will be shared by all of His followers. In this parable, Jesus said, "Enter into the joy of your Lord." The reward of serving Christ will be experiencing that joy of the Lord, joy that lasts forever.

Are you looking forward to that day?

Precious Lord, I praise You today for the joy eternal that You will reward me with someday! In Jesus' name, Amen.

DR. J. KIE BOWMAN, HYDE PARK BAPTIST CHURCH, AUSTIN, TX

WEEK 34—WEEKEND
The Joy of the Holy Spirit

The kingdom of God is not eating and drinking, but righteousness and peace and joy in the Holy Spirit. For he who serves Christ in these things is acceptable to God and approved by men.

ROMANS 14:17–18

This morning I received an e-mail encouraging me to purchase a book written to help new Christians grow. As a pastor, I am constantly on the lookout for quality resources to help new believers mature in their faith. I can't even imagine what it was like when everyone in the church was a new believer!

When the gospel was spreading throughout the ancient world and churches were springing up in places where the gospel message was new, some practical matters had to be addressed. One of the issues was Jewish dietary laws. God had given His Old Testament people specific instructions regarding what they could and could not eat. So the question was asked, "Would the new Gentile believers follow those same dietary regulations when they came to Christ?" Also some food in the Gentile markets had previously been dedicated to pagan gods. Were Christians permitted to eat that food?

The apostle Paul didn't shrink from conversations about the practical aspects of faith. The larger issue, he insisted, was our willingness to sacrifice our freedoms in order to keep our fellow believers from struggling in their faith.

When we think like that, something surprising occurs: the joy of the Holy Spirit floods our lives! It's very freeing to realize that, yes, our Christian lives are about more than what we eat, more than our physical needs. As believers, we are, for instance, able to experience joy that comes from the Spirit of God.

....

Lord, thank You for joy that comes from the Holy Spirit. Pour Your joy into my life as You flood me with Your Spirit. Amen.

WEEK 35—MONDAY
In What Are We Hoping?

Behold, the eye of the LORD is on those who fear Him, on those who hope in His mercy. . . . Let Your mercy, O LORD, be upon us, just as we hope in You.

PSALM 33:18, 22

In our culture the word *hope* implies "wishful thinking." We say, "I hope it's going to rain" or "I hope I get that job." Biblical hope, however, is the future tense of faith. Hebrews 11:1 teaches, "Now faith is the assurance of things hoped for" (ESV). Hope is the assurance of what the future holds. Hope says, "I believe I will receive the promise, and I am looking forward to getting it." This anticipation changes how we live. The future we believe awaits us will greatly impact the decisions we make today.

So what do we believe awaits us? In what are we placing our hope? In Psalm 33, we find how God's people should respond to their enemies. Most nations would trust in their number of troops and their ability to battle. This psalm, however, is not about trusting man but about trusting God.

It is fine to hope that something good will happen: "I hope that I will get the promotion" or "I hope that I will find the right spouse." However, we can desire something so much that our "hope that" turns into "hope in." We begin to live as though that promotion, job, or spouse will be our salvation, our rescuer, the means of righting all the wrongs in our life.

This hope, however, can become idolatry. When we place confidence in that which we hope for, it becomes the object of our faith. Knowing this, the psalmist cried out that the Lord is our only hope.

In what—or whom—are you hoping?

....

Lord, help me to hope only in You. Do not allow what I am hoping for to become what I am hoping in. Amen.

DR. DWAYNE MERCER, CROSSLIFE CHURCH, OVIEDO, FL

WEEK 35—TUESDAY
Waiting Upon the Lord

Oh, love the LORD, all you His saints! For the LORD preserves the faithful, and fully repays the proud person. Be of good courage, and He shall strengthen your heart, all you who hope in the LORD.

PSALM 31:23–24

H ope implies that we are waiting on something that may or will happen in the future. These thoughts of the future can fill us with doubt, worry, and fear, even though it is said that ninety-five percent of the things we worry about never happen. But what about the remaining five percent?

In Psalm 31, the psalmist vacillated between doubt and faith. Although resolute to remain faithful to God in the midst of trials, the psalmist acknowledged that the Lord does not always solve problems instantly.

The existence of hope implies there is something in the future we have not yet received, and the "not yet received" implies waiting. None of us likes to wait. We live in a society that wants instant success, instant answers to prayer, instant relationships, and instant problem solving. Yet waiting is a constant theme in the Bible. And when we wait, we witness the faithfulness of God. Our mandate is to remain faithful to Him, not only in times of trial, but also as we wait for His promises to be fulfilled.

Hebrews 10:36 teaches us, "You have need of endurance, so that when you have done the will of God you may receive what was promised" (ESV). The psalmist declared in Psalm 31:15, "My times are in Your hand," and hope says, "I know 'all things [will] work together for [my] good'" (Romans 8:28 ESV).

....

Lord, help me remain faithful as I wait upon You. I know that by Your grace and in Your power all will work out for Your glory and my good. As I wait, teach me Your ways and strengthen my heart. Amen.

WEEK 35—WEDNESDAY
Hope Amidst Despair

Through the LORD's mercies we are not consumed, because His compassions fail not. They are new every morning; great is Your faithfulness. "The LORD is my portion," says my soul, "Therefore I hope in Him!"

LAMENTATIONS 3:22–24

Whenever we are knocked down, we may be tempted to lose hope. The prophet Jeremiah basically held a funeral for the city of Jerusalem. In the book of Lamentations, his words reflected the heart of God's people who wept over the Babylonian capture of their great city. The verses above show the key moment when Jeremiah went from the lowest point of despair to the heights of hope in God.

In today's passage, Jeremiah told us that God's compassion never fails. In fact, His compassionate acts of love are fresh and new every day. In light of that truth, Jeremiah declared God's great faithfulness: God is reliable and trustworthy. Although we often see circumstances as harsh and even hopeless, that's not the whole truth. Only God knows the complete picture, and since He is totally faithful to us, we can place our hope in Him.

Jeremiah concluded by declaring that God is his "portion," meaning, "The Lord is enough." Jeremiah reached the point of surrendering to the Lord all his needs. As long as he continued worshipping and trusting in God, Jeremiah would have hope.

....

Lord, help me look back over my life and see Your great faithfulness. Help me appreciate what I have in You: You are my portion, and Your presence is the greatest gift in my life. Amen.

DR. DWAYNE MERCER, CROSSLIFE CHURCH, OVIEDO, FL

WEEK 35—THURSDAY
Finding Hope

May the God of hope fill you with all joy and peace in believing, that you may abound in hope by the power of the Holy Spirit.

ROMANS 15:13

When Paul closed his letter to the church at Rome, he invoked "the God of hope," the Source of joy and peace.

This benediction implies that our joy and peace depend on hope. Now, joy is not the same as happiness. We experience happiness when something good happens; we know joy in spite of our circumstances. Finally, peace is inner tranquility even in adversity.

And, according to Paul, we find both joy and peace through hope in Christ. Hope is our faith projected into the future. Our attitude toward the future greatly affects our joy and peace in the present. If we look forward to God's blessing in the future, we more easily have an attitude of joy today. If we trust God with our futures and the futures of our loved ones, we experience peace right now.

We experience hope through the power of the Holy Spirit, and we receive the Holy Spirit the moment we name Jesus our Savior and Lord. The Holy Spirit is the presence of God in our lives. Psalm 16:11 teaches, "In Your presence is fullness of joy; in Your right hand there are pleasures forever." The Hebrew word for *presence* is *panim*, meaning "face-to-face." When we are face-to-face with someone, we are getting to know that person.

When we are in close relationship with God—face-to-face with Him—we experience His presence and His power in our lives, and we find hope.

....

Lord, help me rest in Your presence in my life, so I may know the power of Your Spirit blessing me with hope for my future. Amen.

WEEK 35—FRIDAY
The Hope of Life Eternal

Let us who are of the day be sober, putting on the breastplate of faith and love, and as a helmet the hope of salvation. For God did not appoint us to wrath, but to obtain salvation through our Lord Jesus Christ.

1 THESSALONIANS 5:8–9

Recently, I stood at the bedside of a church member who was near death. As I prayed with the family, I felt their great peace. Although there were tears prompted by the impending loss, these dear people found genuine comfort in knowing that one day they would see their loved one again.

In 1 Corinthians 15:19 Paul said, "If we have hoped in Christ in this life only, we are of all men most to be pitied" (NASB).

For hope to be a reality in our lives, we must believe there is a life with Christ beyond this one. If we make our decisions based on this life only, we aren't being wise, and we risk making the wrong choices.

Do you see your adversities in light of eternity, or do you get anxious when life does not work out as planned? Do you feel bitterness toward or seek revenge on others, or do you believe God will judge all things in the end?

Decisions like these that we make in the present are greatly determined by the future we believe awaits us.

....

Lord, help me to see life from Your perspective. Help me to live today, learning from the past and making godly decisions because I have solid hope in my eternal future with You. I look forward to that time when You right all wrongs and bless those who hope in You. Amen.

DR. DWAYNE MERCER, CROSSLIFE CHURCH, OVIEDO, FL

WEEK 35—WEEKEND
The Anchor of the Soul

After [Abraham] had patiently endured, he obtained the promise. . . . that by two immutable things, in which it is impossible for God to lie, we might have strong consolation, who have fled for refuge to lay hold of the hope set before us. This hope we have as an anchor of the soul, both sure and steadfast, and which enters the Presence behind the veil.

HEBREWS 6:15, 18–19

Why is hope so valuable? Can't we live joyfully and peaceably without it? Maybe. Maybe not.

Consider the Hebrews 6 imagery of hope acting as an anchor to the soul. An anchor is used to steady a ship, to keep it from drifting and floating into troubled waters. When an anchor is "sure and steadfast," it is well grounded, secure, something we can count on.

Then we read that this anchor "enters . . . behind the veil." In the temple the veil separated the Holy Place from the Holy of Holies, the sacred place that housed the ark of the covenant where God resided amongst the Israelites.

Why are these images of an anchor and a veil mentioned together? A ship's anchor digs into the ocean floor, and—as the imagery suggests—the anchor of hope digs deep into our souls. At the same time the ship's anchor hooks itself onto the ocean floor, while still being strongly attached to the ship itself. Similarly, the other end of the chain on our anchor of hope is attached behind the veil, wrapped securely around our Savior, indicating that our hope is attached to Christ.

....

Lord, help me trust You. Help me see You as my Anchor of hope. Help me look toward the future, trusting in You because I know this hope wraps around my soul and Your heart. Amen.

WEEK 36—MONDAY
His Suffering for Our Deliverance

My God, My God, why have You forsaken Me? Why are You so far from helping Me, and from the words of My groaning? . . . [Our fathers] cried to You, and were delivered; they trusted in You, and were not ashamed.

PSALM 22:1, 5

Have you ever felt so completely alone, forsaken, and isolated that you wondered if anyone would ever be there for you again?

These famous words of David in Psalm 22 express a level of anguish and pain that I can honestly say I've never felt before, but maybe you have.

Jesus Himself uttered these same words later as He hung on the cross to pay the penalty for all of our sins. The words seem to express a feeling of total abandonment, but when we look more closely, we see that David knows that God had provided for earlier believers, and David trusted that God would provide for him too.

We also see in this psalm one reason why we can go to Christ for help: we can be confident that He truly understands our suffering and grief because He Himself experienced them. Truthfully, His suffering was much more intense than we will ever be called to endure because, for a short time, Jesus experienced the total abandonment of God, which we will never experience.

Today ask God to grant you the faith to trust Him regardless of your circumstances. Know that Jesus understands your suffering and is always at the throne of God interceding for you.

....

Lord, what You endured on the cross is unfathomable to me. Thank You for Your willingness to suffer and die for my sins. I worship You today as my Lord and Savior. Amen.

WEEK 36—TUESDAY
Resting in His Presence

He who dwells in the secret place of the Most High shall abide under the shadow of the Almighty. I will say of the LORD, "He is my refuge and my fortress; my God, in Him I will trust." Surely He shall deliver you from the snare of the fowler and from the perilous pestilence. He shall cover you with His feathers, and under His wings you shall take refuge; His truth shall be your shield and buckler.

PSALM 91:1–4

Throughout the psalms David referred to God as his Fortress, his Refuge, and his Strength. David faced many physical and spiritual battles throughout his life, and he experienced firsthand how God provides a strong fortress regardless of what attacks come at us.

In the ancient world, a fortress was often walled off from the rest of the city. Its supplies of food, water, and ammunition gave the people a place to be protected and a point from which the city could be defended. David knew that he did not need to fear because in God he found a Fortress stronger than any attack this world could ever muster.

What fortress do you run to when circumstances are overwhelming? Do you turn to people, work, or material distractions? Like David, may we realize that the one true Fortress we have is our one true God. And He is a Fortress that will always protect us and never let us down.

....

Father, I thank You today for bringing to my mind some of the many times You have been my faithful Fortress. Help me this day to rest in Your presence and to be grateful for these memories of Your protection. Amen.

WEEK 36—WEDNESDAY
Where Is Your Dwelling Place?

Because you have made the LORD, who is my refuge, even the Most High, your dwelling place, no evil shall befall you, nor shall any plague come near your dwelling; for He shall give His angels charge over you, to keep you in all your ways.

PSALM 91:9–11

For thousands of years, this psalm has offered inspiration, comfort, and promise to warriors in harm's way.

First, it is amazing to read the psalmist's ancient descriptions of warfare and compare the specifics to what we see in the global war on terror today. Insurgency, snipers, suicide bombers, environmental terrorism—they seem to be aptly described by "fowler's snare," "deadly pestilence," "terror of night," "arrow that flies by day," "pestilence that stalks in the darkness," and "plague that destroys at midday" (vv. 3–6 NIV). What does God say in Psalm 91 that can calm our fears and help us to face these challenges?

God chose to speak words of encouragement through David, a capable warrior who would have had much to share about God's faithfulness in battle. In fact, David might have wanted to pass these lessons on to others as wisdom not just for our physical battles, but for our spiritual battles as well.

Verse 9 begins with the great truth that the people who make God their dwelling place will be protected and guarded. Hear that as God's promise to you as you read today's Scripture passage.

....

Father, I praise You for being my faithful Dwelling Place. May I trust You completely and rest securely in You today. Amen.

WEEK 36—THURSDAY
Jesus Defines Your Value

"Are not two sparrows sold for a copper coin? And not one of them falls to the ground apart from your Father's will. But the very hairs of your head are all numbered. Do not fear therefore; you are of more value than many sparrows."

MATTHEW 10:29–31

At some point, each of us will face what will may seem like mammoth trials and difficulties. When we encounter these hardships, we must know how to embrace the victorious faith that looks beyond what we can see to what God sees.

In times of extreme pressure, God stretches our faith and deepens our dependence on Him. Without a strong abiding faith, we can quickly yield to temptation and fear, especially when the difficulty is intense or prolonged. Every challenge presents many opportunities for God to show how much He loves you. Instead of yielding to thoughts of fear and failure, make a commitment to trust God, even when you do not know what the next day will bring. Jesus said we should not fear because our value to God is great.

Your value in life is secure because of God's ability to cover you with His grace, mercy, and love. You can face any circumstance with confidence and hope because it is not your strength, wisdom, energy, or power that brings victory. When you place your trust in Him, you tap into a force that no one and nothing can successfully oppose. Therefore, let God's love cover you and bless you as you boldly live each moment in His presence.

....

Heavenly Father, I thank You for Your constant love and perfect care. Thank You for valuing me and for showing Your love for me so I may know my value in Your eyes. Amen.

Week 36—Friday
Peace with God

There are many who say, "Who will show us any good?" Lord, lift up the light of Your countenance upon us. You have put gladness in my heart, more than in the season that their grain and wine increased. I will both lie down in peace, and sleep; for You alone, O Lord, make me dwell in safety.

PSALM 4:6–8

Peace in God is the fruit of oneness with God. Every now and then it is helpful for us to take stock of our situation. Right now, you may not be experiencing difficulties during this time of your life. From your perspective, everything may seem sunny and clear; however, storms will come. How do we maintain a sense of peace and spiritual balance when these trials strike?

The answer is found in a close, abiding relationship with Jesus. Fixing our eyes and hearts on Him will give us an unshakable peace. No one but God is equipped to handle our problems. He never meant for us to be strong on our own. He wants us to find courage, hope, and strength in Him and in His Word.

In Psalm 4, David reminds us that when we trust God will provide for us, we can lie down in peace. Accepting God's timetable and our limitations in every situation gives us the peace to release our anxieties into His care. Let Him provide for you in His timing. Tell Him all that you are feeling as you let His peace fill your heart. He has a solution.

When you accept life as a gift from God, you will find mercy and grace, forgiveness and hope, peace and everlasting serenity. Our peace resides in our Savior, who loves us unconditionally. He has promised to help us and to deliver us into the Father's loving arms.

....

Father, I am grateful for Your gifts of gladness and peace today. Thank You for providing me with safety and rest in You. Amen.

Week 36—Weekend
The Promise of His Presence

When you pass through the waters, I will be with you; and through the rivers, they shall not overflow you. When you walk through the fire, you shall not be burned, nor shall the flame scorch you. For I am the LORD your God, the Holy One of Israel, your Savior.

ISAIAH 43:2–3

God is always present with His children, and He draws nearer to us in the midst of our trials. No matter what your struggle or hardship, God promises that He will be with you.

When we walk through fires or pass through the waters of life, sometimes we may begin to doubt God. But God allows certain things to happen to us so that we might lean on Him and grow spiritually. If we trust in the Lord with all of our hearts, He promises never to leave us nor forsake us. When we learn this lesson and apply it in our lives, we will experience a peace that surpasses all understanding. We will be able to stand boldly in faith and speak of our love for Christ with great confidence. Remember that the Holy One of Israel, our Savior, loves us with an everlasting love. The very hairs on our heads are all numbered, and God knows us perfectly from the inside out.

We can fully trust God to stand with us no matter how intense our trials may be. He is present and knows the exact depth of what we're facing. Our greatest fear may be that we can't endure the trials, but God's presence with us gives us strength—and He promises that what we face will not overwhelm or defeat us.

....

Lord, help me to focus on Your presence during life's trials. Thank You for Your ever-present Spirit, who never abandons me. Amen.

Week 37—Monday
Wisdom During Storms

If any of you lacks wisdom, let him ask of God, who gives to all liberally and without reproach, and it will be given to him. But let him ask in faith with no doubting, for he who doubts is like a wave of the sea driven and tossed by the wind.

JAMES 1:5-6

One thing people everywhere and throughout time have in common is this: we all face various trials along this journey called life. No one escapes. What a contradiction to the prosperity gospel that is preached. That false gospel claims a person can live a pain-free, adversity-free life. The school of life, however, teaches that we all face adversity from time to time.

Adversity and trials can challenge our decision-making ability. We may find ourselves desperate to know how to respond in the midst of a storm. We must remember that the purpose of any trial is to mature us as followers of Christ, to make us look more like Jesus.

Trials are a fact of life. They cannot be controlled, but we can control how we react to them. James encouraged us to pray and ask God for wisdom, for Him to tell us how we are to respond. When we approach our heavenly Father, we are to ask Him for help, understanding, direction, and the ability to see His hand in the situation. Remember, God's desire is for us to graduate to the next level of spiritual maturity.

When we ask God for wisdom, He will give it generously. He will hold nothing back, but we must ask in faith, trusting He will show us the next step.

··

God, I ask boldly and without doubting for You to give me help and under-standing in my trials. Amen.

DR. FRANK COX, NORTH METRO FIRST BAPTIST CHURCH, LAWRENCEVILLE, GA

WEEK 37—TUESDAY
Praise the Lord

The fear of the LORD is the beginning of wisdom; a good understanding have all those who do His commandments. His praise endures forever.

PSALM 111:10

I am one blessed man! My heart overflows with gratitude for the blessings God has bestowed upon me. One of those blessings was being born into a pastor's family. Jesus was not an afterthought in our home. No, He was the focus. I've been in church from the first Sunday I was home from the hospital. God placed me in an encouraging home as well as in a nurturing church, where I learned to be a person of worship. I especially love worshipping Jesus.

One of the ways I was taught to worship was through music. My favorite praise song as a child was "Praise Ye the Lord!" Whatever life's circumstances, I was to worship my Lord with praise.

What kind of connection is there between praise and wisdom? The beginning of wisdom is reverence for our Creator. He alone is worthy of our worship and our praise. The psalmist reminded us that worship is our response to God's Word and His works.

In other words, a wise person is one who knows God intimately and has a "good understanding" of His commands. Wisdom is knowing God and doing His will. Obedience to His will shows our judgment to be right and sound. Out of our knowledge of God and our relationship to Him, we sing praise to Him forever. Wisdom prompts praise from God's children. Praise the Lord!

....

Lord, I stand in awe of Your gracious, generous work in my life. May I always praise You with the words of my mouth and the meditations of my heart. Amen.

WEEK 37—WEDNESDAY
Pursue Wisdom

My son, if you receive my words, and treasure my commands within you, so that you incline your ear to wisdom, and apply your heart to understanding; yes, if you cry out for discernment, and lift up your voice for understanding; if you seek her as silver, and search for her as for hidden treasurers; then you will understand the fear of the LORD, And find the knowledge of God. For the LORD gives wisdom; from His mouth come knowledge and understanding.

PROVERBS 2:1–6

Several years ago I found myself single, not by choice, but by the death of my first wife. A few months later I was introduced to a young lady who is now my wife. Instantly, I knew there was something special about Mary, and I knew God was in this relationship. Wanting to know her, I unashamedly pursued a relationship with her. With laser focus I pursued her in order to win her heart. When we were not out on a date, I would call her. When we were apart from each other, I would send her a card expressing my love. There were gifts, candy, and flowers. I spent money, time, and energy to know her.

Solomon encouraged us to pursue wisdom as intensely as I pursued Mary. It is important to know the wisdom of God, and that means understanding the truth found in God's Word.

As you seek God for wisdom and understanding, let His Spirit lead you and listen. When you do this, He will open your heart and give you the peace that passes all understanding.

....

Lord, I want to know You and the wisdom of Your kingdom. Give me the energy and passion to pursue You with all of my heart. Amen.

DR. FRANK COX, NORTH METRO FIRST BAPTIST CHURCH, LAWRENCEVILLE, GA

WEEK 37—THURSDAY
The Priority of Wisdom

Get wisdom! Get understanding! Do not forget, nor turn away from the words of my mouth. Do not forsake her, and she will preserve you; love her, and she will keep you. Wisdom is the principal thing; therefore get wisdom. and in all your getting, get understanding.

PROVERBS 4:5–7

Any parent can tell you that raising a child is costly. In 2014, the estimated cost of raising a child to age seventeen (before college) was $245,300 for the average middle-income American family. This amount of money is staggering, and when you are raising more than one, completely overwhelming. Raising kids is costly!

However, the greatest challenge that parents have is not financial; it is instilling godly wisdom in their children. After I sent each of my three children off to college, I asked myself, "Did I teach them all they needed for life?" I taught them a solid work ethic, how to make eye contact when they shake hands, and how to change a tire. But did they learn godly wisdom? Solomon emphasized, "Wisdom is the principal thing." If children acquire godly wisdom, they are set for life.

The best way to teach wisdom as a parent is through one's relationship with a child. Deuteronomy exhorts parents to teach the truth of God's Word to their children as they experience life together (6:6–9). As parents talk about God and walk according to His wisdom, their children will discern the importance of God's truth. As we teach godly wisdom and live it out in front of our children, they will "get understanding."

....

Lord, help me to make Your wisdom the main thing in my life. Strengthen me to live out the truth of Your Word so others—especially my children—can benefit from Your truth. Amen.

WEEK 37—FRIDAY
The Majesty of Wisdom

Oh, the depth of the riches both of the wisdom and knowledge of God! How unsearchable are His judgments and His ways past finding out! "For who has known the mind of the LORD? Or who has become His counselor?" "Or who has first given to Him and it shall be repaid to him?" For of Him and through Him and to Him are all things, to whom be glory forever. Amen.

ROMANS 11:33–36

Human beings—individually and corporately—have always wondered what makes this world function. We search for knowledge, and there is much out there to be examined.

According to the Global Library Statistics, there are between 500,000 and 1,000,000 libraries in the world. A total of 129,864,880 books have received International Standard Book Numbers (ISBN). A recent report reveals that 60,000 new books are printed annually in the United States and 300,000 worldwide. Now that is impressive.[8]

Many of these volumes are written in man's attempt to share knowledge and gain wisdom. The only book needed for that purpose is the Bible. Its principles and precepts provide all knowledge and wisdom necessary for life and for eternal life. And no one person will never exhaust its content or comprehend all it teaches. Wisdom is applying the truth revealed in the Bible that we do understand.

....

Lord, as I pursue knowledge of You, enable me to wisely apply Your truth. Teach me to walk in wisdom, worship Your greatness, and live humbly before You. Amen.

DR. FRANK COX, NORTH METRO FIRST BAPTIST CHURCH, LAWRENCEVILLE, GA

WEEK 37—WEEKEND
Jesus Is Our Wisdom

*The message of the cross is foolishness to those who are perishing, but to us who are being
saved it is the power of God. For it is written: "I will destroy the wisdom of the wise,
And bring to nothing the understanding of the prudent." . . . But to those who are called,
both Jews and Greeks, Christ [is] the power of God and the wisdom of God. Because the
foolishness of God is wiser than men, and the weakness of God is stronger than men.*

1 CORINTHIANS 1:18–19; 24–25

Our secular society has downgraded the significance of the cross.
Believers wear the cross because of our love for Jesus and because of
our desire to be His ambassadors and witnesses. However, many nonbelievers wear cross necklaces as simply a piece of jewelry. Others whose lifestyles
reflect nothing of Jesus' values may have cross tattoos, and these people make
the cross of "no effect" (1 Corinthians 1:17).

The message of the cross is foolishness to a world that is rebellious and
blinded by the deceptions of Satan. However, those individuals who have
truly heard the message of the cross and responded to its truth have been
changed by its power!

If we are willing to allow God to take charge of our lives, transformation
happens. If we are willing to change what needs to be changed, we will emerge
closer to Christ, more mature as His children, and reflect the love of God to
the world around us.

....

*Lord, You have sent me to preach the message of the cross. It may be foolishness
to a lost world, but I know it has the power to change lives. Enable me to be
faithful with its message. Amen.*

WEEK 38—MONDAY
The Greatest Blessing

Blessed is every one who fears the LORD, who walks in His ways. When you eat the labor of your hands, you shall be happy, and it shall be well with you. Your wife shall be like a fruitful vine in the very heart of your house, your children like olive plants all around your table. Behold, thus shall the man be blessed who fears the LORD.

PSALM 128:1–4

Have you ever wondered how it's possible to be blessed but not feel blessed? How does that happen? How can we know on an intellectual level that we are very blessed but on an emotional and practical level not feel blessed at all?

An unfortunate aspect of not feeling blessed is that we lose the ability to enjoy the blessings right in front of us. We see this fact frequently playing itself out in today's culture. Some of the most blessed people on the planet feel empty rather than blessed. What looks like blessings to outsiders doesn't satisfy or fulfill.

These wealthy but poor individuals are very different from the writer of Psalm 128, who speaks to us of the blessedness of the person who fears God. He spoke of the wonderful ripple effect of fearing God. The psalmist points out that the person who fears God also enjoys his work, his marriage, and his children.

It seems clear, then, that if we are going to know we are blessed, if we are going to feel blessed, and if we are going to enjoy life's blessings, the first step is choosing to live with a healthy respect and reverence toward God. You see, the key to enjoying life's great blessings is first to recognize and enjoy the greatest blessing of all: our heavenly Father.

....

Heavenly Father, You are my greatest blessing! Help me to live consistently in light of this wonderful truth. Amen.

TREVOR BARTON, THE CREEK CHURCH, LONDON, KY

WEEK 38—TUESDAY
Unseen Blessings

Blessed be the God and Father of our Lord Jesus Christ, who has blessed us with every spiritual blessing in the heavenly places in Christ, just as He chose us in Him before the foundation of the world, that we should be holy and without blame before Him in love.

EPHESIANS 1:3–4

Some of the best blessings in our lives are the ones we can see and place our hands on. Of course, I'm speaking about things such as our spouses, children, food, water, shelter, technology, and so forth. Recognizing these as blessings helps us remain grateful to God for them.

The greatest blessings in our lives as Christ followers, however, are probably the ones we can't see or touch. Paul referred to these as "spiritual blessings," those blessings we receive in and through Christ. Paul mentioned many spiritual blessings in his letter to the Christians living in Ephesus.

Consider some of the blessings Paul pointed out. God has chosen us to be His. God has loved us, forgiven us, redeemed us, and adopted us. We have received and continue to receive God's grace, and we have received God's Holy Spirit as well.

Without these unseen blessings received from and because of Christ, nothing else in life really matters. As we noticed yesterday, it is absolutely possible to be blessed but not feel blessed and, consequently, not enjoy the blessings. Let us never allow that to be the case with our spiritual blessings.

Think about it for a moment: you have been chosen by God, loved, forgiven, redeemed, and adopted by your heavenly Father. Do not live unaware and unaffected by your unseen blessings.

....

Heavenly Father, I thank You for the spiritual blessings that are mine because of Jesus. Amen.

THE GIFT OF JESUS

Week 38—Wednesday
The Blessing of Faithfulness

Now may the God of peace Himself sanctify you completely; and may your whole spirit, soul, and body be preserved blameless at the coming of our Lord Jesus Christ. He who calls you is faithful, who also will do it.

1 Thessalonians 5:23–24

Soul-satisfying peace comes with trusting someone completely. Such trust is extremely rare and perhaps entirely impossible since we are part of a depraved humanity. We are too easily suspicious; we too readily expect people to disappoint us. Yes, we trust—but we trust only some people, and we trust them only to a certain point. Our relationships even with those whom we love may be tinged with some disappointment and impacted by unmet expectations.

When writing to Christians in Thessalonica about Jesus' second coming, Paul instructed the letter's recipients to live every day in light of the possibility of Christ's return. Believers are to look forward to Christ's return with great expectation, but the unknown timing of the event could motivate people to live life to the fullest or encourage them to focus on opportunities to make a difference in the world around them.

Paul outlined certain things we should do in light of Christ's promised return: "comfort the fainthearted, uphold the weak . . . pursue what is good both for yourselves and for all, rejoice always, pray without ceasing . . . and abstain from every form of evil" (1 Thessalonians 5:14–17, 22).

No doubt first-century Christians thought, "Easier read than done!" Then Paul told them that God—who had called them to these high standards—would work in and through them to accomplish these things.

. . . .

Thank You, God that we can trust You to enable us to do what You have called us to do. Amen.

TREVOR BARTON, THE CREEK CHURCH, LONDON, KY

WEEK 38—THURSDAY
The Blessing of a Better Way

All of you be of one mind, having compassion for one another; love as brothers, be tenderhearted, be courteous; not returning evil for evil or reviling for reviling, but on the contrary blessing, knowing that you were called to this, that you may inherit a blessing.

1 PETER 3:8–9

Peter was in the Upper Room when Jesus celebrated His last Passover before His death, when He washed the disciples' feet, and when He told them more about His impending death. That meant Peter heard Jesus say, "A new command I give you: Love one another. As I have loved you, so you must love one another. By this everyone will know that you are my disciples, if you love one another" (John 13:34–35).

On an earlier occasion, Jesus had taught that the most important commandment was to love God and the second was to love people. Jesus then said, "On these two commandments hang all the Law and the Prophets" (Matthew 22:40).

After Jesus' resurrection and the launch of the New Testament church, Peter saw how obedience to Jesus' commandment to love began to change the world. So when he instructed other believers in Christian principles, Peter naturally communicated Jesus' message of love. He encouraged believers to be compassionate, tender, courteous, and to treat others kindly even if the kindness would not be reciprocated.

Peter realized there is no greater act of obedience than to love. Consequently, there is no greater blessing than that which results from extending Christ's love to others. Love is a better way to live. In fact, it is a blessed way to live.

....

Heavenly Father, help me love others as You have loved me. Nothing else is more important today or any other day than to love others. Amen.

Week 38—Friday
Bless the Blesser

*Then I looked, and I heard the voice of many angels around the throne, the living
creatures, and the elders; and the number of them was ten thousand times ten
thousand, and thousands of thousands, saying with a loud voice:*
*"Worthy is the Lamb who was slain to receive power and riches and wisdom, and
strength and honor and glory and blessing!"*

REVELATION 5:11–12

Momentarily sit under the weight of this passage. John recorded this
powerful scene, describing a moment in heaven when God held a scroll
sealed with seven seals. John described an angel asking the question: "Who is
worthy to open the scroll and loose its seals?" (v. 2).

Sadly, none was found worthy to open the scroll, and John began to weep.
Then one of the twenty-four elders said to John, "Weep no more; behold, the
Lion of the tribe of Judah, the Root of David, has conquered, so that He can
open the scroll and its seven seals" (v. 5 ESV).

John turned to see the Lion but saw only a Lamb standing as though slain.
This Lamb took the scroll from the hand of God, and heaven responded by
singing a new song in celebration of the Lamb's death and His resurrection
that had redeemed people from every tribe and every nation.

Heaven celebrated the Lamb, declaring that He is worthy "to receive power
and riches and wisdom, and strength and honor and glory and blessing." And
our worship and celebration of Jesus—of His life, death, and resurrection—
are blessings to our Savior. Will you be a blessing today to the One who has
blessed you with forgiveness and redemption?

....

*Jesus, You alone are worthy of all praise and honor and glory! I thank You for
Your life, Your death, and Your resurrection. Amen.*

TREVOR BARTON, THE CREEK CHURCH, LONDON, KY

WEEK 38—WEEKEND
Sharing the Blessing

For when God made a promise to Abraham, because He could swear by no one greater, He swore by Himself, saying, "Surely blessing I will bless you, and multiplying I will multiply you." And so, after [Abraham] had patiently endured, he obtained the promise.

HEBREWS 6:13–15

God's promise changed and blessed Abraham's life; its fulfillment also would eventually change and bless the world. God promised Abraham a son. We now understand that in the line of Abraham would come a Son who would ultimately bless the world and who was Jesus Christ of Nazareth.

We also know that God sent His Son into the world to bless the world because He loves the world. God blessed our world by sending His Son Jesus as Savior of the world. Jesus came to save us from sin. Jesus lived a sinless life so that on the cross, "For He made Him who knew no sin to be sin for us, that we might become the righteousness of God in Him" (2 Corinthians 5:21). On the cross in some cosmic way beyond our imagining, He bore our sins in His body so we could be brought into relationship with God. God poured out His wrath on His Son on the cross so that Jesus might atone for the wages of sins that we may enjoy the gift of life given through grace.

The gospel . . . what a blessing! It is a blessing shared by every Christ-follower. Enjoyment of this blessing involves sharing the gospel message with others as often as possible so those far from God can experience this blessing as well.

....

Father, thank You for sending Your Son to die on the cross for our sins. Give me an opportunity today to share this gospel message with someone who is far from You. Amen.

WEEK 39—MONDAY
The Principle of Delight

Delight yourself also in the LORD, and He shall give you the desires of your heart. Commit your way to the LORD, trust also in Him, and He shall bring it to pass. He shall bring forth your righteousness as the light, and your justice as the noonday.

PSALM 37:4–6

To understand what it means to "delight [ourselves] in the LORD," we must first understand the principle of delight.

Many people quote Psalm 37:4, wanting to believe that God will do for them whatever they desire. But God is not at all obligated to do whatever we want. He is obligated to do only what He has promised in His Word. So what does this verse mean?

First, in Scripture, the word *delight* means "to place yourself in the proper position of humility that you might hear God speak, that God might get access to your entire personhood, in order to mold you and conform you to the image of Jesus Christ." When such delight takes place, God places within your heart His desires for you. In other words, God's desires become our desires when we truly delight ourselves in Him.

Then verse 5 implies that we have the God-given ability to commit our ways to Him and trust Him to bring to pass the plans He initiated. God will always bring to pass what He initiated as, by faith, believers cooperate with Him. What a wonderful and freeing principle: we are not responsible to perform *for* God, but in simple faith—in responding to what God reveals—we are simply to cooperate *with* God. When we do, God will bring to pass those desires that He has placed in our hearts and that we are embracing.

....

Lord, today I humble myself so that I might hear You speak, so that I can by faith join You in what You desire to do in my life. Amen.

STONEY BENFIELD, PROSPECT BAPTIST CHURCH, ALBEMARLE, NC

WEEK 39—TUESDAY
The Pathway of Delight

Blessed is the man who walks not in the counsel of the ungodly, nor stands in the path of sinners, nor sits in the seat of the scornful; but his delight is in the law of the LORD, and in His law he meditates day and night. He shall be like a tree planted by the rivers of water, that brings forth its fruit in its season, whose leaf also shall not wither; and whatever he does shall prosper.

PSALM 1:1–3

Today's passage speaks of two pathways that we can choose between for a possible source of delight. We can choose to walk in the pathway of an ungodly environment or a godly environment. We choose that godly path when our "delight is in the law of the LORD." This word *delight* means "to take pleasure in or to desire with hunger."

What does it look like to delight in God's Law? First, we must meditate on the Word. This means to read it, and think about over and over again until the Word has captured our hearts and is directing our steps. Second, we must appropriate the Word. We must apply the Word in our lives. We are to live in such a way that the truth of God's Word is clearly reflected in what we say and how we act.

Are you allowing the truth of God's Word to be planted in your life and rooted deeply into the soil of your heart? When you appropriate the Word in your life, you will bear the fruit of God's righteousness.

....

Lord, today I ask You to grow in me the desire to delight in Your pathway. Please enable me and empower me to learn as well as appropriate the truths of Your Word, so my life might bear the fruit of Your righteousness. Amen.

WEEK 39—WEDNESDAY
The Protection of Delight

The steps of a good man are ordered by the LORD, and He delights in his way. Though he fall, he shall not be utterly cast down; for the LORD upholds him with His hand.

PSALM 37:23–24

So far this week, we have seen the principle of delight, the pathway of delight, and now the protection of delight. Psalm 37 reveals the protection that God places around the person who delights in Him and in His Law.

We who delight in God are protected the sovereignty of God. The first verse says our steps are "ordered by the LORD": God goes ahead in order to arrange the steps of the godly person. As my mentor Dr. Ron Lynch put it, "God either authors or allows everything that happens in my life." We can rest in the fact that we serve a sovereign God. This is the reason we can learn to rest in Jesus Christ. I am in Christ and Christ is me, and He who lives in me, orders my day-to-day steps!

We who delight in God experience the safety of God. You and I will stumble from time to time because we still live in fleshly bodies. When God saves us from the consequences of our sins, He doesn't remove our fleshly nature, but He does deposit within us His divine nature. Even when we stumble and fall, God upholds us with His hand! What safety!

Be encouraged today that when you truly belong to Him, the sovereignty and the safety of God will protect you!

....

Lord, today may I cooperate with You so that Your divine nature that resides in me will enable me to overcome my fleshly nature. And may I abide in You so I can experience Your protection. Amen.

STONEY BENFIELD, PROSPECT BAPTIST CHURCH, ALBEMARLE, NC

WEEK 39—THURSDAY
The Person of Delight

"Behold, I send My messenger, and he will prepare the way before Me. And the Lord, whom you seek, will suddenly come to His temple, even the Messenger of the covenant, in whom you delight. Behold, He is coming," Says the LORD of hosts.

MALACHI 3:1

Malachi was a prophet of God who foretold the coming of Jesus Christ, the Messiah. Many scholars believe Jesus is "the Messenger of the covenant" mentioned in today's passage. John the Baptist is the messenger of verse 1, sent to "prepare the way" for the coming Messiah. Jesus Christ did come: He humbled Himself, took on a human body, lived a perfect, sinless life, died a brutal death, and was resurrected for our salvation. Clearly, we have many reasons to delight in this Person!

We delight in His love for us. The people of Malachi's day were guilty of perverting temple worship and cheating God out of what was due Him. The priests of that day were also corrupt. Yet God, in His amazing love, sent Jesus Christ so that all of our sins and failures would be forgiven through His sacrificial death!

We delight in His life in us. The New Testament teaches that when a person is truly born again, God literally deposits His very own Spirit inside that believer. We have the Spirit of God dwelling in us and enabling us to live the Christian life that we cannot live using our own strength.

I believe the key to Christianity is knowing that on my own, I cannot live the kind of life God wants me to live. I must surrender myself to Jesus, allowing Him full access to my entire life, so His Spirit can live through me.

....

Lord, I choose today to delight in Your love for me! Help me choose to allow Your Spirit in me to guide my life this day. Amen.

WEEK 39—FRIDAY
The Promise of Delight

Who is a God like You, pardoning iniquity and passing over the transgression of the remnant of His heritage? He does not retain His anger forever, because He delights in mercy. He will again have compassion on us, and will subdue our iniquities. You will cast all our sins into the depths of the sea.

MICAH 7:18–19

Today we are going to look at a promise God makes to those who delight themselves in the Lord. Remember to delight yourself in God is to position yourself to hear Him and respond to Him.

Micah said, "Who is a God like you?" The answer: there is no God like Jehovah God! The Bible is full of promises that reveal to us the character and nature of God; this passage from Micah teaches that when we delight in God, He does something for us that we could never do ourselves.

God forgives our sins. God's willingness to forgive us, whose sins nailed His Son to the cross, is truly amazing grace. To forgive means "to lift and bear a person's sin and to remove it from his or her record." This action is possible only because of God's mercy: He chooses not to give us what we deserve.

God forgets our sins. In other words, God will not pour out His anger on us; instead, He will have compassion on us. The Bible says that He "cast all our sins into the depths of the sea." Jeremiah 31:34 adds, "And their sin I will remember no more." We will not be judged according to our sins because at the cross, God poured out His wrath on His Son to forgive those of us who choose to delight in our great God!

Lord, today I delight in You and thank You for Your forgiveness! Amen.

STONEY BENFIELD, PROSPECT BAPTIST CHURCH, ALBEMARLE, NC

WEEK 39—WEEKEND
The Practice of Delight

Thus says the LORD: "Let not the wise man glory in his wisdom, let not the mighty man glory in his might, nor let the rich man glory in his riches; but let him who glories glory in this, that he understands and knows Me, that I am the LORD, exercising lovingkindness, judgment, and righteousness in the earth. For in these I delight," says the LORD.

JEREMIAH 9:23–24

We have talked all week about Jesus being our delight. Once we believe in Jesus and come to delight in Him, our delight will be seen in our behavior. It seems that one of the missing elements in Christianity today is behavior that supports what we say we believe. In these verses, Jeremiah told the people not to glory themselves in wisdom, might, or riches, but to glory in the truth that they understood who God is. We should know God so much that His Spirit can work through us to reveal Himself to others. How does our relationship with Jesus become our delight?

We will love others. Jesus said the best way for the world to know that we are His disciples is by our love. In order to love others, we must be in a love relationship with God so that He enables us to love others with His love. Apart from Jesus Christ living in us, we simply don't have the ability to love others. Whom will we extend love to today the way Jesus extended love to us?

We will live righteously before God. Righteous living is evident in our loving God supremely and our loving our neighbors as ourselves. Righteous living, in simple terms, is the Holy Spirit living in and through us as we choose daily to delight in Him.

....

Jesus, allow Your Spirit to work through me today so others may see and believe! Amen.

WEEK 40—MONDAY
The Indescribable Gift

Thanks be to God for His indescribable gift!

2 CORINTHIANS 9:15

I f you think about it, love has many languages. In his excellent book *The Five Love Languages*, Gary Chapman does a wonderful job of explaining, in practical terms, how we communicate and interpret love. My primary love language is words of affirmation, while my wife's primary language is gifts. I think the greatest gift I ever gave her was on her fiftieth birthday when I flew our oldest son home for a surprise party. When he walked into the room, she was absolutely speechless. She wept and was overjoyed. She later told me that I could not have given her a more special gift.

Have we ever experienced something so wonderful that we had difficulty finding the words to describe it? Our relationship with Jesus is like that at times. God often works in our lives in ways unnoticed by even those people who are closest to us, yet we see with spiritual eyes the work His Spirit is doing in our minds and hearts. And try as we may, sometimes words fail when we try to describe the impact Jesus and our salvation have had on our lives. The apostle Paul said it well: "eye has not seen, nor ear heard, nor have entered into the heart of man the things which God has prepared for those who love Him" (1 Corinthians 2:9).

There truly aren't enough words or glorious enough words in the English language to describe it adequately. Spend some time today reflecting on and rejoicing over this indescribable gift.

....

Father, thank You for the gift of Jesus. Thank You that my relationship with You is more wonderful than I can communicate. You are truly an awesome God, and I praise You for all You are doing in my life. In Jesus' name, Amen.

DR. LEE SHEPPARD, MABEL WHITE BAPTIST CHURCH, MACON, GA

WEEK 40—TUESDAY
Reconciliation: It's Important

"If you bring your gift to the altar, and there remember that your brother has something against you, leave your gift there before the altar, and go your way. First be reconciled to your brother, and then come and offer your gift."

MATTHEW 5:23–24

I saw a bumper sticker that read, "Jesus loves you, but everyone else thinks you're a jerk." It's funny—and true. Scripture tells us that God loves us all the time, even when we're jerks, and all of us do act like jerks sometimes. That's not how God wants us to live.

Jesus made it clear that if we know someone (to whom we've been a jerk) has something against us, we are to go to that person and try to be reconciled. Our reconciliation with others is our response to being reconciled to God through the death of Jesus Christ on the cross. As Paul wrote, "[God has] reconciled us to Himself through Jesus Christ, and has given us the ministry of reconciliation" (2 Corinthians 5:18). The good news of the gospel is that we have been reconciled to God; therefore, we can be reconciled to others.

But what does reconciliation with others look like? It's important to remember that Jesus said, "Be reconciled to your brother," not "Reconcile your brother to you." A good way to start moving toward reconciliation is to say these simple words: "I'm sorry. I was wrong. Please forgive me." Don't offer excuses or disclaimers. Just make a simple apology. Doing so will go a long way in jumpstarting the process of reconciliation.

Father, thank You for sending Jesus to die so I could be reconciled to You. Thank You for Your unconditional love and ongoing forgiveness. Give me the discernment and grace to reconcile with those I've wronged. Amen.

WEEK 40—WEDNESDAY
Keep Praying!

"Ask, and it will be given to you; seek, and you will find; knock, and it will be opened to you. For everyone who asks receives, and he who seeks finds, and to him who knocks it will be opened. Or what man is there among you who, if his son asks for bread, will give him a stone? Or if he asks for a fish, will he give him a serpent?"

MATTHEW 7:7–10

My wife, Gina, suffered a massive stroke. The doctors told me that she wouldn't live through the day. As I called our children and other family members, I thought about what Jesus said about persistent prayer: if we ask, seek, and knock, our prayers will be answered. So all day long I prayed, and prayer warriors all across the nation and even around the world were notified, and they prayed. Tens of thousands of people were praying, and God answered our prayers. Gina lived through that day, and a year later—after nine surgeries and months of rehab—she is, according to medical professionals, a living miracle.

Persistent prayer is not easy. It requires work and perseverance. We have to keep at it until God answers! We have to be like a child who wants to ask his mother for something. If she is not nearby, the child seeks. And if she is in a room and the door is shut, the child knocks on the door until she opens it.

The process of asking, seeking, and knocking reminds us that we need God and are dependent on Him. We bow before His throne, ready to accept His kingdom purposes, and we keep praying. Regardless of the circumstances, we must keep praying!

. . . .

Father, thank You that You don't tire of our prayers. Give me strength to keep praying and grace to accept the purpose You are accomplishing when life is difficult. In Jesus' name, Amen.

DR. LEE SHEPPARD, MABEL WHITE BAPTIST CHURCH, MACON, GA

WEEK 40—THURSDAY
Finding True Peace

"These things I have spoken to you while being present with you. But the Helper, the Holy Spirit, whom the Father will send in My name, He will teach you all things, and bring to your remembrance all things that I said to you. Peace I leave with you, My peace I give to you; not as the world gives do I give to you. Let not your heart be troubled, neither let it be afraid."

JOHN 14:25–27

We live in a dark and troubled world. Political corruption, natural disasters, war, and terrorism have many people living in a perpetual state of fear and uncertainty. Untold multitudes clamor for peace in this chaotic and confusing world.

In Scripture *peace* refers to a quiet spirit despite our circumstances. Peace is a gift from God, and we experience true peace when we know Him. The closer we draw to God, the more peace we experience as our minds and spirits begin to rest in His power and wisdom. In His presence we remember His sovereign power and good plans for us.

We can't receive God's peace, however, without trusting Him, without setting our hearts to love and follow Him whatever happens in our lives. When we insist on being in control, when we choose worry rather than faith, we can't know peace. Worry is the enemy of peace.

God invites us to cast our cares upon Him rather than hold on to them. He wants to be our Refuge and our Strength. When we cry out to God, we experience His peace that truly does pass all human understanding.

Father, thank You that I can run to You and trust in You. Make me aware of Your presence so that fear and worry don't control me. In Jesus' name, Amen.

WEEK 40—FRIDAY
A Marvelous Gift

The judgment which came from one offense resulted in condemnation, but the free gift . . . resulted in justification. For if by the one man's offense death reigned through the one, much more those who receive abundance of grace and of the gift of righteousness will reign in life through the One, Jesus Christ.

ROMANS 5:16–17

What is the most special gift you've ever received? Did you receive it on your birthday, for Christmas, or on another occasion? Through the years I've received some amazing gifts, but Jesus is the most marvelous gift ever given. And it is the most needed gift ever given.

The apostle Paul taught that by one man—Adam—sin entered the world, and death was pronounced upon all, for in Adam all have sinned. On the other hand, grace entered the world through Jesus, and a forgiven life and eternal life are available to all who believe. Adam brought into the world sin, offense, judgment, condemnation, disobedience, and eternal death. Yet Christ brought grace, justification, righteousness, obedience, and eternal life.

Christ's death saved us from God's wrath. We now live with hope of eternal life rather than under the curse of death. We rejoice in God who, in His Son, atoned for our sins. Our justification is complete and irrevocable; there is no condemnation in Christ Jesus. And Paul confidently wrote that "he who has begun a good work in you will complete it until the day of Jesus Christ" (Philippians 1:6). What a marvelous gift!

....

Father, thank You for the gift of Jesus. Thank You that because of Him I will one day stand before You cleansed of my sin, welcomed by You, and not condemned. In Jesus' name, Amen.

DR. LEE SHEPPARD, MABEL WHITE BAPTIST CHURCH, MACON, GA

WEEK 40—WEEKEND
The Benefits of Eternal Life

Having been set free from sin, and having become slaves of God, you have your fruit to holiness, and the end, everlasting life. For the wages of sin is death, but the gift of God is eternal life in Christ Jesus our Lord.

ROMANS 6:22–23

C hristians often hear certain terms used again and again, and we can easily become desensitized to their meaning and power. The gift of eternal life, for instance, is something about which we sing, preach, and teach, yet it is difficult for us to comprehend the concept of eternity. A lifetime is a long time, but eternity is difficult to get our minds around. When does eternity begin? When does it end? I once heard that if each grain of sand on every beach in the whole world represented one million years, that incredible span of time would not put even a dent in eternity.

Having considered the scope of eternity, let's now reflect on the numerous and wonderful benefits of eternal life. Eternal life is ours because, through Jesus, our sins are forgiven and His righteousness has been credited to us. We, therefore, have peace with God, a new standing before Him, and personal access to Him. We can rejoice in the hope of glory, a hope that is sure and steadfast, strengthened by the love of God that fills our hearts. Eternal life also means we have received the Holy Spirit and are no longer spiritually dead. Additionally, we are saved from the wrath of God and receive atonement and an abundance of grace. Eternal life is ours only because of our total justification in God's eyes. And that justification is God's amazingly gracious gift to us.

....

Father, I am overwhelmed by Your goodness and grace. You have given me the marvelous gift of eternal life, and I am grateful for all You have done in my life. In Jesus' name, Amen.

WEEK 41—MONDAY
Giving Glory to God

Whether you eat or drink, or whatever you do, do all to the glory of God. Give no offense, either to the Jews or to the Greeks or to the church of God, just as I also please all men in all things, not seeking my own profit, but the profit of many, that they may be saved.

1 CORINTHIANS 10:31–33

Your life can be busy with many things this week. You could focus on your financial portfolio, a favorite sports team, an upcoming business decision that may catapult your career, or spending time with your family. While those things are not unworthy of your time, why not choose to focus on something entirely different this week?

Why not focus on giving glory to God in everything this week? Refuse to get tangled up in the details of life that drain your energy and joy. Rise above the frustrating details and exhausting demands of everyday life by keeping your eyes and heart looking to heaven.

Don't let trivial details weigh heavily on you this week. Make important choices this week. Decide, for instance, to give glory to God in everything you do. When you do so, people will see Christ in you, and God may even use you to lead someone to salvation.

Yes, live this week giving glory to God! Pass on any praise you receive to Jesus, who will one day receive all praise and glory!

O Lord, I accept this challenge. I choose to give glory to You at every opportunity! In Jesus' name, Amen.

DR. RONNIE FLOYD, CROSS CHURCH, NORTHWEST ARKANSAS

WEEK 41—TUESDAY
Believing God Brings Him Glory

Jesus said to [Martha], "Did I not say to you that if you would believe you would see the glory of God?" Then they took away the stone from the place where the dead man was lying. And Jesus lifted up His eyes and said, "Father, I thank You that You have heard Me." . . . Now when He had said these things, He cried with a loud voice, "Lazarus, come forth!" And he who had died came out bound hand and foot with grave clothes, and his face was wrapped with a cloth. Jesus said to them, "Loose him, and let him go."

JOHN 11:40–41, 43–44

Will we choose to believe God today? Every day we face various decisions, many of which come down to acting with faith in God or faith in ourselves, doing what God wants us to do or doing what we want to do. It is essential that we look at these decisions through the lens of this key question: will we choose to believe God today?

Jesus told Lazarus' sisters and friends that if they trusted Him, they would see the glory of God demonstrated—and they did! Jesus raised Lazarus from the dead. At the command of His voice, Lazarus came back to life.

Today, in the twenty-first century, we can see amazing demonstrations of power in microchips, smartphones, the Internet, fracking, and nuclear energy. Yet nothing is more powerful than the Lord Jesus Himself. His words bring life—physical as well as spiritual.

Remember that when you open the Bible, the Word of the living God. Choose this day and every day to read it, to think about it, and, in faith, to base your life on what you learn. Choose to believe God. When you do, you give Jesus glory!

....

Lord God, I choose to believe You in all that I do today. Amen.

Week 41—Wednesday
Focus on Jesus, the Glory of God

When [the elders and scribes] heard these things they were cut to the heart, and they gnashed at [Stephen] with their teeth. But he, being full of the Holy Spirit, gazed into heaven and saw the glory of God, and Jesus standing at the right hand of God, and said, "Look! I see the heavens opened and the Son of Man standing at the right hand of God!"

ACTS 7:55–56

When the elders and scribes heard Stephen boldly proclaim the Word of God and accuse them of killing the prophets as well as the One about whom they prophesied, they killed Stephen. And in this tragedy, the first Christian martyr taught us something about how to live and how to die. Basically, Stephen lived and died focusing on Jesus Christ.

Stephen was such a unique man of God that in his death, Jesus enabled Stephen to see Him standing at God's right hand as he died for his faith.

Was Jesus applauding Stephen for the way he lived and the way he died? Did Jesus enable Stephen to see Him in order to encourage Stephen about the glory of heaven? I'm not sure, but here is something I do know.

It is the middle of the week. Distractions have abounded, constantly drawing you away from the eternally important. Surprises and interruptions have occurred. What now? Will you give up or will you continue to try to give God glory in all that you do?

Learn from Stephen: focus on Jesus now. In life keep your eyes where they should be continually: on Jesus! You cannot change your circumstances, but you can refocus your heart and mind.

....

The blood of Stephen motivates me to want to live like him. Lord, help me keep my eyes on You! Amen.

DR. RONNIE FLOYD, CROSS CHURCH, NORTHWEST ARKANSAS

WEEK 41—THURSDAY
Trusting God for the Impossible

[Abraham] did not waver at the promise of God through unbelief, but was strengthened in faith, giving glory to God, and being fully convinced that what He had promised He was also able to perform. And therefore "it was accounted to him for righteousness."

ROMANS 4:20–22

As Abraham neared one hundred years of age and Sarah was long past childbearing years, he still trusted God for the impossible. Humanly speaking, pregnancy was impossible. But divinely choreographed, nothing is impossible! That is why Abraham did not waver in unbelief. Abraham knew that God was able to do anything. He had seen it before, and he knew he would see it again. Trusting in God alone, Abraham stood on the Lord's promises and trusted God for the impossible!

We cannot think ourselves into a deeper walk with Christ. We cannot feel our way into a deeper walk with Christ. We must instead simply place our faith in Christ alone for every aspect of life.

After all, God can do more in a moment than you and I can do in a lifetime. Do you need a breakthrough in your life? Or a miracle? Do you need God to step in and do what man says is absolutely impossible?

Read God's Word now. Hear His voice today. When He speaks through His Word to you, stand on the promises you find there. The Lord's promise is all Abraham had, and you have that too. The Lord's promise is sufficient; it is all you need whatever you face.

Remember that God can do anything at any time. And God can do more in a moment than you can do in a lifetime. So trust Him!

....

Lord, You are a Promise Maker and a Promise Keeper with whom nothing is impossible. I want to live my life totally trusting You. Amen.

WEEK 41—FRIDAY
Accepting Others

Receive one another, just as Christ also received us, to the glory of God. Now I say that Jesus Christ has become a servant to the circumcision for the truth of God, to confirm the promises made to the fathers, and that the Gentiles might glorify God for His mercy.

ROMANS 15:7–8

If you've traveled to the Middle East, you've seen how most Jews and Gentiles struggle to accept one another. This is not a new problem, and nothing suggests it is going to be resolved anytime soon. Yet God's plan to redeem the world—through the death of Christ on the cross—is a plan to redeem both Jews and Gentiles. Jesus died for the sins of *all* people.

When we ask Christ to be Lord of our lives, He receives us as we are. We don't have to clean ourselves up before He will save us. We simply go to Him in repentance and faith, and He does for us what no one else can do for us: Jesus forgives us and accepts us just as we are at the time, and all the glory of this grace goes to God.

So who are we not to accept others? We need to love and accept all people. In one hand we hold the truth of God, and in the other, the love of God. And we extend both to people. We gently but clearly speak the truth about the consequences of sinful choices . . . and we love them.

After all, if it weren't for the grace of God helping us recognize the truth about Jesus and the truth about ourselves, we would still be right where unbelievers are today.

Jesus, thank You for opening my eyes to both the truth of who You are and the truth that I am a sinner in need of a Savior. Help me to accept others with Your love. Amen.

DR. RONNIE FLOYD, CROSS CHURCH, NORTHWEST ARKANSAS

WEEK 41—WEEKEND
Caring About Others

All things are lawful for me, but not all things are helpful; all things are lawful for me, but not all things edify. Let no one seek his own, but each one the other's well-being. Eat whatever is sold in the meat market, asking no questions for conscience' sake; for "the earth is the LORD's, and all its fullness."

1 CORINTHIANS 10:23–26

The big idea in this challenging text is to think about other people rather than about ourselves. Doing so gives God glory!

In today's passage, Paul addressed the complicated issue of living out our religious convictions without offending people who either do not know Christ or who are weaker brothers. Paul discouraged legalism that adds to God's Word. He encouraged liberty in Christ that is found when we live within the parameters of God's Word. But not all issues are clear-cut.

Within the parameters of Christian liberty, we are called to consider others when we make choices: we want our choices to build up rather than weaken their faith. We never want to make choices that offend a brother or alienate a person who needs Jesus. We should refuse our own self-gratification in order to choose something much better: building up another person's faith and confidence in the Lord.

This weekend, what can you do to live this out in your family? In your neighborhood? In your church?

Think about others when you make choices. This weekend focus on others. This brings God glory!

Lord, I want to die to myself today. Help me choose to care about others and serve them with Your love. Amen.

WEEK 42—MONDAY
Father God Watches over Us

Blessed is the nation whose God is the LORD, the people He has chosen as His own inheritance. The LORD looks from heaven; He sees all the sons of men. From the place of His dwelling He looks on all the inhabitants of the earth; He fashions their hearts individually; He considers all their works.

PSALM 33:12–15

Have you ever wanted a magic wand that gave you the ability to shape your future or a crystal ball to get a glimpse of what's ahead? When it comes to shaping your future, though, who could do a better job than the all-wise, all-loving, all-powerful Creator God?

Our heavenly Father not only created us, but He also chose us as His inheritance (Psalm 139:14; 33:12). In other words, He has adopted us as His children, making us "joint heirs with Christ" (1 John 3:1; Romans 8:17). That means, among other things, that we are always under the watchful eye of our heavenly Father. Absolutely nothing can escape His loving oversight of His people.

The psalmist also taught that God has created us to honor and serve Him as Yahweh. In His total sovereignty and supremacy over all creation and its inhabitants, God rules rightfully and with authority (Psalm 24:1–2). The psalmist honored the nation Israel as God's chosen people, as His inheritance among the nations.

I'm grateful that even today our heavenly Father continues to adopt people into His family inheritance according to His plan and purpose.

. . . .

Father God, thank You that You have chosen to watch over Your people the way a shepherd watches over his sheep. And thank You for truly blessing us with an eternal inheritance in You. May we as a nation always bless You. Amen.

DUSTY MCLEMORE, LINDSAY LANE BAPTIST CHURCH, ATHENS, AL

WEEK 42—TUESDAY
Hang in There! We Win!

The Lord knows the days of the upright and their inheritance shall be forever. They shall not be ashamed in the evil time, and in the days of famine they shall be satisfied.

PSALM 37:18–19

Do you ever have days when you feel as though you are losing? Christians know that they ultimately win, but it sure doesn't appear that way sometimes! The world around us seems to be falling apart, and evil too often seems to triumph over good. We may feel like crying out, "Hey, God! We're the good guys!"

The prophet Habakkuk must have felt that way when he wrote, "O LORD, how long shall I cry and You will not hear?" (Habakkuk 1:2) or "The law is powerless and justice never goes forth. For the wicked surround the righteous" (v. 4). David had similar thoughts at times, but here in Psalm 37, David encouraged fellow believers by expressing his confidence that God's sovereign hand would prevail.

In this psalm, David also exhorted us about how to live even as God watches over and protects us. The Lord "knows the days of the upright" (v. 17), and Jesus later taught "the very hairs of your head are all numbered" (Matthew 10:30). The psalmist went on to remind us that God never forgets His children or the inheritance He has promised us. Even when—like today—evil is all around, God's Word promises that things are not quite what they seem. The Lord has sovereignly determined the days of the wicked. Even though the righteous suffer temporarily while they're in this world, "the steps of a good man are ordered by the LORD" (Psalm 37:23). In other words, we win!

....

Lord, thank You that Satan is a defeated foe and that we have victory in Jesus! Amen.

WEEK 42—WEDNESDAY
It's All About Life "In Him"

In Him also we have obtained an inheritance, being predestined according to the purpose of Him who works all things according to the counsel of His will, that we who first trusted in Christ should be to the praise of His glory.

EPHESIANS 1:11–12

Over the next couple of days, our devotions will be based on Ephesians 1:11–19. We'll observe God's sovereign plan of salvation for His people and the eternal inheritance He has reserved for us in heaven.

The apostle Paul often used the term *mystery* to refer to God's truth that was once hidden but is now revealed. Christians have not only been blessed with the promise of eternal life (John 3:16), but we have also inherited God's eternal truth . . . through His eternal Word (John 8:32; 1 Peter 1:25). Specifically, it was God's plan from the beginning to send His Son, to be the sacrifice for our sins and the One to save us from our sins.

This life-changing truth is the gospel's mystery, which Paul alluded to with his often-used phrase "in Him." Paul taught, for example, that "in Him we have redemption, the forgiveness of sins" (Ephesians 1:7); "in Him we have obtained an inheritance" (v. 11); and "in Him you also trusted after you heard the word of truth" (v. 13). Clearly, our eternal inheritance as described in the Word of life is all about being "in Him," our Lord and Savior, Jesus Christ!

In His sovereignty, God predestined and transformed all "who first trusted in Christ . . . to the praise of His glory" (v. 12). What a blessing to be among His chosen people! May we never forget the price God paid to redeem us and claim us as His inheritance.

....

I praise You, heavenly Father, for choosing me in Christ to be part of Your eternal inheritance! Amen.

DUSTY MCLEMORE, LINDSAY LANE BAPTIST CHURCH, ATHENS, AL

WEEK 42—THURSDAY
Signed, Sealed, and Delivered

In Him you also trusted, after you heard the word of truth, the gospel of your salvation; in whom also, having believed, you were sealed with the Holy Spirit of promise, who is the guarantee of our inheritance until the redemption of the purchased possession, to the praise of His glory.

EPHESIANS 1:13–14

Years ago, my wife and I were shopping for a new bicycle for our oldest daughter. We found just the right one at Kmart, but we didn't have the money to pay the total price of the bicycle. So we made a down payment and had the bike placed on layaway: the store placed our name on the bike and stored it in the back of the store. The bicycle belonged to us, but we couldn't take it home until we brought Kmart the final payment and redeemed our purchased possession.

This Kmart shopping experience illustrates what the apostle Paul taught in this passage. God created us to worship and glorify Him, but we became tainted by sin in the garden of Eden. Sin separated us from God. So God did for us what we could never do for ourselves, and that was to pay the cost of our redemption from sin (Hebrews 10). God did this by sending His Son to die in our place (Romans 5:8). Therefore, Jesus Christ paid the full price for our salvation through His blood which was shed to redeem us from our sin! Then to "guarantee . . . our inheritance" as joint heirs with Jesus, God sealed every believer with His Holy Spirit as a promise that we'll forever be His adopted children.

Thank You, Father God, for sending Your Son, Jesus, to be the redemption price for my sins, for sealing me with Your Holy Spirit, and for guaranteeing my inheritance. Amen.

WEEK 42—FRIDAY
Confident in the Call

[I make] mention of you in my prayers: that . . . the eyes of your understanding [be]
enlightened; that you may know what is the hope of His calling, what are the riches of
the glory of His inheritance in the saints, and what is the exceeding greatness of His
power toward us who believe, according to the working of His mighty power.

EPHESIANS 1:16, 18–19

I love people with passion! To see someone clearly excited about something
not only excites me, but inspires me as well. I feel confident that the apostle
Paul was a man of passion.

What was Paul so elated and passionate about? His Damascus road
encounter with Jesus was the reason (Acts 9:11–22). Now, in Ephesians, Paul
the Evangelist once again praised God, this time for the saints in Ephesus, as
he interceded on their behalf. As soon as Paul heard of their faith in the Lord
Jesus, he immediately began praising God and thanking Him for the saints at
Ephesus (vv. 15–16). Paul went on to pray that God might grant these believers
spiritual wisdom and divine revelation about "the hope of [God's] calling."
Paul desired that "the eyes of [their] understanding [be] enlightened" and
their knowledge of almighty God strengthened and increased.

In sharp contrast to the passion of Paul, atheists today attest that there
is no such God, and agnostics proclaim that even if there is a God, we can't
know Him. But there is no doubt that Paul knew God personally through
Jesus Christ! People may try to defame, discredit, or even deny that there's a
God. But one thing people can never silence is the personal and passionate
testimony of one who has met King Jesus!

....

Father, thank You for Jesus. Make me passionate about my relationship with
Your Son, so I may be a powerful witness for You and Your love. Amen.

DUSTY MCLEMORE, LINDSAY LANE BAPTIST CHURCH, ATHENS, AL

WEEK 42—WEEKEND
Jesus, Lamb of God

If the blood of bulls and goats and the ashes of a heifer, sprinkling the unclean, sanctifies for the purifying of the flesh, how much more shall the blood of Christ, who through the eternal Spirit offered Himself without spot to God, cleanse your conscience from dead works to serve the living God? And for this reason He is the Mediator of the new covenant, by means of death, for the redemption of the transgressions under the first covenant, that those who are called may receive the promise of the eternal inheritance.

HEBREWS 9:13–15

I magine coming to worship on Sunday and seeing several bulls and goats at the altar. Well, that was ordinary worship for an Old Testament saint. The temple priest would sacrifice the animals and sprinkle the blood seven times upon the temple altar. This ritual sacrifice was a sin offering for the Jews.

Then entered Jesus Christ, who "came as [our] High Priest" (Hebrews 9:11). All the Old Testament sacrifices were a foreshadowing of the once-and-for-all-sacrifice of Jesus, the sinless Lamb of God. Shed at Calvary, Jesus' precious blood made atonement for all of mankind's sin—with one key difference.

The Old Testament sacrifices focused on external ceremonial cleansing, on "the purifying of the flesh," but these sacrifices could do nothing to cleanse the internal spirit or conscience. The old covenant rituals could not change a person's heart. The New Testament sacrifice of God's own Son, however, focused on the internal. With this new covenant sacrifice, the Lord would now "put [His] laws into their mind and write them in their hearts" (Hebrews 8:10).

By His sinless life, sacrificial death, and glorious resurrection, Jesus secured both our "eternal redemption" (9:12) and our "eternal inheritance."

....

Jesus, You are my Savior and my High Priest, the Mediator of the new covenant through Your sacrifice on the cross—and I am grateful. Amen.

WEEK 43—MONDAY
Jesus, All We Need for Life

His divine power has given to us all things that pertain to life and godliness. . . . [We] have been given . . . exceedingly great and precious promises, that through these you may be partakers of the divine nature, having escaped the corruption that is in the world through lust. But also for this very reason, giving all diligence, add to your faith virtue, to virtue knowledge, to knowledge self-control, to self-control perseverance, to perseverance godliness, to godliness brotherly kindness, and to brotherly kindness love. For if these things are yours and abound, you will be neither barren nor unfruitful in the knowledge of our Lord Jesus Christ.

2 PETER 1:3–8

I often hear these words: "it is hard to live the Christian life." Usually the person means that it's difficult to live a moral life in an extremely immoral world. And it's getting harder. Christians around the globe face difficulty, suffering, persecution, and even death for one simple reason: they follow Christ.

Following Jesus offers soul-satisfying fulfillment. Our Lord saves us from the corruption of sin and equips us to live for Him. He has given to us all we need to live a godly, God-honoring life.

Pursuing godliness and following the Lord Jesus are synonymous. We are to discipline our lives in submission to the Lord. We are to apply God's truth to life and, by His Spirit, experience transformation and become more like Christ. This is all possible because, by His grace, God has "given to us all things that pertain to life and godliness." Out of love for our Lord, we submit to Him and obey His Word. By His power we live for Him—and more and more that may mean we face persecution and death for Him. But we must never waver in our committment to Him.

. . . .

Lord, I depend on You to empower me to live for You and, if necessary, to die for You. Amen.

REV. MICHAEL ORR, FIRST BAPTIST CHURCH, CHIPLEY, FL

WEEK 43—TUESDAY
Jesus, Companion for Life

"You denied the Holy One and the Just, and asked for a murderer to be granted to you, and killed the Prince of life, whom God raised from the dead, of which we are witnesses. And His name, through faith in His name, has made this man strong, whom you see and know. Yes, the faith which comes through Him has given him this perfect soundness in the presence of you all."

ACTS 3:14–16

Have you ever noticed how pleasant it is to be around someone who is beautiful on the inside? A person of great integrity and a pure heart, a person living for the Lord, resting in His grace, and shining for His love refreshes our soul. Yet no one's beauty compares to the beauty of the Lord Jesus. He is holy and perfect in all His being and all His ways. He will never do anything other than what is right and just. Being with the Lord is the ultimate source of joy and of refreshment and blessing for the soul.

In today's passage Peter referred to Jesus as "the Holy One," a reference to our Lord's perfect character and complete commitment to the will of the Father. Second, Peter described Jesus as "the Just [One]," a reference to our Savior's innocence and purity. Third, Peter called Jesus "the Prince of life." Jesus is the giver of life, both physical and eternal.

All who have faith in the risen Jesus have in Him a perfect Companion for life. In addition, He gives us the gift of eternal life. Thus we will have everlasting fellowship with Him as well.

....

Father, may I enjoy perfect fellowship with Your Son, my Savior and Lord, today and always. Amen.

WEEK 43—WEDNESDAY
Jesus, Our Savior

"The God of our fathers raised up Jesus whom you murdered by hanging on a tree. Him God has exalted to His right hand to be Prince and Savior, to give repentance to Israel and forgiveness of sins. And we are His witnesses to these things, and so also is the Holy Spirit whom God has given to those who obey Him."

ACTS 5:30–32

The longer I walk with Jesus, the clearer the truth becomes that salvation is completely of the grace of God.

Also the older I grow in the Lord, the more aware I have become of the sinfulness of my heart. No human being could ever overcome such spiritual deadness on his own. I need a Savior; we all need a Savior.

Jesus is that Savior, cursed on behalf of your sin and mine. He was punished for you and for me so that forgiveness of sins could be ours. Jesus chose to be punished for our sins in order to satisfy the just penalty for sin that God requires. What Jesus did for us is truly amazing.

Now when we confess our sins to Jesus and call on Him to save us, our sins are completely washed away. We are declared righteous because God has credited Jesus' righteousness to us (Romans 4:22–25). God seals us with His Holy Spirit as a guarantee of our salvation (Ephesians 1:13–14).

And since we are saved by the grace of our Lord Jesus Christ, we respond in love for Him by telling people about His grace. We are witnesses of His love and hope to the desperate and sinful world around us.

....

Lord, thank You for Your saving grace, and empower me, I ask, to testify effectively to others of Your grace. Amen.

REV. MICHAEL ORR, FIRST BAPTIST CHURCH, CHIPLEY, FL

WEEK 43—THURSDAY
Jesus, Our Assurance

God is not unjust to forget your work and labor of love which you have shown toward His name, in that you have ministered to the saints, and do minister. And we desire that each one of you show the same diligence to the full assurance of hope until the end, that you do not become sluggish, but imitate those who through faith and patience inherit the promises.

HEBREWS 6:10–12

I t seems too easy. I confess my sins, I recognize Jesus as God's Son, I admit my need for a Savior, and I am saved from the consequences of my sin. Wouldn't it be nice to have evidence that the transaction truly happened? The writer of Hebrews pointed to two kinds of evidence that can assure us of our salvation. The indications are God's justice and our works. First, God's justice refers to His grace revealed in the atoning work of the Lord Jesus. Bible-believing Christians know that redemption cannot be earned, that it is freely given to all who believe that Jesus paid the price for our sins.

Second, of course our works don't save us, but they serve as evidence that we have indeed been saved by God's grace. Once we are saved, one of the assurances that we have been converted is our works. Our lives change and we obey the Word of God. This lifestyle of Christlikeness shows people around us that we have truly met Christ.

What evidence of your genuine conversion do you see in your life? If you're not sure, ask someone you trust who knows you well. If that person doesn't identify some specifics, maybe you need to call on Jesus to save you. If evidence is present, rejoice in the assurance of your salvation.

....

Lord God, thank You for salvation through Jesus' death on the cross for my sins. Amen.

WEEK 43—FRIDAY
Jesus Alone

You are all sons of God through faith in Christ Jesus. For as many of you as were baptized into Christ have put on Christ. There is neither Jew nor Greek, there is neither slave nor free, there is neither male nor female; for you are all one in Christ Jesus. And if you are Christ's, then you are Abraham's seed, and heirs according to the promise.

GALATIANS 3:26–29

I have experienced many wonderful moments in my life. My wedding day was one of those special times. It was amazing to see my beautiful bride come down the aisle, her raven black hair, soft brown eyes, and olive skin highlighted by a gorgeous gown. I thought to myself, "You are blessed, dude!" The day our daughter was born was another significant moment in my life. I was overwhelmed with emotion as I took her in my arms for the first time. What a gift from God!

Of all the significant times in my life, however, nothing compares to my conversion. When I recognized my sins and learned about Jesus' sacrificial death for my sins, when I placed my faith in Jesus as my Savior and Lord, I was adopted into God's family. I became a son of the living God. Everyone who is saved is part of my spiritual family now, and we are all heirs of God. The wonder of redemption is unfathomable.

I am grateful today to be a son of God through my faith in the resurrected Jesus Christ, the Victor over sin and death.

....

Father, thank You for enabling me to see the truth about Jesus and about my need for a Savior. Thank You for making me one of Your children. My desire is to live for You today. Amen.

REV. MICHAEL ORR, FIRST BAPTIST CHURCH, CHIPLEY, FL

WEEK 43—WEEKEND
Jesus, Not the Law

The promise that he would be the heir of the world was not to Abraham or to his seed through the law, but through the righteousness of faith. For if those who are of the law are heirs, faith is made void and the promise made of no effect, because the law brings about wrath; for where there is no law there is no transgression. Therefore it is of faith that it might be according to grace, so that the promise might be sure to all the seed, not only to those who are of the law, but also to those who are of the faith of Abraham, who is the father of us all.

ROMANS 4:13–16

The Law has never been the means of salvation from the consequences of our sin. On the contrary, the Law brings God's wrath because no human being can keep the Law.

God gave the Law to awaken us to our sins and rebellion against Him. Our failure to keep the Law also helps us understand the coming wrath—described in Revelation—that we all justly deserve. God's grace that we appropriate by our faith is the only way we can be justified and have a relationship with God. Jesus satisfied God's just wrath toward our sins when He died. His resurrection—His victory over death and sin—assured forgiveness and righteousness to all who believe in Him.

Then, after our salvation, we are to live according to God's standards with the help of His Spirit. The Spirit is also at work developing Christlike character in us and enabling us to share the message of grace with others. We should praise God for His grace, rest in it, and share it.

....

I thank You, Father, for Your perfect plan of salvation. Thank You for the Law that helps me see my sin and for Your grace that saves me despite my inability to keep the Law. Amen.

Week 44—Monday
Godly Sorrow

I rejoice, not that you were made sorry, but that your sorrow led to repentance. For you were made sorry in a godly manner, that you might suffer loss from us in nothing. For godly sorrow produces repentance leading to salvation, not to be regretted; but the sorrow of the world produces death.

2 Corinthians 7:9–10

Have you ever said something you regretted? That is how Paul felt. His first letter to the Corinthian church was a strong rebuke: he pointed out the ungodly divisions within the fellowship, the immoral activity occurring among the members, their lack of love for one another, and their self-centered service. Paul regretted sending the letter—until Titus returned and shared with him how the Corinthians had responded.

The believers in Corinth were not merely sorry for being rebuked for their sins. That would have been worldly grief, which typically produces a prideful desire to justify one's behavior. In this case, it would have also prompted great animosity toward Paul. But Paul was elated to learn that the Corinthians had experienced "godly sorrow." They recognized their sin as offensive to God, and they repented. They experienced a change of mind and heart that grew within them a desire to repent.

Am I causing or encouraging divisions among the fellowship I attend? Am I involved in any immoral activity? Do I lack genuine love for anyone in my church? Do I serve in order to be recognized for my gifts?

If you answered yes to any of these questions, repent. Your sin offends God. If you truly experience true godly sorrow, true repentance will result.

....

Father, show me my sin that I am too comfortable with to see. Help me experience godly sorrow that leads to genuine repentance. Amen.

DR. LEVI SKIPPER, CONCORD BAPTIST CHURCH, CLERMONT, GA

WEEK 44—TUESDAY
You Think the Locusts Were a Big Deal?

"Now, therefore," says the LORD, "Turn to Me with all your heart, with fasting, with weeping, and with mourning." So rend your heart, and not your garments; return to the LORD your God, for He is gracious and merciful, slow to anger, and of great kindness; and He relents from doing harm.

JOEL 2:12–13

God's covenant people had rebelled against Him, and their disobedience prompted His discipline. In Joel 1, the prophet recalled an invasion of locusts that destroyed their produce. These locusts served as an object lesson as Joel warned the people of the enemy invasion they would experience if they did not repent.

Joel encouraged the people of God to repent wholeheartedly. The Lord did not want merely a display: he didn't want people ripping their shirts and saying, "Woe is me!" God wanted their hearts truly to turn from sin and be realigned with His purposes. Joel spoke of God's patience and His willingness to turn from cursing them to blessing them. But the people did not repent. So God sent a pagan army to invade the land and carry His people into captivity.

The locust invasion served as a picture of this army's invasion, and this pagan army is a lesson to the unrepentant people in our day. The apostle Peter described the great and terrible day of the Lord when He will unleash the full fury of His wrath upon unbelievers. No plant could escape the locust, no person could escape the pagan army, and, likewise, apart from Jesus, no one will escape the just wrath of God. God is patient, "not wishing for any to perish but for all to come to repentance" (2 Peter 3:9 NASB). But the unrepentant will perish.

....

Father, thank You for helping me see my sin and prompting me to repent. Give me courage, I pray, to warn unbelievers in my life of Your coming wrath. Amen.

WEEK 44—WEDNESDAY
Band-Aids® Will Not Work

"Those who are well have no need of a physician, but those who are sick. But go and learn what this means: 'I desire mercy and not sacrifice.' For I did not come to call the righteous, but sinners, to repentance."

MATTHEW 9:12–13

The religious people of Jesus' day did not need Him. They had created rules and kept those rules as others watched. With prideful hearts, they pointed fingers at those who didn't live up to their standards of righteousness and avoided such people at all costs. Their so-called spiritual lives kept them feeling superior to others and gave them a false assurance that their activity was pleasing to God.

Jesus, however, did not adhere to the man-made rules and traditions of the Pharisees, Sadducees, and scribes. Whenever people flocked to Jesus, He was quick to spend time with the worst of the worst. The religious mocked Jesus as defiling Himself by eating and drinking with tax collectors and sinners.

Imagine the bewildered looks on their faces when Jesus said He had come for those who were sick. Indeed, the religious elite were sick spiritually, just as the tax collectors and other sinners were. The difference was that the religious sought to cover their sickness with Band-Aids® of religion, while others were quick to realize that they needed Jesus and that they could do nothing to bring about their own spiritual healing.

Jesus did not come to mock sinners, but to extend mercy to these who were spiritually sick. Only people who recognize their sin before God and repent will experience the merciful healing of the Savior. Band-Aids® will not work.

Lord Jesus, thank You for helping me recognize my spiritual sickness and bringing me to spiritual health. Amen.

DR. LEVI SKIPPER, CONCORD BAPTIST CHURCH, CLERMONT, GA

Week 44—Thursday
Joy in Heaven

"What man of you, having a hundred sheep, if he loses one of them, does not leave the ninety-nine in the wilderness, and go after the one which is lost until he finds it? And when he has found it, he lays it on his shoulders, rejoicing. And when he comes home, he calls together his friends and neighbors, saying to them, 'Rejoice with me, for I have found my sheep which was lost!' I say to you that likewise there will be more joy in heaven over one sinner who repents than over ninety-nine just persons who need no repentance."

LUKE 15:4–7

Jesus told this parable when the Pharisees were grumbling about Him. They spoke negatively of Jesus because He apparently enjoyed welcoming sinners and tax collectors into His company. With this parable, Jesus hoped that the religious elite might compare their reactions to the reactions in heaven when one sinner repents.

Jesus began by stating the obvious: if you've lost a sheep, you go and find that sheep. Then, after finding the lost sheep, you gather others together and rejoice that you have found the lost one. If you hadn't found the sheep, you likely would have had to pay the owner of the flock for the one sheep that was lost on your watch.

If the shepherd in the parable seeks out a lost sheep with such passion, how much greater will be Jesus' passion as He seeks out lost souls? If the shepherd and his friends experience such excitement after finding a lost sheep, how much greater the excitement in heaven must be when a lost soul is found?

Clearly, a sheep is hardly disposable, so can any human—created in God's image—be treated as disposable?

....

Father, give me the joy of heaven when souls are found and brought into Your flock—and please use me in that effort. Amen.

THE GIFT OF JESUS

263

WEEK 44—FRIDAY
Make Disciples Everywhere

"It was necessary for the Christ to suffer and to rise from the dead the third day, and that repentance and remission of sins should be preached in His name to all nations, beginning at Jerusalem."

LUKE 24:46–47

God the Father predetermined by His divine foreknowledge to give His Son over as a substitute upon the cross. Jesus was the Righteous given for the unrighteous. He bore in His body God's full wrath against sin. But then, like an incompetent employee, death did not have the necessary skill set to keep Jesus in the grave. Jesus' resurrection was proof from heaven that God the Father had accepted His sacrifice.

Jesus' death and resurrection dealt with two major problems. First, the problem of sin was handled: we deserved to die for our sins, but Jesus paid the death penalty for our sins. Now all who trust Him by faith are—by His grace—granted forgiveness. Second, Jesus also dealt with our significance problem: upon trusting Jesus as Savior, we are adopted into the family of God. This new status gives our lives meaning and purpose. Apart from a relationship with God the Father through Jesus the Son, we are still in our sins and have no purpose in this life.

This is the message Jesus commanded that we are to share with others. If we are followers of Jesus, we are missionaries. People where we live, work, and play—family members, neighbors, other team parents, cashiers at the grocery store—need to hear the good news of Jesus. Whom will we to talk to this week?

....

Father, help me make disciples in my circles of influence—for the people's good and Your great glory. Amen.

DR. LEVI SKIPPER, CONCORD BAPTIST CHURCH, CLERMONT, GA

WEEK 44—WEEKEND
Don't Be Mean

A servant of the Lord must not quarrel but be gentle to all, able to teach, patient,
in humility correcting those who are in opposition, if God perhaps will grant them
repentance, so that they may know the truth.

2 TIMOTHY 2:24–25

Every follower of Jesus is a missionary—and if you're reading this book, that probably means you. Therefore, your life must represent Jesus well. The number-one attack on the message of the gospel of Jesus is false teaching. You do not have to look far to find someone who is watering down the message, adding to the message, or creating a new message altogether. It is incumbent upon you to know the truth and be ready to give a defense of the truth.

Paul warned that when giving a defense of the truth, we must make sure to watch our attitudes. We may say the right biblical things, but if we deliver it with a sour attitude, we may turn people away from Jesus.

Also we must work not to clash severely with unbelievers. We can and need to be bold but without being mean. We can be kind as we present the truths of the gospel: those truths stand on their own merit when they're compared to that which is false. Like the Lord, we must be patient and not pompous as we share the truth. We must not answer opposition in a way that might harm our relationships with others.

Trust the Lord to bring to repentance those with whom you live, work, and play. Ask the Holy Spirit to open the eyes of the blind that they may see the truth of the gospel.

....

Father, help me be patient, articulate, kind, and humble when I share the good
news with people who need to hear it. Amen.

WEEK 45—MONDAY
Charity That Pleases God

"When you do a charitable deed, do not let your left hand know what your right hand is doing, that your charitable deed may be in secret; and your Father who sees in secret will Himself reward you openly."

MATTHEW 6:3–4

Look again at the verses above. You might even read through the three chapters that contain Jesus' Sermon on the Mount. If you do, you'll realize that nowhere in that sermon did Jesus explicitly command His followers to be generous or charitable. Why? Because He likely assumed they already were: "When you do a charitable deed," He began. So instead of issuing a command, Jesus offered principles to guide His followers in a lifestyle of generosity. Specifically, Jesus said that one's giving is to be humble, discreet, and completely uninterested in recognition from others.

Jesus makes it clear that we should not seek praise from others for our generosity because God will reward us publically. Anyone promising us an immediate or tangible return for our generosity in this life is not preaching the gospel of Jesus Christ. The only promise Jesus made was that our heavenly Father is fully aware of our acts of charity and will reward each one in His own time and manner.

This absence of an immediate or tangible reward for doing what is right leaves us with a question to ponder: "Is the approval of my heavenly Father enough for me, or do I require recognition from others as well?"

Father, free me from the trap of seeking the praise of men. Help me know soul-satisfying contentment in simply pleasing You. In the name of Jesus I pray, Amen.

WEEK 45—TUESDAY
What Will Matter Most on the Day of Doom?

The LORD rewarded me according to my righteousness; according to the cleanness of my hands He has recompensed me. For I have kept the ways of the LORD, and have not wickedly departed from my God. For all His judgments were before me, and I did not put away His statutes from me. I was also blameless before Him, and I kept myself from my iniquity. Therefore the LORD has recompensed me according to my righteousness, according to the cleanness of my hands in His sight.

PSALM 18:20–24

At the day of doom, the question will be whether or not you were a doer or a talker. James, the half-brother of Jesus, made a similar point in his epistle: "what does it profit, my brethren, if someone says he has faith but does not have works? Can faith save him? . . . Faith by itself, if it does not have works, is dead" (James 2:14, 17).

James and David, writer of the psalm above, each said that saving faith would manifest itself in a life surrendered to God in active service to Him and others. No one has ever been saved by works, but the saved have always proven their faith by their works.

Furthermore, God constantly rewards faith that acts, does, and serves. The reward may not come in the time and manner we would choose, but the reward is God's guaranteed response to faith in Him.

The greatest reward for our faithfulness will not be fame, wealth, or happiness. It is intimacy with the Creator and Sustainer of the universe.

....

Father, You who know my heart, please give me contentment in the truth that You are my highest reward for living a life of active service to You. Amen.

WEEK 45—WEDNESDAY
How Will We Handle the Persecution?

"Blessed are you when they revile and persecute you, and say all kinds of evil against you falsely for My sake. Rejoice and be exceedingly glad, for great is your reward in heaven, for so they persecuted the prophets who were before you."

MATTHEW 5:11–12

Theologian John Stott once said, "Persecution is simply the clash between two irreconcilable value systems." If this is true, then persecution is unavoidable for a follower of Jesus Christ. After all, our value system is diametrically opposed to the value system of this world. That means persecution is not a matter of *if*, but of *when, how,* and *to what extent.*

Throughout church history—and it's happening around the world today—faithful followers of Jesus have endured unspeakable violence, relentless oppression, and brutal deaths. Because the United States has respected the right of individuals to practice the faith of their choice, American Christians have been insulated from this kind of persecution. But this rare protection could potentially come to an end, and Jesus tells us how to respond properly: with joy and gladness.

Only by having a proper and eternal perspective will we be able to rejoice and be glad when we are persecuted for our faith. Jesus said, "Great is your reward in heaven." In other words, persecution may be all we experience in this life; we may receive no reward until we get to heaven. In the meantime, though, we have the presence of Jesus as our reward. Is that enough for us?

. . . .

Father, please give me contentment in the truth that You are my highest reward for serving You and for being persecuted for my faith in You. In Jesus' name I pray, Amen.

PASTOR JOHN WELBORN, CROSSLINK COMMUNITY CHURCH, HARRISONBURG, VA

WEEK 45—THURSDAY
Are You Ready for Judgment Day?

"Behold I am coming quickly, and My reward is with Me, to give to every one according to his work. I am the Alpha and the Omega, the Beginning and the End, the First and the Last." Blessed are those who do His commandments, that they may have the right to the tree of life, and may enter through the gates into the city.

REVELATION 22:12–14

A recent poll found that eighty-five percent of Americans said they believe in heaven, and more than 87 percent of Americans said they believe they are headed there. So what about the two percent who believe themselves to be headed to a place they don't think really exists?

Besides making us smile, these humorous findings illustrate the amount of confusion surrounding heaven, hell, and judgment. According to Jesus, heaven is a real place. It isn't a product of religious imagination or some pie-in-the-sky fantasy.

Heaven is the place where God dwells and where Jesus sits today at His right hand. As Jesus said, "I go to prepare a place for you. And if I go and prepare a place for you, I will come again and receive you unto Myself; that where I am, there you may be also" (John 14:2–3). Simply put, Jesus is coming back, and we can get ready for His return by—if we haven't already—turning from our sin. Jesus is coming back, and He will judge the lost according to their sins and the saved according to their works. Are you ready?

....

Father, in preparation for Christ's return, please speak to my heart about repentance, faith, and works, and give me the courage to act on what You reveal to me about myself. In the name of Jesus I pray, Amen.

WEEK 45—FRIDAY
Let's Go to War!

"What profit is it to a man if he gains the whole world, and loses his own soul? Or what will a man give in exchange for his soul? For the Son of Man will come in the glory of His Father with His angels, and then He will reward each according to his works."

MATTHEW 16:26–27

Abraham Neuman once said, "The soul is the place where man's supreme and final battles are fought." We cannot afford to relinquish this battle-field of the soul, for that is where the flesh and the spirit go to war every single day of our lives.

Those of us who live in the lavishly affluent culture unique to America may find it quite enticing to "[gain] the whole world" at the expense of our souls. However, the stakes of that battle are very high. If we exchange the gospel of Jesus Christ for the temporary fame, fortune, and personal comfort that the world offers, the effect on our eternal destinies will be catastrophic.

Years ago we often heard it said, "He who dies with the most toys wins." However, the temporary joy that worldly possessions bring will evaporate before the God of the universe and His righteous judgment. Furthermore, it is hardly "winning" to sacrifice an eternity in heaven on the altar of short-lived luxuries on earth.

Clearly, winning the battle of the soul looks a lot less like "he who dies with the most toys wins" and more like Jesus' call to "deny [yourself] and take up [your] cross daily, and follow Me" (Luke 9:23).

....

Father, thank You for opening my eyes to the truth of Your gospel and the reality of heaven. Thank You for rescuing me from the grip of this world. Help me keep that eternal perspective and be ready to celebrate Your return someday. In the name of Jesus I pray, Amen.

WEEK 45—WEEKEND
How to Handle Hatred

"Blessed are you who hunger now, for you shall be filled. Blessed are you who weep now, for you shall laugh. Blessed are you when men hate you, and when they exclude you, and revile you, and cast out your name as evil, for the Son of Man's sake. Rejoice in that day and leap for joy! For indeed your reward is great in heaven, for in like manner their fathers did to the prophets."

LUKE 6:21–23

Pastor and Nazi war victim Dietrich Bonheoffer said, "When Christ calls a man, He bids him come and die." This statement is consistent with what Jesus said in Mark 8:35, "Whoever desires to save his life will lose it, but whoever loses his life for My sake and the gospel's will save it." So we should not be surprised when—as we follow the Person who once said, "If the world hates you, you know that it hated Me before it hated you" (John 15:18)—we encounter opposition.

The Luke 6 verses above come from the Beatitudes section of Jesus' famous Sermon on the Mount. These are some of Christ's promises to the faithful:

If we hunger for God, He will fill us with the Holy Spirit.

If we will mourn over our sins, we will experience the joy of freedom from them.

If we are despised for following Jesus, we should be hope in the promise of heaven.

For every moment of persecution we experience in this life, Jesus promises joy in return. May the presence of Jesus and our hope of heaven enable us to endure the pain, problems, and persecution of this life.

....

Father, give me the courage to embrace the cost—whatever it may be—of following Jesus. In His name I pray, Amen.

THE GIFT OF JESUS

WEEK 46—MONDAY
A Beautiful, Self-Giving Life

I beseech you therefore, brethren, by the mercies of God, that you present your bodies a living sacrifice, holy, acceptable to God, which is your reasonable service. And do not be conformed to this world, but be transformed by the renewing of your mind, that you may prove what is that good and acceptable and perfect will of God.

ROMANS 12:1–2

A Muslim had been coming to our church for several years when he asked a perceptive question: "if God accepts me by grace—if His acceptance of me has nothing to do with how I live—then why not live any way that I want?" We don't have to be a Muslim to ask this question. It's a question everyone asks.

Some people are motivated to live better because they want to be the best people they can be. Advertising today appeals to this kind of motivation with slogans such as "Achieve your personal best! Be beautiful, wealthy, strong, rich, famous!" Other people are motivated to live a good life in the hopes that God will forgive them for the sins they have committed. Even many religions of the world teach: live a good life, and God will be pleased with one's efforts.

The Bible, however, presents another way: Live life not simply for yourself. Live not just hoping for God's acceptance. Instead, live a beautiful, self-giving life because—as the love of Jesus on the cross illustrates—God has accepted you. Live your life in gratitude for Christ's extraordinary mercy. While you should never attempt to pay God back for His grace, you should live with an inner joy and in obedience to Christ because of His great mercy.

．．．

Father, thank You for Your great mercy. How can I not give myself completely to You, who offered Your Son completely to me as a sacrifice for my sins? Amen.

WEEK 46—TUESDAY
Heaven Without God?

The scribe said to [Jesus], "Well said, Teacher. You have spoken the truth, for there is one God, and there is no other but He. And to love Him with all the heart, with all the understanding, with all the soul, and with all the strength, and to love one's neighbor as oneself, is more than all the whole burnt offerings and sacrifices."

MARK 12:32–33

Anna, a woman no older than thirty, listens repeatedly to the gospel message. After many weeks of listening to carefully crafted sermons and months of study, she comes to a conclusion. She approaches the church's pastor and explains that, after careful consideration, she has decided that it is to her benefit that she makes a decision about Jesus. Anna has realized that she doesn't want to experience pain throughout eternity, and she wants the peace that many others have experienced as result of their religious experience.

Years go by, during which she marries and later divorces. All alone now and after a long absence, she reenters the church, and that is when she hears Jesus' teaching that loving God is the most important commandment. As if she were hit by a lightning bolt, Anna realizes that her religious experience has not been authentic. Brokenhearted, she discovers that she has loved God for His gifts rather than loving the Giver Himself.

Do you love God or His gifts? To help you answer that question, consider these: Could you enjoy heaven's streets of gold and gates of pearl if God weren't there? If you could choose an eternity with your family and friends but without God Himself, would you go?

Father, I know that You first loved me in order that I can respond in love to You. Please teach me to love You—and not just Your many blessings and gifts—with all that I am. Amen.

WEEK 46—WEDNESDAY
An Undetected Need

Every high priest taken from among men is appointed for men in things pertaining to God, that he may offer both gifts and sacrifices for sins. He can have compassion on those who are ignorant and going astray, since he himself is also subject to weakness. Because of this he is required as for the people, so also for himself, to offer sacrifices for sins. And no man takes this honor to himself, but he who is called by God.

HEBREWS 5:1–4

Headlines report still one more effort to make peace in the cauldron of boiling animosity in the modern Middle East. Police officers tell of the call they especially hate: a need to respond to domestic violence, where anything can happen. And then there is the heartbreaking suicide rate: on average, one person dies by suicide every forty seconds somewhere in the world.[9]

Alienation—between countries, between spouses, and even within ourselves—is evident throughout the world. Clearly, each person needs to be reconciled to God and made holy.

What is holiness? It is being set aside exclusively for God.

If we could lay everything our hearts desire before us on a table for analysis, we would realize that our hearts want lots of contradictory things. In a word, our hearts are not holy. We are not living exclusively for one purpose: we aren't living for God alone, the purpose for which we were created.

We who are sinful can't approach a holy God. We cannot enter His presence as we are. We need a priest to go before God on our behalf, and there is no priest as qualified as Jesus Christ.

. . . .

Father, I am humbled to be reconciled to You through Jesus Christ. Enable me more and more each day to live for You alone, to live a holy life, a life set apart for You. Amen.

WEEK 46—THURSDAY
Can You Open the Door?

It was necessary that the copies of the things in the heavens should be purified with these, but the heavenly things themselves with better sacrifices than these. For Christ has not entered the holy places made with hands, which are copies of the true, but into heaven itself, now to appear in the presence of God for us.

HEBREWS 9:23–24

Peter's impeccable grades enable him to graduate *summa cum laude* from one of our nation's best schools. Carissa's fledgling acting career takes off when she suddenly lands a starring role in a successful movie. Many doors open to both of these people.

We spend much of our lives seeking open doors, looking for opportunities for our careers or our social lives, and there are various keys for each. But what about the door of heaven? Will it open for us? What kind of key does it take?

One day you will stand before a pure and holy God. Among other reactions, you may realize that throughout your life you have focused on your happiness, and you are sharply aware of the immense gulf between you and God. Before the raw presence of God, you realize fully and finally just how very different He is from you.

Only One can open the door of heaven. Only One has the key that allows access to the very presence of God. And it is only through Him—it is only through the self-sacrifice of Jesus, the Great High Priest—that you and I can enter into the very presence of God.

....

Father, only Your Son has the ability to open the door of heaven for me—and He has done that. I praise You for Your grace and Your love! Amen.

Week 46—Friday
Extra Payments and a Wasted Cross

Every priest stands ministering daily and offering repeatedly the same sacrifices, which can never take away sins. But this Man, after He had offered one sacrifice for sins forever, sat down at the right hand of God, from that time waiting till His enemies are made His footstool. For by one offering He has perfected forever those who are being sanctified.

HEBREWS 10:11–14

It was a little more than a year ago that we paid off my wife's car. It was the most expensive car we had ever bought, and it was the perfect family vehicle for us. After we spent four years making monthly payments, the car was completely paid for. After we made the last payment, the bank sent us the title to the car.

If, when the next month rolled around, I authorized the bank to withdraw the amount of the monthly car payment from our account, you'd think I was foolish. People don't make extra car payments. Once a car is paid for, the hard-earned cash goes toward something else.

Just as you would question me about extra car payments, I want to question you about why you are trying so hard to earn God's acceptance and ignoring Jesus' grace. Why are you trying to be your own savior? Open your eyes and see the amazing grace of God. Jesus offered Himself as the complete payment for your sins.

Father, I want to know Your grace and rest in Your acceptance of me. Remind me often that I obey Your commands to show You my love, not to earn Your love. I am deeply humbled by and grateful for Your grace. Amen.

Week 46—Weekend
Visible Worship

By Him let us continually offer the sacrifice of praise to God, that is, the fruit of our lips, giving thanks to His name. But do not forget to do good and to share, for with such sacrifices God is well pleased.

HEBREWS 13:15–16

Look again at the passage above and follow its logic. Because of Jesus' sacrifice for us sinners, we experience God's great love. In response to His sacrifice, we are to praise God and share with others.

In light of what Jesus' sacrifice means to us—forgiveness, adoption in God's family, abundant life, eternal life—how could we do anything but live a life of constant gratitude to Him? The primary way to show our gratitude is to praise Him, and praise is simply bragging about what we love or enjoy. We recommend restaurants after a great meal, and we wear our favorite NFL player's jersey on game day. Praise is a natural thing to do when we love someone or something. May it truly become second nature to praise Jesus once we have experienced His mercy.

But Jesus' sacrifice also calls for us to demonstrate that our treasure is in heaven. Because we have experienced mercy, we then extend mercy to the Bible's vulnerable quartet: the widows, the fatherless, the immigrants, and the poor (Zechariah 7:10–11). People who truly experience mercy cannot help but extend mercy to others.

When you offer sacrifices of praise and service, God is pleased with you.

....

Father, in gratitude for Your grace, forgiveness, and love, I offer You both the song of my heart and the actions of my hands. Amen.

Week 47—Monday
The Necessary and the Best

As for God, His way is perfect; the word of the LORD is proven; He is a shield to all who trust in Him.

PSALM 18:30

O ur son has played sports since he was ten, and he is now in his final season of college football. Every team he played for supplied the *necessary* equipment, but it was not necessarily the *best* equipment. That's why his mother and I always purchased his helmet and shoulder pads. We wanted him to have state-of-the art protection that met the highest standards of quality and provided the greatest degree of protection. Of course we parents haven't always done everything right, but we always did whatever we could to protect our children from harm.

Just as our son needs protection on the football field, we need protection in life, and the psalmist declared that God is our Shield and Protector. Unlike the efforts of earthly parents, His way for us—His children—is perfect. He has always done everything right. He never fails. His Word is true, and everything He says will come to pass in exactly the way He says it will. Our God is trustworthy and dependable, all the time and in every situation. Because He is perfect in every way, we can trust in Him. He is indeed our Shield of protection, and we could not have a better one.

When you face uncertainty, fearful situations, and even real danger, you may wonder if you need to upgrade your shield to something bigger, better, or stronger. But with God as your Shield, you can do no better. You can trust Him. He will never let you down.

....

Father, thank You for Your hand of protection over me today. You are my Shield, you have never failed me, and I trust in You. Amen.

DR. DAVID FLEMING, CHAMPION FOREST BAPTIST CHURCH, HOUSTON, TX

WEEK 47—TUESDAY
A Shield That Surrounds Us

You, O LORD, are a shield for me, my glory and the One who lifts up my head. I cried to the LORD with my voice, and He heard me from His holy hill.

PSALM 3:3–4

I watch people riding motorcycles on the open road, hair flying in the wind, and, they're seemingly carefree. It looks like fun, but I will not be joining them. One reason is that I live in Houston where there are not many open roads to ride and there are far too many other cars to share the road with. While I might like to experience that feeling of freedom, I need a little more metal surrounding me to feel safe and truly to be protected from danger all around.

The Lord is a Shield of protection for us. As our Shield, He is for us and all around us. The psalmist celebrated this fact that we are surrounded by God's almighty hand of protection. He is our Glory, meaning "victory," and the Lifter of our head, meaning "encourager." Because He is our all-encompassing Shield of protection, we can live in and move through this dangerous world with confidence and courage.

David faced many dangerous situations, and we will too. But the Lord is with us, and He hears us when we cry out to Him for help. As our Shield, the Lord surrounds us and protects us.

If you are feeling vulnerable and insecure, call out to Jesus. He is with you, and He will lift you up.

....

Lord, You are a Shield for me. Surrounded by Your protection, I am safe and secure. Restore my courage; rebuild my confidence. I am blessed to be cradled in Your loving arms and protected by Your almighty power. Amen.

WEEK 47—WEDNESDAY
Staying Behind the Shield

The LORD God is a sun and shield; the LORD will give grace and glory; no good thing will He withhold from those who walk uprightly. O LORD of hosts, blessed is the man who trusts in You!

PSALM 84:11–12

I once had the opportunity to preach in Kenya, and toward the end of the trip, I had the experience of a lifetime. Camera in hand, I went on an African safari into the Maasai Mara. What I didn't count on was sleeping on the ground in a tent each night in an area where lions and tigers lived. But our guide built a fire in the middle of the camp, and a Maasai warrior kept watch throughout the night. I stayed close to both! And between the light of the fire, the Maasai's protection, and the Lord's grace, I slept like a baby.

The psalmist also knew the Lord's protection. He said that the Lord is "a sun and shield," and the Lord does indeed light up the darkest night and keep watch over us. When we move, He goes before us and protects us. By His grace, He gives us everything we need to walk in a right relationship with Him. Trusting in Him, staying close to Him, and obeying Him are the keys to both a life of abundant provision and His almighty hand of protection.

It's not surprising that Christians get into trouble when they venture out on their own. If you have wandered away from His light, repent and return. The Lord will be gracious to you, and He will restore you. Stay very close to Jesus, your Sun and your Shield!

....

Lord, You are my Sun and Shield. Thank You for the blessing of Your provision and protection. Guide and direct my steps today. Help me to walk with You. Amen.

DR. DAVID FLEMING, CHAMPION FOREST BAPTIST CHURCH, HOUSTON, TX

Week 47—Thursday
A Wall of Protection

He shall cover you with His feathers, and under His wings you shall take refuge; His truth shall be your shield and buckler. You shall not be afraid of the terror by night, nor of the arrow that flies by day . . . A thousand may fall at your side, and ten thousand at your right hand; but it shall not come near you.

PSALM 91:4–5, 7

As a quarterback, our son depends on his offensive linemen to protect him. While playing, the other team is charging toward him with one thought in mind: sack the quarterback! His offensive linemen form a wall of protection to keep the defenders out and the quarterback safe. We are grateful for those young men and for the fact that the wall usually holds. But even on their best day, the wall occasionally collapses, and the quarterback is definitely in harm's way.

Psalm 91 gives us a beautiful picture of God's intimate, sufficient, and never-failing protection. He covers us with His feathers when we take refuge under His wings. God's faithfulness is the source of our security; it forms a shield around us, and it functions as a wall of protection behind which we can hide. That is why we need not fear what we know or what we cannot see.

We feel vulnerable at times because we are. In this fallen world, bad things do happen to good people. But we are not alone. The Lord is our Shield, and we can trust in His providential, unfailing care for us.

....

Lord, thank You that I am safe and secure, surrounded by the Shield of Your protection. I will not be afraid. I will trust in You. Amen.

Week 47—Friday
Enough Good Sense

He stores up sound wisdom for the upright; He is a shield to those who walk uprightly; He guards the paths of justice, and preserves the way of His saints. Then you will understand righteousness and justice, equity and every good path.

Proverbs 2:7–9

Growing up in Florida, we could pretty much always count on an afternoon rain shower to cool off a hot summer day. Usually we played on in spite of it, and when we did, my dad said we lacked the good sense to come in out of the rain. But sometimes that gentle rain would turn into a fierce thunderstorm. When it did, our good sense kicked in, and we scrambled for shelter. Suddenly, taking cover was the right thing to do.

God "stores up sound wisdom for"—He gives good sense to—those who are willing to exercise it. Wisdom is more than intelligence. Wisdom is the exercise of good judgment and the ability to do the right thing every time. As we make wise and godly decisions, the Lord guards our path and preserves our ways. He is like a shield that protects those who have the good sense to carry it into battle.

We have two daughters away from home. We were apprehensive about sending them off to college, but we raised them "in the nurture and admonition of the Lord" (Ephesians 6:4 KJV). They have good, godly sense, and we know they will make wise decisions. We also know that God will be their shield and protection.

How is your good sense? Could you use a little more wisdom today? Go ahead and ask Him for it now.

....

Lord, thank You for the wisdom You provide me so I can make good decisions. Thank You too for being my Shield of protection today and always. Amen.

DR. DAVID FLEMING, CHAMPION FOREST BAPTIST CHURCH, HOUSTON, TX

WEEK 47—WEEKEND
Worthy of Our Trust

Every word of God is pure; He is a shield to those who put their trust in Him. Do not add to His words, lest He rebuke you, and you be found a liar.

PROVERBS 30:5–6

I ride a mountain bike. And I wear a helmet. We may not have the Rocky Mountains in Houston, but we have plenty of dangerous roots and rocks to ride over. I was racing through the woods one day, and suddenly the bike stopped. I went flying over the handlebars and landed on my head. Fortunately, I wore a good helmet, a tested helmet certified as reliable. I'd paid more for it, and that day I was glad I did.

Proverbs 30:5 tells us that "every word of God is pure." That means that every promise He has made has been tested and certified as reliable. So if the Lord tells us that He is a shield to those who put their trust in Him, to those who depend on Him, then we can indeed trust in Him. His words are true, and His promises can be trusted. You are His, and He has promised to protect you always!

I will not get on my bike without a helmet on my head. Nor will I get out of bed without putting my trust in Jesus and declaring my dependence on Him. How about you? Jesus is your shield. You can always trust in Him.

....

Lord Jesus, thank You for watching over me today and every day. Thank You for always showing Yourself faithful, reliable, and true to Your promises. I put my trust in You. Amen.

WEEK 48—MONDAY
Be Prepared

"A disciple is not above his teacher, nor a servant above his master. It is enough for a disciple that he be like his teacher, and a servant like his master. If they have called the master of the house Beelzebub, how much more will they call those of his household! Therefore do not fear them. For there is nothing covered that will not be revealed, and hidden that will not be known."

MATTHEW 10:24–26

My wife, Tonya, a teacher by occupation, asks her students' parents this question: "are you trying to prepare your child for the road ahead, or are you trying to prepare the road ahead for your child?"

We often see parents running ahead trying to repair the potholes so that their child won't experience any discomfort. The problem with that method of parenting is that the day will inevitably come when the parent (teacher) is not around to smooth things over for the child (disciple). All good teachers will do anything they can to equip those under their tutelage to be prepared for the future.

Jesus recognized that He would not be with His students on this earth forever. So Jesus warned the disciples that there would be bumps ahead and that they would face the same false accusations that He had faced. The Master Teacher prepared His followers for what they would encounter. As Jesus' modern-day followers, we should not be surprised when the world accuses, rejects, and persecutes us. When that happens, we can find comfort in the truth that Christ shared: a day coming when all truth is revealed.

Lord, help me to recognize and even anticipate the potholes in the path of my life. Help me to teach those whom You have entrusted to me to navigate—if not avoid—trouble and to stay the course. Amen.

REV. TIM SIZEMORE, LIGHTHOUSE BAPTIST CHURCH, MACON, GA

WEEK 48—TUESDAY
The Perfect Teacher—and a Difficult Lesson

Now behold, one came and said to Him, "Good Teacher, what good thing shall I do that I may have eternal life?" So He said to him, "Why do you call Me good? No one is good but One, that is, God. But if you want to enter into life, keep the commandments."

MATTHEW 19:16–17

Having played and coached high school football, I can assure you that few things in this world are more exciting than the experience of Friday night lights.

The small Christian school where I coached never seemed to have an adequate number of players to be successful. Many students wanted to be on the team and reap the benefits that come along with it, but few loved the game enough to make the heavy sacrifices necessary to wear the jersey.

Like most of the students at that school, the young man in this passage had a real desire for something, but a misunderstanding kept him from achieving it. Specifically, this young man wanted to live forever, but he misunderstood the meaning of eternal life. Christ laid the foundation for the lesson by letting him know that only God is without sin. Notice the words that our Teacher so masterfully chose: "if you want to enter into life." In order to *enter* something, you must first be *outside* of it. And this man was.

This young man had all that life could offer him, and he wanted simply to extend his current experience for a similar eternity. But Jesus explained that true life is not of this world at all. In verse 21 we see that eternal life required more than this rich young ruler was willing to give.

....

Lord, give me the desire and the strength to lay down my life—my very self— daily to follow You. Amen.

WEEK 48—WEDNESDAY
Priestly Divas

"[The scribes and the Pharisees love] greetings in the marketplaces, and to be called by men, 'Rabbi, Rabbi.' But you, do not be called 'Rabbi'; for One is your Teacher, the Christ, and you are all brethren. Do not call anyone on earth your father; for One is your Father, He who is in heaven. And do not be called teachers; for One is your Teacher, the Christ. But he who is greatest among you shall be your servant. And whoever exalts himself will be humbled, and he who humbles himself will be exalted."

MATTHEW 23:7–12

A saying in the South goes something like this: "I wish I could buy him for what he is worth and sell him for what he thinks he is worth."

The scribes and Pharisees of Jesus' day thought they were worth a lot. Jesus said they had come to enjoy the attention of "greetings in the marketplace" and being called "Rabbi." Such special recognition contributed to their thinking more highly of themselves than was warranted.

But rather than judge, let's realize how easily a position of authority can inflate our opinion of ourselves. That's one reason why Jesus called us to be humble. All that we have is from God, so why would we arrogantly act as if we have accomplished anything on our own? What did anyone do to deserve being born of a sound mind and healthy body, in a country where freedoms are many and poverty is low? Regardless of how many people seek our advice or how many Twitter followers we may have, all we have, all we know, and all we are come from Christ. Jesus is our Teacher.

....

Lord, give me the humility and the vision to see around me the constant reminders that I am nothing without You. Amen.

REV. TIM SIZEMORE, LIGHTHOUSE BAPTIST CHURCH, MACON, GA

WEEK 48—THURSDAY
Getting on Our Knees

"You call Me Teacher and Lord, and you say well, for so I am. If I then, your Lord and Teacher, have washed your feet, you also ought to wash one another's feet."

JOHN 13:13–14

O ne of a football coach's most gut-wrenching tasks is the pre-game speech. All of the preparation has been done. He has spent countless hours teaching his players all that he can. To the best of his ability, he has prepared them for battle. No more practicing plays or running drills. This speech is the last opportunity the coach has to influence his team. He must capitalize on this chance to communicate the things he wants them most to remember as they battle the enemy.

Like that football coach, in the passage above Jesus was in His last hours with His team. Jesus was well aware that the moment of His arrest was near, that this very night the apostles would experience chaos, that they were about to clash with the enemy. Christ wanted to remind His followers of teachings they could fall back on when He was no longer present with them to give them direction.

Knowing that pride is one of man's greatest enemies, Jesus spent a few minutes reminding His disciples of the divine call to serve. As Jesus' followers today, we are to serve as many people as we can, not rule over as many as possible. We are to follow the example of our Savior: Jesus came to serve, not to be served.

....

My Teacher and my Lord, thank You for Your daily instruction in my life. Keep me mindful that it's difficult to wash someone's feet if I don't get on my knees first. Amen.

Week 48—Friday
We Are the Body

You are the body of Christ, and members individually. And God has appointed these in the church: first apostles, second prophets, third teachers, after that miracles, then gifts of healings, helps, administrations, varieties of tongues. Are all apostles? Are all prophets? Are all teachers? Are all workers of miracles? Do all have gifts of healings? Do all speak with tongues? Do all interpret? But earnestly desire the best gifts. And yet I show you a more excellent way.

1 Corinthians 12:27–31

My father currently has forty stents carefully placed inside his heart to maintain adequate blood flow. We can't live without an effective heart, and that fact holds true about other vital organs, like our lungs. Although some injuries may not be fatal, our effectiveness would certainly be diminished with, for instance, the amputation of a limb.

Likewise, the body of Christ functions in a fashion similar to the human body. (It should really be no surprise, given the fact that God created both bodies.) In 1 Corinthians 13, Paul made the point that even if we gain the position we much desire but do not love others, then we have accomplished nothing. God created each of us with particular gifts for the purpose of the effectiveness of the church, not so that we could boast.

How helpful to his body would it be if my father's doctor decided to replace his heart with a perfectly good lung? How effective would the church be if everyone tried to function as the pastor? Likewise, we must all embrace our own indivual roles in the body of Christ.

....

Lord, I need You to help me respond to Your calling to me and not to Your calling to other people. Then, Lord, help me to serve in love. Amen.

REV. TIM SIZEMORE, LIGHTHOUSE BAPTIST CHURCH, MACON, GA

WEEK 48—WEEKEND
The Blind Leading the Blind

"Can the blind lead the blind? Will they not both fall into the ditch? A disciple is not above his teacher, but everyone who is perfectly trained will be like his teacher."

LUKE 6:39–40

Years ago I attended a class at a drug rehabilitation facility run by the Georgia Baptist Convention. The class was required for anyone who wanted to visit the residents. The one thing I remember from that class was the director's teaching on this passage.

The director talked about how often addicts get involved in relationships with other addicts, always intending to help one another, and defending that plan by saying that only addicts can understand one another's struggles. But, the director continued, these relationships never end well. They result in both addicts returning to the grips of substance abuse, both individuals falling into the ditch.

Jesus' point with this teaching was that a student can only expect to be like his or her teacher. It would stand to reason, then, that I would seek a teacher who represents the person I strive to resemble. I know a lot of people who could help me improve my golf game, and many individuals could teach me to be a better writer and scholar. But Jesus is the One I turn to in my efforts to be a better Christian.

I am blessed to have spiritual mentors in my life, but I make sure that they are closer to God than I am. I want them to point me to the Master, and they can only do that if they know the way to Him.

As valuable as my mentors are, in the end Jesus is my Teacher.

....

Thank You, Jesus, for the perfect instruction You offer me and for having patience with me even when I struggle. Amen.

THE GIFT OF JESUS

WEEK 49—MONDAY
Treasures on Display

"'If you will indeed obey My voice and keep My covenant, then you shall be a special treasure to Me above all people; for all the earth is Mine. And you shall be to Me a kingdom of priests and a holy nation.' These are the words which you shall speak to the children of Israel."

EXODUS 19:5–6

I srael has been—and always will be—the chosen people of God. This promise from God, given to Moses, was contingent upon the Israelites' obedience and faithfulness to Yahweh. Their faithfulness and obedience make them a special treasure to God. By grace through faith in Jesus Christ, those of us who are Gentiles have been grafted into this covenant of blessing, with all the privileges and rights as the people of God. In light of this truth we, too, are special treasures to God. We are "a chosen race, a royal priesthood, a holy nation, a people for his own possession" (1 Peter 2:9 ESV).

The apostle Paul said we are "his workmanship, created in Christ Jesus for good works" (Ephesians 2:10 ESV). This is possible only because of Jesus! We are the treasures, God's masterpieces, that have been set on display for the world to see.

What is the purpose of a masterpiece? To reflect the glory and exhibit the good care of its master. As one of God's masterpieces, are you reflecting His glory? As His treasure, are you living in such a way that your life shines bright with the glory of God in a world of darkness? Today strive to be a Philippians 2:15 believer—"shine like stars in the world" (HCSB).

Father, thank You for making me one of Your special treasures. Help me to shine brightly in this world of darkness—and to do so for Your glory. Amen.

PASTOR KELLY BULLARD, TEMPLE BAPTIST CHURCH, FAYETTEVILLE, NC

WEEK 49—TUESDAY
Chosen and Loved

"You are a holy people to the LORD your God; the LORD your God has chosen you to be a people for Himself, a special treasure above all the peoples on the face of the earth. The LORD did not set His love on you nor choose you because you were more in number than any other people, for you were the least of all peoples; but because the LORD loves you, and because He would keep the oath which He swore to your fathers, the LORD has brought you out with a mighty hand, and redeemed you from the house of bondage, from the hand of Pharaoh king of Egypt."

DEUTERONOMY 7:6–8

Everyone likes to be chosen. Boys dream of being chosen for the football team. Young women desire to be chosen as a wife. Adults in the workplace long to be chosen for a job promotion. Being chosen feels good.

God chose the line of Abraham—the nation of Israel—to be His people, and He set them apart to be unlike other nations. Why did He choose them? Not because of anything they did, but simply because He loved them.

This truth applies to your life as well. Like Israel, you have been chosen by God (Ephesians 1:3–5). And why did He choose you? He chose you not because of anything you've done but simply because He loves you!

Regardless of your present circumstances, remember that you are chosen by God and loved by Him. Jesus reiterated in the New Testament, "You did not choose Me, but I chose you" (John 15:16). You did not do anything to earn God's favor, but you are a recipient of His blessings. Spend some time today thanking the Lord that you have been chosen and not overlooked!

....

Thank You, Father, for choosing me and loving me! Amen.

Week 49—Wednesday
The Apple of My Eye

My son, keep my words, and treasure my commands within you. Keep my commands and live, and my law as the apple of your eye. Bind them on your fingers; write them on the tablet of your heart.

PROVERBS 7:1–3

I am always intrigued by the origins of phrases and clichés. Have you ever wondered where the phrase *apple of the eye* originated?

Some scholars have credited this phrase to Shakespeare's *A Midsummer Night's Dream*, but the truth is it originated long before Shakespeare. In fact, its first usage is found in Deuteronomy 32:10 where Moses "spoke in the hearing of all the assembly of Israel the words of this song" (31:30). The phrase is also used in Psalm 17:8 and Zechariah 2:8. In Proverbs 7:1 (above), Solomon used this phrase to describe our ideal attitude toward God's commands: "[his] law should be as the apple of your eye."

Just as the apple of your eye, whatever it may be, is pleasant and adds joy to your life, obeying the commands of God should bring joy. Walking in obedience to the commands of God brings peace, joy, and His blessings. Walking in disobedience brings burdens and cursings (Deuteronomy 28:15–69).

Are you treasuring—and obeying—the commands of God? Are they the apple of your eye?

....

Father, help me to treasure Your Word and walk in obedience to Your commands. May I find my delight and joy in You. Amen.

PASTOR KELLY BULLARD, TEMPLE BAPTIST CHURCH, FAYETTEVILLE, NC

WEEK 49—THURSDAY
A New Heart

"A good tree does not bear bad fruit, nor does a bad tree bear good fruit. For every tree is known by its own fruit. For men do not gather figs from thorns, nor do they gather grapes from a bramble bush. A good man out of the good treasure of his heart brings forth good; and an evil man out of the evil treasure of his heart brings forth evil. For out of the abundance of the heart his mouth speaks."

LUKE 6:43–45

As a pastor I often counsel people struggling with anger, temptation, pride, jealousy, envy, and so forth. The truth is that on some level all of us deal with these issues. While these may seem like problems, they are actually symptoms of a much deeper issue—a sinful heart.

Someone once said, "What's down in the well comes up in the bucket," and Solomon understood this truth. In Proverbs 4:23 he wrote, "Watch over your heart with all diligence, for from it flow the springs of life" (NASB). The picture here is of guarding or placing fortresses around our hearts. While this is good to do and can be done by abiding in God's Word and living lives of prayer, we must be sure that we are not just watching over and protecting wicked hearts. The truth is that we need new hearts!

As David said in Psalm 51:10, "Create in me a clean heart." The beauty of the gospel is that God is in the heart transplant business (Ezekiel 36:26; 2 Corinthians 5:17)! Through Jesus Christ, we can have new hearts and live in ways that bear good fruit to the glory of God.

....

Father, create within me a clean heart. Enable me to bear good fruit for Your glory in every aspect of my life. Amen.

Week 49—Friday
Where's Your Heart?

"Do not lay up for yourselves treasures on earth, where moth and rust destroy and where thieves break in and steal; but lay up for yourselves treasures in heaven, where neither moth nor rust destroys and where thieves do not break in and steal. For where your treasure is, there your heart will be also."

MATTHEW 6:19–21

David Livingstone was a medical missionary to Africa. After serving and ministering among the village people of Africa, Livingstone died of malaria and other medical complications. The villagers were so fond of Livingstone that upon his death, they removed his heart from his body and buried it under a tall Mvula tree, to be near the people whom he loved so greatly. His body was shipped to London for burial at Westminster Abbey.[10]

Jesus said, "Where your treasure is there your heart will be also." Our most treasured possessions and our deepest desires are inseparable. If your heart were to be buried in the place you love most, where would it be? Would it be buried in your wallet or safe deposit box? Would it be buried among all of your possessions? Are your treasures on earth or in heaven?

Set your heart and affections on the things of God—things that have eternal significance. It has been said all that matters in this life are God, His Word, and the souls of people. Investing in these will give your life eternal significance and God's reward!

....

Father, set my heart and affections for what matters most in life. Help me to love You more, treasure Your Word, and make an eternal impact in the lives of other people. Amen.

WEEK 49—WEEKEND
Living with an Open Hand

Jesus said to [the rich young ruler], "If you want to be perfect, go, sell what you have and give to the poor, and you will have treasure in heaven; and come, follow Me." But when the young man heard that saying, he went away sorrowful, for he had great possessions.

MATTHEW 19:21–22

John Wesley, the founder of Methodism, was away from home one day when his house burned to the ground.

When others shared the news with him of what had happened, Wesley said, "That's impossible. You see, I don't own a house. God gave me a place to live in. I only managed that house for Him. If He didn't put the fire out, then that's His problem. He'll have to put me somewhere else."[11]

If your house burned to the ground, how would you react? If your car were totaled or your boat sank, how would you react? Your attitude during situations like these reveals much about your walk with the Lord and your trust in Him.

Are you living with a tight grip on your possessions, or are you living with an open hand, realizing that all you have belongs to God?

....

Father, help me to live my life with an open hand, not holding too tightly to the things I have, but living and giving generously so I can be a blessing to others. Amen.

Week 50—Monday
Jesus' Truth Frees Us from Sin

"If you abide in My word, you are My disciples indeed. And you shall know the truth, and the truth shall make you free."

JOHN 8:31–32

Many people believe that personal liberty is being able to choose freely matters like vocations, possessions, and lifestyle, but Scripture shows that genuine freedom is found only in Jesus and His truth. Living according to the whims of fallen humanity is actually a form of slavish bondage (Romans 6:16), but Jesus offers real freedom (John 8:36).

By accepting Christ and His truth, one can experience liberty from sin and its accompanying consequences (Romans 8:2). The truth in view here involves the realities concerning God, creation, and man, as detailed in Scripture. This truth is given through God's revelation of His Son, Jesus (John 1:14; 14:6).

We are most free when we align our lives with God's truth, because we have been created in the image of God in order to enjoy Him and glorify Him forever (Genesis 1:26–27; Matthew 5:16).

Have you foolishly followed after a false form of freedom by seeking an identity apart from the truth of Jesus? Has a hobby, a habit, a secret sin, pride, an inappropriate relationship, or a numbing addiction robbed you of the liberating life of the gospel? Understand that true freedom comes when you live according to the realities of who you are, who God is, and how He has created you to live. Live by Jesus' truth, and you will live a liberated life!

....

Father, thank You that I can be free through Your truth. Help me to experience this freedom. Amen.

DR. PATRICK LATHAM, FIRST BAPTIST CHURCH LAWTON-FORT SILL, LAWTON, OK

WEEK 50—TUESDAY
Jesus' Truth Changes Us for His Glory

For the word of the LORD is right, and all His work is done in truth. He loves
righteousness and justice; the earth is full of the goodness of the LORD.

PSALM 33:4–5

Jesus' truth is dynamic and powerful (Hebrews 4:12). When we cherish His truth, it can effect extraordinary change in the ways we live.

Our personal holiness is obtained positionally at the moment of salvation (Romans 3:21–22), but believers are called to pursue holiness throughout their Christian journeys (1 Peter 1:15–16). At the end of the day, all righteous living is a result of a heart devoted to God's truth (Psalm 119:9).

The psalmist spoke of this in his description of the Word of the Lord. After describing the Bible as trustworthy and dependable, he remarked on how the Lord "loves righteousness and justice." Together, these two terms call us to do what is right in the eyes of the Lord, to live a holy life.

Since our Creator is the God of truth and since He loves righteousness, His truth will naturally lead us to live holy lives. Second Timothy 3:16 teaches that Scripture provides "instruction in righteousness."

If you want to live rightly, regularly ingest God's Word. His truth will enlighten your mind as well as show you the path of moral and spiritual living. As God's principles and precepts change you, He will subsequently use your changed life as a light for His glory in a dark world.

....

Father, help me to read, to understand, and to obey Your Word so that You
might be glorified in my life. Amen.

WEEK 50—WEDNESDAY
Jesus' Truth Helps Us in Adversity

Teach me Your way, O LORD; I will walk in Your truth; unite my heart to fear Your name. I will praise You, O Lord my God, with all my heart, and I will glorify Your name forevermore. For great is Your mercy toward me, and You have delivered my soul from the depths of Sheol. . . . You, O Lord, are a God full of compassion, and gracious, longsuffering and abundant in mercy and truth.

PSALM 86:11–13, 15

Psalm 86 contains a prayer King David possibly offered while he was on the run, fleeing from his treasonous and murderous son Absalom. In this psalm, David expressed his desire for spiritual restoration.

Do you, like me, sometimes find yourself praying similar prayers? One of my most repeated supplications is this: "Dear Lord, help me to love You and live for You."

But I often wrestle with this matter: what can I do to encourage my heart to change? David's prayer in Psalm 86 contains an important insight. After declaring his commitment, he recognized that all of his abilities to live devotedly were derived from the character of God—His mercy, compassion, truth, and grace.

Maybe you feel like you can't live fully devoted to the Lord. Perhaps you have experienced moral failure, the betrayal of a loved one, difficulties at work, or family problems. David faced all of these hardships and more, yet he still sought after God.

Less-than-ideal life circumstances can make spiritual energy seem an impossible ideal. Yet David's testimony shows that our abilities to live for God aren't based on our track records or merits. Instead, our abilities to live for God are founded on His truth and mercy.

Father, help me to grow in the experience of Your grace! Amen.

WEEK 50—THURSDAY
Jesus' Truth Enlightens Us with Wisdom

"Everyone practicing evil hates the light and does not come to the light, lest his deeds should be exposed. But he who does the truth comes to the light, that his deeds may be clearly seen, that they have been done in God."

JOHN 3:20–21

During my college years, I waited tables to pay for tuition. That experience taught me—among other things—that restaurants often keep the lighting low to hide crumbs on the carpet and other undesirable sights. Darkness masks things, but light exposes.

Such is true in the spiritual realm as well. In his writings, the apostle John used the concepts of light and darkness as metaphors for truth and error, right and wrong. Recounting how Jesus came to live among humanity, he used images of light and darkness to describe how many rejected God's Son.

People who live with themselves as the guiding principle of life don't want to be convicted of their ungodliness, so they stay away from the light of Jesus. When people do draw near to God's Son, they experience the Lord's gracious illumination (1 John 1:7).

People who refuse the truth of Jesus stay in spiritual darkness. They live unaware of the way their sin robs them of the real life and joy found in living by God's truth (Proverbs 4:19).

Don't live in the darkness of deception. Let Jesus turn His spiritual light on in your life. Regularly look to Him and His Word for truth. He will help you see yourself, Himself, and all of life according to His divine realities.

....

Father, thank You for the illuminating power of Your Word. Help me to live in its light. Amen.

WEEK 50—FRIDAY
Jesus' Truth Equips Us for Worship

"The hour is coming, and now is, when the true worshipers will worship the Father in spirit and truth; for the Father is seeking such to worship Him. God is Spirit, and those who worship Him must worship in spirit and truth."

JOHN 4:23–24

During His ministry, Jesus introduced a new type of worship. Both the Samaritans and Jews of His day debated the best place to worship God (John 4:20). For Christ, geography wasn't really important. Spirit and truth mattered most.

According to Scripture, the Lord is a Spirit, and He cannot be isolated to a certain locale, as religious leaders of Jesus' day assumed. Further, when people trust in God's Son for salvation, they receive His Spirit (John 3:6). Thus they receive the presence of God.

Truth is also essential to worship: praise of God is to take place in light of His revelation of Himself. Worship that isn't grounded in God's Word isn't real worship. Believers in Christ have continual access to the Father. In all situations, at all times, and in all places, they can worship Him through His Spirit and in His truth.

Are you availing yourself of the opportunity of personal and corporate worship? Are God's Spirit and His truth at the heart of your praise? Or has your worship became dull, meaningless, and stale, guided mostly by form, style, schedule, or cultural custom? Make sure that both the Spirit of God and the Word of God fuel your worship. God's truth equips you for worship, so seek Him according to His precepts.

....

Father, help me to learn to worship You through Your Spirit and Your truth. Amen.

WEEK 50—WEEKEND
Jesus' Truth Saves Us from Sin

"I am the way, the truth, and the life. No one comes to the Father except through Me."

JOHN 14:6

When referring to Himself as "the way," Jesus identified Himself as God's special path to Him. Jesus wasn't just a good teacher, leader, example, or person. He was God's only Son, who died as a perfect Sacrifice to make a way—the only way—for imperfect people to enter into a relationship with God.

No other leader, so-called prophet, religious figure, political authority, cultural icon, prolific author, or philosopher has ever done such. Jesus alone paved a path so that sinners might travel to their loving heavenly Father.

Jesus described His "way" with the words *truth* and *life*. In other words, Jesus is the only way to God. Fallen humanity supposes many paths to God, but only one true path to God exists (Acts 4:12).

Finally, the word *life* shows that Jesus' way contains a quality found nowhere in any other worldview. Our Lord didn't just teach about God; He actually provided life—abundant life—as God (John 10:10).

Are you trusting in Jesus as "the way, the truth, and the life," or have you become distracted by the busyness of life? Refresh your perspective concerning the Lord. Seek to walk in His way and to live His life. Flee religion that is based on merely doing good. Radically commit to your relationship with the One who gives real life.

....

Father, thank You that You have provided the only path for salvation and enabled me to recognize it. Help me to walk in Jesus' way. Amen.

WEEK 51—MONDAY
Knowing the Word Is Knowing Jesus

In the beginning was the Word, and the Word was with God, and the Word was God.
He was in the beginning with God. All things were made through Him, and without
Him nothing was made that was made. In Him was life, and the life was the light of
men.

JOHN 1:1–4

Recently a man came by my office who wanted my counsel about a particular situation. As the conversation unfolded, he started telling me about one of the sweetest times in his life. Interestingly enough, it was perhaps the most difficult time as well.

My friend had been diagnosed with tuberculosis and was in the hospital for more than a year. While he was there, he developed a strong love for reading the Bible. Each night the lights were to be turned out at 9:00 so everyone could go to sleep. However, his desire to read the Bible was so strong that many nights he would go into the bathroom with his Bible so he could continue to read. He said to me, "You know the story about Moses's face having to be covered up because it was glowing? Well, that's how I felt" (Exodus 34:29–35).

What turbulent situation, if any, are you facing right now? Go to the Word! Get to know Jesus and allow His Word, His Person, to fill you and shine through you. To know the Word is to know Jesus.

....

Lord Jesus, develop in me a deep thirst for knowing Your Word. Please give me
a passion to know You! Amen.

JAY THOMASON, FIRST BAPTIST CHURCH, DAWSON, GA

WEEK 51—TUESDAY
The Unpardonable Sin

"Anyone who speaks a word against the Son of Man, it will be forgiven him; but whoever speaks against the Holy Spirit, it will not be forgiven him, either in this age or in the age to come. . . . But I say to you that for every idle word men may speak, they will give account of it in the day of judgment. For by your words you will be justified, and by your words you will be condemned."

MATTHEW 12:32, 36–37

The thought of committing the unpardonable sin has tortured the hearts of many. In today's passage, however, when Jesus referred to speaking against the Holy Spirit, He was referring to the Pharisees' rejection of the works that Jesus had done. They had witnessed the miracles of Jesus and seen prophecies fulfilled, yet they claimed Jesus had done these works by the power of Satan. This was the very essence of blasphemy.

If a person today is concerned that he has committed the unpardonable sin, I would say that he has not. Clearly, his heart is longing for the assurance that his sin has indeed been forgiven. Friend, if you are concerned about your condition before God, cry out to Him right now! Settle the fact that Jesus will be faithful to forgive you, save you, and cleanse you from all unrighteousness. God's truth is far more reliable than your feelings.

....

"Let the words of my mouth and the meditation of my heart be acceptable in Your sight, O LORD, my rock and my Redeemer" (Psalm 19:14 NASB). In Jesus' name, Amen.

WEEK 51—WEDNESDAY
Good Ground Is Broken Ground

"He who received seed on the good ground is he who hears the word and understands it, who indeed bears fruit and produces: some a hundredfold, some sixty, some thirty."

MATTHEW 13:23

From the cotton fields of the Mississippi Delta to the peanut patches of southwest Georgia, I have been around farmers and farming for as long as I can remember. Jesus often alluded to farming to teach lessons of His kingdom. Today's verse comes from His parable of the soils.

Of the four types of ground that Jesus mentioned, only one was good for producing fruit, and that was broken ground. Just as the farmer uses a plow to break up the ground so it will be a good seedbed, the Lord often allows trials in our lives to break up the hardened ground of our hearts in order that His Word can be planted deep in our souls.

A broken heart is one longing for comfort. For a Christian, encouragement from Jesus can bring comfort like nothing else can. Jesus is the only One who can make a broken heart better and stronger than it was in the beginning.

Spend time reading the Bible. Watch with anticipation to see what kind of fruit the Lord brings from your life. When it's "a hundredfold, some sixty, some thirty," there is plenty to share with others. May many taste and see from your life that the Lord is good!

....

Lord, break my hard heart so it will be good ground for the seeds of Your Word to grow and produce a harvest for Your kingdom. In Jesus' name, Amen.

JAY THOMASON, FIRST BAPTIST CHURCH, DAWSON, GA

Week 51—Thursday
Praising God for His Word

Assuredly, I say to you, this generation will by no means pass away till all these things take place. Heaven and earth will pass away, but My words will by no means pass away.

MARK 13:30–31

Among the many great gifts Jesus has given His children is His Word. By His Word we know Him as Creator, Savior, and Sustainer of all that belongs to Him. Jesus truly is worthy of all the praise that we can ever give Him.

We know we should praise Him and have many reasons to praise Him. So let's not just talk about what we should do, only to fail in carrying out our good intentions. Instead, in regard to praising and worshipping Jesus, let us move beyond our good intentions. Psalm 33, in particular, calls us to praise God because of His power in creation. So I invite you to pray with me as I offer this prayer of praise to our God and King:

Father, I praise You because You are my Creator. You knew me before I was conceived in my mother's womb. You took pleasure in making me for Yourself. Thank You for knowing me better than anyone and loving me anyway!

Father, I praise You for allowing Jesus to suffer to save me from my sins. Because of Your Son, I do not have to go to hell. Thank You for Your Word too. May I learn it and follow its teachings.

....

Father, thank You for sustaining me moment by moment in this life. As Your child, no matter what I face, nothing can separate me from You and Your love. Father, help me to live as Your grateful and obedient child. In Jesus' name, Amen.

WEEK 51—FRIDAY
Don't Lose Focus

"Now these are the [seeds of God's Word] sown among thorns; they are the ones who hear the word, and the cares of this world, the deceitfulness of riches, and the desires for other things entering in choke the word, and it becomes unfruitful. But these are the ones sown on good ground, those who hear the word, accept it, and bear fruit: some thirtyfold, some sixty, and some a hundred."

MARK 4:18–20

Today we consider the warning that emanates from this Mark 4 text. In addition to the reality of being separated from God for all eternity in a place called hell, a person's greatest fear should be coming to the end of this life and having nothing to show for it. First John 2:28 warns us readers that Christians should abide in Jesus so we can have confidence and not be ashamed at His appearing.

If we are not careful, though, this life will pass us by, and our opportunity to make a difference will be gone. Many believers will go to heaven, but they will go empty handed because they did not heed the warning in Mark 4. So they will be embarrassed to meet the Savior and have no gift to give Him.

One danger of life in this busy world is that we can easily be distracted and lured away from the things of God. Let us not suffer losses in eternity because we focused too much of our attention and energy on the temporary things of this world.

....

Lord, help me listen to and follow the sweet voice of Your Word. May I believe You when You say, "Great is your reward in heaven" (Matthew 5:12). Help me to remember that my citizenship is found in heaven with You. This world is not my home! Amen.

JAY THOMASON, FIRST BAPTIST CHURCH, DAWSON, GA

WEEK 51—WEEKEND
Difficult Words

"It is the Spirit who gives life; the flesh profits nothing. The words that I speak to you are spirit, and they are life."

JOHN 6:63

Jesus had just declared to the Jews and His disciples that they must eat His flesh and drink His blood for eternal life (John 6:54), and the disciples' responded with "This is a hard saying; who can understand it?" (v. 60). Thus Jesus was gracious and took the opportunity to teach a lesson about the gospel.

In verse 54, Jesus was not saying that His followers would literally eat His flesh and drink His blood. But just as our physical body gains life-sustaining nutrients from the food that we eat, our souls gain eternal life from the words that Jesus speaks. The truth of His death, burial, and resurrection serves as the source of soul-sustaining assurance that we have eternal life. If we trust anything other than the broken body of Jesus and His shed blood to pay for our sins, we are probably motivated by a works-based effort to be saved.

Some decided that they could no longer follow Jesus and heed His difficult words, so they walked away. That's when Jesus asked the Twelve, "Do you also want to go away?" (v. 67). Peter's answer revealed his faith in Jesus as he confessed that he had nowhere else to go. Peter had come to believe that Jesus—and Jesus alone—had the words of eternal life.

There comes a point in everyone's life when he or she has to determine whether or not to believe or to walk away from the truth that Jesus proclaimed, the truth presented in Scripture. Commit today to a belief that the Bible is the inspired and infallible Word of God.

....

Father in heaven, give me a heart to walk according to Your Word. Amen.

WEEK 52—MONDAY
Sovereign Power, Sovereign Goodness, Sovereign Love

To everything there is a season, a time for every purpose under heaven: A time to be born, and a time to die; a time to plant, and a time to pluck what is planted; a time to kill, and a time to heal; a time to break down, and a time to build up.

ECCLESIASTES 3:1–3

Today we hear from the wisest man who ever lived, and Solomon told us that not only are there times and seasons in this world, but there is also an overruling providence in our lives. From before our births to the moment of our deaths, God is accomplishing His divine purposes in our lives even though we may not always understand what He is doing.

These truths defy theories of fatalism (the belief that all events are determined by fate and, therefore, inevitable) and deism (the belief that God exists and created the world but is not actively involved in it). The Bible's truth is this: the almighty God created the whole world and controls it. He is compassionate toward us and sovereign in His lordship over creation, history, and our lives.

Consider how His sovereignty is reflected in this passage's comparisons:

Born/Die: God's care for us is comprehensive. As the psalmist wrote, "All the days ordained for me were written in your book" (Psalm 139:16 NIV).

Plant/Pluck: God uproots us and plants us He according to His good plans for us.

Kill/Heal: God permits some to die and others to be healed. He gives, and He takes away. Blessed be His name.

Break down/Build up: this counsel applies to family members, friends, neighbors, and nations.

....

Lord, You are in control of all of creation, all of history, all of my life, and I'm grateful. In Your name, Amen.

DR. JOHNNY HUNT, FIRST BAPTIST CHURCH WOODSTOCK, WOODSTOCK, GA

WEEK 52—TUESDAY
Faith That Moves Mountains

"Have faith in God. For assuredly, I say to you, whoever says to this mountain, 'Be removed and be cast into the sea,' and does not doubt in his heart, but believes that those things he says will be done, he will have whatever he says. Therefore I say to you, whatever things you ask when you pray, believe that you receive them, and you will have them."

MARK 11:22–24

Every verse of God's Word contains truth for us. At times, I hear a gentle rebuke from my heavenly Father. At other times, His Word compels me to look at my sins or encourages me to trust Him more.

In Mark 11:22–24, Jesus challenged His disciples to consider the measure of their faith, and that is a good exercise for you as well. You should ask yourself, "Do I really trust God? Is He truly able to do what He says?"

To have faith in God—to trust Him for something—often calls us to step out of our comfort zones and believe God.

In Jewish literature, the term "rooter up of mountains" was used to describe leaders who could solve problems and do the apparently impossible. We have no record of Jesus' uprooting mountains, but His point is clear: through His glorious power, He can do in our lives things that seem impossible.

Think right now about a time when God came through for you, a time when He did that which only He could have done. And then thank and praise Your sovereign and loving Lord.

....

Lord, may the fact that You are the sovereign Doer-of-the-Impossible lead me to pray big prayers! Amen.

Week 52—Wednesday
Abiding in Christ

"If you abide in Me, and My words abide in you, you will ask what you desire, and it shall be done for you. By this My Father is glorified, that you bear much fruit; so you will be My disciples."

John 15:7–8

Today we will reflect on concepts that are fundamental to abiding in Christ. To abide means "to remain," and it can speak of perseverance. As we abide in God and His words abide in us, our desires really become His desires for us. We know what to ask for because our abiding in His Word has readied our hearts to both ask for His guidance and hear His voice when He responds.

Abiding is rooted in our devotion. We can't keep God's Word if we don't know His Word. God's Word must abide in us, and we must be devoted to hearing what He says to us through His Word.

Dependence speaks of our relationship with Christ and our acknowledgement that we need Him and His guidance all our days.

When we abide, we make decisions based on hearing from Him after we've asked Him for what we desire. Remember, those desires have resulted from our abiding. Our relationship with Him has given us the ability to know Him and trust His desires for us.

As already mentioned, our desires result from our meditating on the Lord. During such times He gradually changes our hearts, and we start to desire for ourselves what He desires for us. Abiding is not about a relationship that allows us to get whatever we desire; abiding is about a relationship that allows God to have His (far better) way in us.

....

Heavenly Father, teach me to abide in Your Son and in Your Word. In Jesus' name, Amen.

DR. JOHNNY HUNT, FIRST BAPTIST CHURCH WOODSTOCK, WOODSTOCK, GA

WEEK 52—THURSDAY
Chosen by God and for God

Blessed be the God and Father of our Lord Jesus Christ, who has blessed us with every spiritual blessing in the heavenly places in Christ, just as He chose us in Him before the foundation of the world, that we should be holy and without blame before Him in love.

EPHESIANS 1:3–4

The apostle Paul was full of praise as he reflected on his relationship with the Lord Jesus Christ and on "every spiritual blessing." Paul was grateful for the natural and spiritual blessings—both works of the Lord—that he was already enjoying. Paul put on display the rich life he knew as a result of the grace God bestows on believers. Indeed, it is a privilege to be a child of God.

In these two verses Paul also celebrated the doctrine of election. He realized that he did not choose God, but rather God chose him. Almighty God took the initiative in the relationship. Furthermore, Paul understood that he was chosen not only by God but also for God. Pastor and writer Adrian Rogers would often say, "He chose me, that I could choose Him." Pastor and writer John MacArthur said, "God's election or predestination does not operate apart from or nullify man's responsibility to believe in Jesus as Lord and Savior."

We are blessed to realize that there was nothing in us to commend us to God, no human goodness or merit, yet He saved us from our sins. Through Jesus' work on the cross, God declared righteous those of us who were unrighteous. The good and generous God did all this and more "to the praise of the glory of His grace" (Ephesians 1:6).

Almighty and sovereign God, You alone are worthy of praise. Teach me to praise You with all that I am. Amen.

WEEK 52—FRIDAY
Loving God and One Another

Beloved, if our heart does not condemn us, we have confidence toward God. And whatever we ask we receive from Him, because we keep His commandments and do those things that are pleasing in His sight. And this is His commandment: that we should believe on the name of His Son Jesus Christ and love one another, as He gave us commandment.

1 JOHN 3:21–23

Since the heavenly Father—through His Son—has given us such love, we are able to love others. More than fifty-five times in the New Testament we find the term "one another." In this passage, for instance, we find the command "love one another." Such loving becomes a reality when we are found believing and obeying the Word of God.

At times we find it difficult to love others, a difficulty that is often due to our own insecurities and doubts. However, when we allow the love of God to fill our hearts, love eradicates self-condemnation and "we have confidence toward God."

He answers our prayers due to the fact that we "keep His [Word] and do those things that are pleasing in His sight." We do—what He in His Word has called us to do.

In essence, Christ and His Word are active in our lives as we pray, trust, and obey. Our belief on "the name of His Son Jesus Christ" is in line with the first of the Ten Commandments: "you shall have no other gods before Me" (Exodus 20:3). At the same time, our belief is an aspect of loving the Lord with all our hearts, minds, souls, and strength. When we do, He changes our hearts from feeling condemned to feeling confident as we obey His commands.

Lord, Your Word works in my heart, and I am grateful. Amen.

WEEK 52—WEEKEND
Yielded to the Almighty

Now to Him who is able to do exceedingly abundantly above all that we ask or think, according to the power that works in us, to Him be glory in the church by Christ Jesus to all generations, forever and ever. Amen.

EPHESIANS 3:20–21

Hear the buoyant confidence of Paul's words as he praised God for His omnipotence. I remember the question posed to Abraham: "Is anything too hard for the LORD?" (Genesis 18:14), and I can confidently say no. Nothing is too hard for our God.

We should look back over your life for evidence of that truth. Describe the most recent time the Lord came through for you. Review in your mind when He did what seemed impossible and took down a giant. The Lord provides for us in ways that are above and beyond our needs—and what a great source of encouragement and strength. Another way to look at this passage is to think of God Himself as more than we can imagine, more wonderful than we could ever conceive!

Notice, too, that God's power "works in us." He will do for us and through us to the degree we let Him in us. To what degree will we yield ourselves to the Holy Spirit? Know that we limit God's working to the degree we are not yielded to Him.

So right now yield yourself to Him. Then watch His promise become His provision in you and for you in far greater ways than you can ask or imagine.

....

Lord, You are a mighty God, and it's a joy to serve You. In Christ's name, Amen.

Contributors

Notes

WEEK 8

1. Christianity.com, "George Mueller, Orphanges Built by Prayer," http://www.christianity.com/church/church-history/church-history-for-kids/george-mueller-orphanages-built-by-prayer-11634869.html.

WEEK 22

2. Pulpit Helps, "Look What I Did!" http://www.pulpithelps.com/www/docs/1157-9275.

3. Adventists Affirm, "Why We Need the Holy Spirit," http://www.adventistsaffirm.org/article/136/previous-issues/volume-18=numbers3/why-we-need-the-holy-spirit.

4. My Wintersong, "Headstone Humor . . . Here Lies:" https://wintersong.wordpress.com/favoritequotations/headstone-humor-here-lies.

WEEK 25

5. European-American Evangelistic Crusades, http://www.eaec.org/faithhallfame/dlmoody.htm.

WEEK 27

6. Gerald H. Wilson, *The NIV Application Commentary: Psalms,* vol. 1 (Grand Rapids, MI: Zondervan, 2002), 595.

WEEK 28

7. Grace to You, "The Man of God," http://www.gty.org/resources/sermons/54-47/the-man-of-god.

WEEK 37

8. https://www.oclc.org

WEEK 46

9. Suicide.org, "International Suicide Statistics," http://www.suicide.org/international-suicide-statistics.html.

WEEK 49

10. Wikipedia, "David Livingstone," http://en.wikipedia.org/wiki/David_Livingstone#Death.

11. Tony Evans, Tony Evans' *Book of Illustrations* (Chicago, Moody Press, 2009), 311.

SCRIPTURE INDEX

ACTS

ROMANS

JAMES

1 PETER

2 PETER

1 JOHN

JUDE

REVELATION